Born 1949 in Calcutta India, to an Armenian father and Czech mother, John Gasper, grew up in London. He survived ten years of boarding school before studying Architecture at Kingston University (Surrey UK). Upon graduation in 1974, John went on a working holiday to Australia. He decided to settle in Adelaide, where he lives with his French wife, Dominique, and their three-legged cat, Pudd.

Dilijan

A story of survival

John M Gasper

Published John M Gasper
Gasperian@outlook.com

First published 2023
Reprinted 2024

A catalogue record for this book is available from the National Library of Australia

ISBN 978 0 6457830 0 1 (pbk)
ISBN 978 0 6457830 1 8 (ebk)

Designed and typeset by Helen Christie, Blue Wren Books
Cover photo of Khor Virap Monastery at sunrise with hazy Mount Ararat in the background by Anton Andreev/iStock
Sunflower images from iStock and Shutterstock
Back cover wedding photo is the author's paternal grandparent's wedding in Istanbul (circa 1902) supplied by the author
Printed by Ingram Spark

This book is dedicated to:

My Armenian father, who enthused me with his art of storytelling.

My Czech mother, who endowed me with a sense of gratitude and respect for life.

My French wife, who has supported me with tender love, care, and her exquisite cooking.

I would also like to express my sincere gratitude to the late Sir Nicolas Winton MBE. He not only saw the dark clouds of war over the horizon, but with tireless dedication for others, did something about it.

Contents

PART 3

Never say never

PART 4

A Journey to the Never Never Lands

Author's Notes

This novel has been inspired by real people and actual incidents. It is based on the lives of four generations of my family and how they survived the Armenian Massacres, and the Jewish Holocaust. It tells of how these traumatic events scattered the family all over the world, how they struggled, how they survived, how they flourished, and how by chance, they came together again.

The names, and in some cases even the gender, of the people have been changed. There has also been a healthy dose of embellishment and a generous sprinkling of my own imagination.

I owe much to both my Czech, and my Armenian heritage. Both sides of my family suffered greatly under tyrants and despots. Yet my parents spoke little of their pasts, but instead, have looked to the future.

* * *

The picturesque township of Dilijan is set in the lush foothills near the northern end of Lake Sevan, Central Armenia. Armenia, with its chequered and turbulent past, is now a small landlocked country in the southern Caucasus. Today it covers an area of about the size of Belgium, South Carolina or just slightly larger than Wales. Under the reign of Tigranes the Great, 95–55 BC, 'The Kingdom of Armenia' was ten times the size of what it is today, stretching from the Mediterranean through to the Caspian Sea.

The ancient, rugged terrain harbours many hidden mysteries and sacred sites. For many centuries, Mount Ararat was the geographical and symbolic centre for the Armenian peoples. The Old Testament tells of a dove that led Noah and his Ark to the foothills of Mount Ararat and how a new beginning emerged from the devastating floods.

After Christ's crucifixion, many of his followers, persecuted for their religious beliefs, fled towards Armenia and other outposts of the Roman Empire. Armenia claims to be the 'Cradle of Christianity', and the first country to adopt Christianity as its national religion.

Armenia straddles both eastern and western cultures. Under great pressure, it has managed to maintain its Christian beliefs, much to the chagrin of its predominately Muslim neighbours. After the collapse of the Soviet Union in 1989, Armenia once again became a separate Republic.

The Armenian people are survivors. Many have been forced to flee their homeland and have sought shelter in other parts of the world. They have adapted well to their new environments, taking on the language of their new country, and adding to the culture of their adopted lands. They are well known for their artistic and musical talents, while many have prospered as traders with astute business acumen.

My Czech heritage has also been subjected to turmoil. My maternal grandparents were academics, and social democrats with Jewish connections. Recognising the dangers that Hitler and his Third Reich were posing, my grandparents managed to send their only child, my mother, to safety in the West Midlands township of Stourbridge in Britain. They were later to perish at Auschwitz.

My story tells of the turbulence suffered by my forebears, making comparison with the relative safety and ease of my own journey through life. The delicate threads of existence and the intricate webs that are woven, are often subject to the strains of wars and invasions. Somehow, the resilience of the human spirit continues to shine through unconquered.

PART 1

And never the twain shall meet

West   East

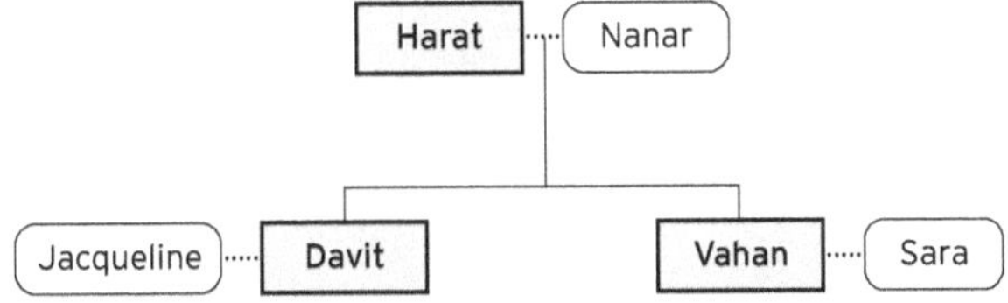

1

Harat Kaspar

My mother always told me that I was a most considerate child. Well, that is compared with my younger sister Ann, who apparently came into this world like an explosion. When I asked my mother what she meant by 'considerate', she replied that I was born at 11:10am, just in time for both of us to have lunch. Food it seems has always played an important part in both of our lives.

I was born in Calcutta, now Kolkata, India on 23rd September 1947, in time for both lunch and the partition of the sub-continent, happening all around us. India was certainly a turbulent place, but having just been born, I did not really know too much about the partition of a nation and the separation of religious groups. I was, I suppose, much more concerned about lunch, rather than the political or religious issues. Being born on the autumn equinox meant that the world was also in the balance from an astronomical perspective, but that didn't seem to register with me either.

Some couple of years later, I was baptised at the Armenian Holy Church of Nazareth in Calcutta and given the name Michael Kaspar. My father Hovhannes Kaspar was proud to be of Armenian descent as was my mother Hana Kaspar (née Kohl) proud of her Czech origins. The result has been that I am a product of a mixture of cultures and that mixture has become even more layered as time has gone by.

* * *

But enough of my birth and about me. My story starts more than a century before my birth and even before the birth of my paternal grandfather Vahan Kaspar in Constantinople now Istanbul. My great-grandfather, Vahan's father, was a successful merchant with Armenian origins but as far as we know came from a lineage that had been living in Constantinople for centuries.

At birth, my great-grandfather had been given the grand-sounding name of Haratyun Asdvadzadour Kasparian. He was always known as Harat by the immediate family and most of his friends, but soon after his birth, his father changed the family name. His father believed that having a surname Kasparian in Constantinople was sounding too much like an Armenian, and that was bad for business. It was decided to change their surname to Kaspar, which seemed to have a more neutral sound and could come from anywhere. Having -ian, -yan or -jan at the end of the surname was a dead giveaway for being Armenian so changing the surname to Kaspar was in hindsight, a good idea. Apparently Harat used his surname like a Christian name. People in business called him Kaspar; only his direct family and close friends ever called him Harat. Business was his life. He loved the cut and thrust of haggling and striking a deal. He always said that the making of money was more important than having money. He was very generous, giving away large sums of money and jewellery to what he considered worthwhile charities. He preferred giving gifts to charities rather than individuals as he did not want individuals pestering him. He never showed his wealth, making the distinction between being rich and being wealthy. He always said, 'Only rich people show the world that they have money, so they don't stay rich for very long. Whereas wealthy people stay wealthy because no one knows how much money they really have.'

Harat had a strong baritone voice and wasn't afraid to use it. He was a great admirer of Italian opera and often burst out into song. His favourite composer was Giuseppe Verdi, as he loved his use of the grand chorus.

He was a larger-than-life character, always impeccably attired. He wore a lot of silk and soft shoes that we today would consider more like carpet slippers. From the only photo I have seen of him he looked like a Middle Eastern Father Christmas with a beaming smile through a somewhat grey fog of a beard. A smile that says, 'You know you can trust me.' Heavy, hooded eyebrows with dark, piercing eyes that were no doubt always on the move. I don't know of his total integrity, but it was said that no one ever got the better of him. Most gamblers usually boast about their winnings, never telling you about their losses. I suspect that Harat was a huge gambler, especially within his business deals. As my father used to say to me, 'Gambling in your business is what business is about. Gambling for pleasure can lead to an addiction, and that is bad for your business.' My father, like his grandfather was a big gambler, and although they never physically met, I am sure the gambling gene was passed down through the blood.

In those days, a merchant handled all types of goods, creating deals to provide goods or services. There was always a special price, 'Especially for you, sir.' His clients ranged from all over the Middle East. It did not matter your nationality, religion, colour, or class, as long as you had the money to pay. He worked effortlessly among the Iranians, Americans, British, Dutch or any other Europeans. He sometimes for a fee acted as a negotiator of deals between people. His language skills were excellent, and it was said that he fully blended into the language that he was speaking. He spoke seven languages fluently and could flip from one to another in mid-sentence. As he had learnt the various languages in the street, he understood and used the local idioms as a native speaker would. He was once asked which language he dreamt in and he simply replied, 'I always dream in colour, and usually dream in the language of the country in which I sleep.'

By all accounts, Harat was certainly a colourful character and was renowned for his magnificent telling of a story. This gift came naturally and was handed down through each generation of the family. Telling a story is more than just relating the content. As all good actors or musicians would know, the telling of a story or the playing of a piece of music, is more about capturing, then holding the attention of an audience, while transporting them to another consciousness. In the live performance, storytelling can be more akin to magic or hypnosis. The audience is spellbound as the narrator weaves the content of the story; the spell becomes ever more intense as the transportation is completed. All stories need a beginning, a middle, and an end. They are all vital links in a chain of events. Timing of the words, the use of the voice and sometimes facial expressions, especially the eyes, are the only tools to be used. The silences say it all. No complicated technology is required, not even a pen. The story can be passed from generation to generation and from culture to culture. To some, storytelling comes quite naturally; to others, they are simply the recipients of the spell. Children are wonderful recipients of stories as they enter other worlds with ease. They do, however, relate to the magic of the storytelling rather than the content.

Harat was brought up in Constantinople, which is located at the meeting point of Europe and Asia Minor. His travels took him both east and west; he felt at home in either direction. His success was to quickly assess his audience, and then become the wise outsider. When in Tehran, he would play his refined European card to his predominately Persian audience. But when in Paris, he would be the exotic Middle Eastern gentleman. His understanding of both the Persian and Parisian ways gave him that enticing mystique. This was an art, that he had passed on to his friend and compatriot Calouste Gulbenkian, who used it to great success in the negotiations of the Persian oil reserves. Harat would say, 'Negotiations are like being a double agent; both sides believe that you are acting exclusively for them. The truth is, you are playing on both sides of the fence, but ultimately working for yourself.'

Harat had been sent to England to complete the last two years of his schooling at an English Public school in Gloucestershire, with the hope that he would be transformed into a proper 'Gentleman'. There he gained many influential friends from around the world and would later use the 'old school tie' tradition to his advantage. He acted in numerous school plays, making a fine 'Bottom' in Shakespeare's *A Midsummer Night's Dream*. He played rugby in the 2nd XV as a powerful prop forward and was given the nickname 'The Bull'. He was never promoted to the top team as he failed to grasp the finer points of the game, so was subjected to numerous fouls and referees' whistles. In cricket he opened the batting for the 1st XI. With an open stance similar to that of W.C. Grace, he used his cricket bat as a club to thrash at the ball. He was often reprimanded by the sports master after the opposition had complained about the deafening roar he bellowed as he ferociously struck the ball. At Lords cricket ground, he had made ninety-eight runs in his first innings against Marlborough College, when he took a risky run and tripped mid-pitch.

'It's there to be hit,' he would say loudly in earshot of the opposition bowler, to an incoming batsman joining him at the crease. 'Hit it hard to clear the boundary and you won't be caught.' This was the way he played his cricket, and how he would meet life's challenges.

Harat was not the most academic of young men and considered that 'life' should be his university. He was sent to University College London to study economics but found it all too rigid for his liking. He enjoyed reading essays by John Stuart Mill and the likes of David Ricardo or Thomas Mathus but putting theories into written words did not fully agree with him. He was more interested in commerce and the making of money than academic studies.

Reluctantly his father finally agreed that Harat should return to Constantinople to start his career in the family's 'Trading Company'. It was agreed that as Harat had not completed his academic studies, he would have to start his business career as a junior errand boy, working his way up the ladder on merit rather than favour. Harat always suspected that even if he had completed his degree with 1st class honours, he would have had to start at the bottom and work his way up. As Harat always said 'Any son of mine will have to start at the bottom because that's where he will learn respect for his fellow man.'

* * *

Not much is known of Harat's wife Nanar. She appears to have been totally overshadowed by her husband's exuberance and preferred to stay at home while Harat was on his business trips. Not that Harat took advantage of or suppressed his wife. The roles of their marriage had been clearly defined and accepted by both parties. Harat was the breadwinner whilst Nanar would be the homemaker. They worked as a team, and both were happy to fulfil the others' expectations of them. I would like to be able to say that Nanar was beautiful but in truth no account to date can lead me to categorically state this to be true or false. Even though the marriage had been arranged and was part of a consolidation of two separate companies, suffice it to say that the partnership was a loving, uncomplicated, and fruitful marriage that bore two sons.

<h1 style="text-align:center">2</h1>

<h2 style="text-align:center">March 1879</h2>

It was on 23 March 1879, when Harat, away on business in Baghdad, heard that his wife was about to give birth. He rushed home and was delighted to find that Nanar had given birth to not one but two identical boys. The twins were born 10 minutes apart and were so identical that no one could distinguish which one was which. They were both born healthy, with black wispy hair, and beaming smiles. Harat was ecstatic; it was beyond his wildest dreams. 'Two for the price of one,' he chuckled. As he entered the room and saw Nanar with one of his sons on each of her breasts, his thoughts went to pieces. 'Good job we didn't have triplets,' he said as he burst out laughing, much to the dismay of his wife.

* * *

Nanar was much calmer than Harat and had already examined both boys for any distinguishing markings but couldn't find anything. The length of their fingers was identical, the toes curled up in the same way, the lips and cheeks on their chubby little faces smiled that same smile. They even had the same birthmark behind their left ear. This was the same marking that their father Harat had been born with, a feature handed down from father to son. It was this inherited birthmark that assured Harat that both boys were in fact his own. Not that he was in any doubt about the matter – his wife Nanar wasn't the type to stray.

Nanar and Harat had previously discussed a name for their child. If it was a boy, Harat had chosen Davit, the Armenian version of the biblical name David. If it was a girl, Nanar had chosen Azniv meaning 'gentle'. They had never in their wildest dreams considered that it could possibly be twins, and that they would need two boys' names. Harat wanted to stay with the Old Testament theme, suggesting that the second son be called Goliath. Nanar didn't get the joke and would have nothing of it. She said that as Harat had chosen one name, she would call her second son Vahan. So Vahan it was, and Harat was happy to oblige. Davit and Vahan had come into the world together, bringing great joy and merriment.

The problem of distinguishing the two boys remained. As a temporary measure, Nanar tied a blue ribbon around Davit's left ankle and a red one around Vahan's right ankle. This solved the immediate problem and would remain the preferred method of distinction, until the boys were of an age to identify themselves.

Davit was older by only ten minutes, but these ten minutes made all the difference. They had just turned six years old when the notion of age entered one of their heads and they started to squabble about who had been born first. Nanar without thinking, told them that Davit was indeed ten minutes older than Vahan. It was too late. As she said it, she realised she couldn't retract her statement. These ten minutes brought about an imbalance that would affect both of them for the rest of their lives.

Up to the age of six years old, the boys' characters were also indistinguishable. Both displayed a cheeky enthusiasm making Harat immensely proud. As Nanar had uttered the words 'Davit was born first and is older ….', Vahan physically withered, never to fully recover. Through the years, Nanar tried all manner of ways to console Vahan, but without success. She said that Vahan would live at least twenty minutes longer or things like, 'But you know, Vahan was conceived first.' She knew this was not necessarily true but justified her comment by saying to Harat, 'The boys won't be able to grasp the concept of conception.' He laughed at her unintentional play on words. As Vahan seemed to wither, Davit appeared to flourish. Vahan went further and further into himself, making Davit appear even more confident. And so, the vicious cycle escalated. One small comment from a mother had borne such grave consequences, especially for Vahan. Sibling rivalry can crush the weaker sibling whilst the stronger one goes from strength to strength.

In the July of 1885 something happened that brought all this to a head. A British-American adventurer visited Constantinople as part of his heroic travels around the world on his penny farthing bicycle. His remarkable journey had started the previous year in San Francisco and was to take him around the world. As remarkable as the journey, was the comprehensive account of his travels in the form of a diary that he kept. This account was first published in 1887 and gives a clear insight into life around the world at that time.

Harat, as a prominent English-speaking gentleman, was asked to welcome the young adventurer to Constantinople. He admired greatly the young man's attitude to life and to his unswerving motivation to complete his journey. Harat's congenial personality, his fluency in English, and his understanding of British customs and etiquette, allowed the young man to feel comfortable in his company. They soon became quite familiar, chatting away on a first name basis.

Harat invited Thomas to his house for lunch and to meet his family. The invitation was accepted, and a date was agreed for the following Tuesday. Harat was keen to create a favourable impression upon his guest. 'We must put on quite a feast for this young man,' Harat told Nanar. 'He looks like he needs fattened up a bit for the next leg of his journey.'

As arranged, Thomas the cyclist arrived at the house riding his penny farthing dressed in plus four pants, chequered waist coat and deerstalker shooting hat. The front wrought iron gates had been opened for Thomas to ride around the fountain in the front courtyard calling out 'Hello everyone,' in several different languages. On his way, Thomas had attracted quite a crowd, running after him through the streets and screaming with delight. A man riding a penny farthing bicycle was quite a novelty in Constantinople, especially a man with sparking blue eyes, blonde moustache and wavy hair bursting out from under his peculiar deerstalker hat.

The twins Davit and Vahan, each holding a hand of their nanny Sevan, came to see the spectacle. They joined the street crowd that had gathered in a large circle, clapping, and cheering as Thomas threw both his arms in the air while somehow managing to steer his cumbersome contraption, using just his knees. A group of local musicians had been employed for the occasion and appeared on the front balcony playing Turkish music, faster and faster as Thomas completed numerous circuits, with more and more daring bicycle stunts. The crescendo of sound came to a climax, as Thomas, performed a handstand on his trusted penny farthing, holding his pose for a good fifteen seconds and pretending to wobble from time to time, the gathered crowd was stunned into complete silence. Finally, a glissando on a violin as Thomas dismounted gracefully by pushing up like a gymnast alighting from a static horse. A loud beat on the drum to accentuate the final landing back to earth was the signal for further cries of joy from the enthralled crowd. Thomas had been an acrobat in a circus back home in San Francisco and was using every trick in his repertoire. To the continued cheering and clapping, Thomas completed his bowing to the crowd whilst holding onto his bicycle. One of the servants then came forward to take charge of the contraption while Thomas made his way up the steps to the awaiting Harat and Nanar who were dressed in full traditional Armenian costumes. He shook Harat's hand vigorously and then turned towards Nanar bowing as he took her hand and kissed it gently as if she was royalty. Harat then raised his arms as a signal for the crowd to stop their applause while he made a welcoming speech. The crowd obeyed without question, Harat addressed the crowd in the local Turkish dialect, turning to Thomas at the end of each sentence to translate each phrase into English. He finished his welcome with a blessing. First for Thomas, then for his family and finally for the crowd. He turned to the front door and said to Thomas, 'Come let us eat for we have prepared a feast for your delight.' The feast was something to behold and went on late into the night with music, dancing, and merriment, all with a typical middle eastern flavour.

The two young boys Davit and Vahan had noticeably started to grow apart. Davit had eagerly taken up the challenge to ride Thomas's bicycle, even though there was no way that he could reach the pedals. Thomas held onto Davit, slowly pushing the bicycle some ten feet or so. 'Now it's Vahan's turn,' bellowed Harat, but Vahan just buried his face deeper into his nanny's skirt.

The next day Nanar sought to find out what was troubling Vahan.

Finding a private moment with Vahan she asked him, 'Son, why didn't you want to ride on the bicycle? Davit did it so well didn't he?'

'I don't like Davit,' replied Vahan abruptly bursting into tears.

'Why don't you like him? What has he done wrong?' asked Nanar in her soft maternal manner.

'He's ten minutes older than me,' snivelled Vahan. 'I wanted to be the older one,' he sobbed trembling.

That night, Nanar told Harat what had transpired and asked for his advice. She blamed herself for letting the cat out of the bag as to who was the older twin, and only wished she could turn back the clock. Harat said that he had the solution and would sort it out in the morning. Harat slept well but Nanar hardly slept at all.

The next day Harat brought up the subject at breakfast. He explained to the two boys that when they were just babies, Nanar, their mother, had tied a blue ribbon around Davit's left ankle and a red one around Vahan's right ankle, so they could be distinguished at a glance.

'One day, your mother decided that she was going to give both of you a bath,' he explained as Nanar and the twins listened intently. 'She took off the ribbons from your ankles so they wouldn't get wet. She carefully placed the ribbons by the side of the bath and began to bathe both of you. She went to get a towel but when she returned, you were both playing in the water, one on top of the other. "Goodness gracious," she exclaimed. "Which one is which?" She couldn't tell you apart. So finally, she picked up one of you, saying, "You can be Davit," and tied the blue ribbon onto your left ankle. 'Then she picked you up,' continued Harat, turning to Vahan. 'She dried you off and said proudly, "And you can be Vahan," as she put the red ribbon around your left ankle.' A big grin came upon Harat's face as he turned to Nanar. She tried to conceal her surprise as nothing of the kind had actually happened, but she knew where this might be leading.

'So, you see,' continued Harat. 'We don't actually know which one of you is Davit and which one of you is Vahan. All we know is that Davit is ten minutes older and that could be either of you. Now I'll hear nothing more of which one of you is the older or which one is the younger but if I do, I will have your names switched over. Do I make myself clear?'

Both boys smiled but Vahan's smile beamed the most. 'I could be the older one,' he thought to himself.

'Now off you go and play as I have some important things to discuss with your mother,' said Harat and the two boys went off happy.

'What did you say that for?' snapped Nanar, 'Now they will both grow up with an identity crisis not knowing who they really are.'

* * *

Harrat's ploy worked for a while. Davit no longer felt superior for being ten minutes older, but Vahan couldn't overcome that niggling thought that he could be ten minutes younger. He lived with this negative burden for the rest of his life, and even though he had tried hard to bury it, it lurked deep in his subconscious mind, mysteriously surfacing to play havoc and destruction.

3

The Art of the Deal

Life in Constantinople during the 1880's became somewhat of a growing struggle. This was especially true for a wealthy Armenian family that didn't hold back their demonstration of wealth. Harat had no problem with making money as he had business interests throughout the Middle East. He often thought that it would be wise to move out of Constantinople, but he enjoyed the richness of life that the city offered. He enjoyed the cosmopolitan flavour with its hustle and bustle, crowded intimate markets, and the many friends that greeted him with true affection. They came from all walks of life, as he held no issue regarding their status. A visit to the market was often a full day event. It was his other home, his office, and his inspiration. On strolling down the market laneways, he would call out to friends and stall holders who in turn would call out to him as a brother. He made friendships easily and was known for his generosity, with both his time and money. He always asked for a special discount, and always offered one in return. 'For you my friend a very special discount. Don't tell anyone as they will all ask for it and I would have to put up my prices.' He wouldn't even buy a bucket without asking for a discount.

* * *

It was on one of these many occasions, while buying some cheese from his favourite cheese merchant, that he bumped into a good friend called Arman Galutian. Arman was a young man in his early thirties and had branched out from the Galutian family carpet business, to become a small-time builder and developer. The Galutian family had been an honourable Armenian family and well known within the community. Arman's father and brothers sold high quality Persian carpets and at one time Harat had negotiated on their behalf with some Persian carpet merchants from Isfahan. Both parties had thought he had got them a special deal and both parties had paid him handsomely, as well as throwing in a carpet as a gift. The Galutian's felt that they were getting a heavily discounted bulk price whilst the Persians were only too pleased to be moving some of their difficult stock. After meeting with both parties separately and then together, Harat had told the Persians that they needed to put a certain kind of label on the back of their carpets to show authenticity, while he told the Galutian's that they should promote the fact that the label meant quality, and without it, the carpets would fall apart within a couple of years.

'Just show your customers a worn-out carpet that doesn't have a label and tell them look what happens,' said Harat.

The carpets sold well, and all were pleased with the outcome.

* * *

'Wonderful to see you on this delightful afternoon,' Harat said to Arman giving a gentle peck on both cheeks. 'How is business going? How are your brothers? And how is that gangster father of yours?' He used the term 'gangster' with some affection as old man Galutian was as straight as they come. Harat didn't give Arman a chance to answer but continued, 'Come let's have a coffee and you can tell me all your problems.' Harat had somehow sensed that Arman wasn't at ease within himself. Arman had done his best to hide his problems, but the disguise certainly was no match for Harat's radar.

They found a little coffee shop and the owner was delighted to see Harat, exclaiming. 'Why haven't I seen you? For so long I have been waiting. Come, have some coffee.' The owner showed them to the back corner, Harat offered Arman the choice of seat. They sat on the floor on big, plump cushions. Harat made his cushions spread out a bit so he could lie stretched out rather than sit upright. This gave Harat the subservient position and allowed Arman to take the higher standing. Harat wanted to let Arman feel in control. Harat wanted information rather than to strike a deal from an authoritative height.

After accepting a refill of thick black coffee, and then taking a swig from the bottle of water on the table, Harat put on a beaming smile saying, 'So what has been happening? Tell me your problems. How can I help if I don't know what it is that is troubling you?'

Arman's guard dropped as he started to let it all out. 'Well, you see I've become involved with a Syrian man who owned land in an uninhabited bay near the small town of Turan.'

'So where is this Turan?' enquired Harat.

'It's a small town across the Sea of Marmara. Bandirma direction.'

'Okay. I think I know where it is. So go on, tell me what's happened,' replied Harat.

'Well, I agreed to pay for half the cost of the land so together, the Syrian and I, could develop five houses. He would put in 20% of the cost of materials and I would put in the rest. Then I would be able to charge him for the labour component at agreed stages of construction of each house. I would construct one house at a time and the profits of the sale of a house would help to build the next one.'

'Well, what seems to be the problem?' asked Harat throwing out both his hands in an enquiring gesture. Harat used his hands and eyes to enhance his desired emotion while his voice uttered the content.

'You see, I haven't quite completed the first house and now this Syrian says he can't afford to pay his 20%. I can't afford to do the project by myself so I'm up to here with debt and the banks want their money back,' stuttered Arman in a forlorn whimper.

Harat had listened patiently and then asked Arman. 'Have you got any more that you need to tell me?'

'No, except do you know anyone who wants to buy an unfinished house?' Arman asked pleadingly. 'I wished I had never got myself into this mess. I would be better off in my family's carpet business. Building work just isn't for me. There are too many rogues about.'

'I can't think of anyone off the top of my head,' replied Harat adjusting himself to a more dominant position. 'Perhaps I will need to know a few more details. In fact, I might need to have a look at this house before

I start putting the word out for a quick sale. I'm not in the business of misrepresentation. Anyway, tell me the name of this Syrian fellow and where I might find him. Once I have seen the property, I will need to check him out.'

Arman told him the name of the Syrian and where he could be found.

'Fine,' said Harat writing down the name and address of the Syrian. 'So I will meet you at 6:30am tomorrow at the entrance to the fisherman's jetty and together we will get ourselves a boat to this little bay of yours. Don't be late as we will need to make an early start.' With that he rose from his sitting position, gave Arman a hug saying 'Don't worry my friend; I'm sure we can sort all this out. Don't be late. We will need our wits about us as this could prove to be quite a dangerous mission.'

* * *

The next morning Arman arrived at the dock well before 6am. He certainly didn't want to be late. There were three or four colourful fishing boats tied to the dock, bobbing up and down in the water. Arman waited patiently while a group of swarthy, weather-beaten fishermen played cards on one of the boats. Harat arrived at exactly 6:30am. As usual he was dressed in a fine waist coat, silk shirt and cravat with a gold pin. He looked very dapper except for his soft house shoes that he always wore. Under his arm he carried a box like flat briefcase. Arman assumed that Harat had brought plenty of reading material that he could read on the boat trip. As Harat arrived, one of the swarthy fishermen threw in his cards and jumped onto the jetty saying 'Mr Kaspar your boat awaits you. Please come this way.'

Harat greeted the man asking him his name and telling him to call him Harat.

'Mr Smulian, Vazrick Smulian at your service' the man said shaking Harrat's hand profusely.

'Well, I would like to call you Vaz if that is alright with you. This is my friend Arman Galutian, he will be coming with us,' responded Harat with gusto.

'Fine,' said the fisherman 'I have brought plenty of supplies, so we won't go hungry. My wife is on board preparing breakfast,' he added pointing to his little boat. With that Harat very nimbly jumped on board and beckoned for Arman to follow. Even though Harat was a large man, dressed in fine attire, nothing hampered his ability to jump on board a fishing boat. He was a skilled yachtsman and as a schoolboy at an English boarding school had sailed small racing craft in numerous regattas around the coast of Cornwall. He had proudly won the regatta from Falmouth to Penzance and on accepting his trophy vowed that one day he would circumnavigate the world as a solo yachtsman. He liked to aim high.

Arman was somewhat astounded and asked Harat what was happening. 'Through some contacts I organised our trip for today. Hope you don't mind. Thought it would save some time rather than wasting time looking for a boat. Vaz has agreed for a small fee to take us to Turan and back. Said he would throw in a breakfast on the outbound trip and lunch for us on the way back. Come let us sit out of the way at the front of the boat. The first rule of sailing in someone else's boat is to sit out of the way but always be ready to carry out any orders from the skipper. Vaz is in charge so we can make ourselves scarce and have a bit of a chat.' Vaz had very efficiently set sail and soon Yeva his somewhat wizened wife served up a delicious breakfast with lashings of hot coffee to follow.

'This is the life isn't it,' said Harat wiping his mouth with the back of his hand.

'Yes, indeed it is,' said Arman feeling a lot happier now that Harat was involved. The waters were calm but there was enough wind to sail at quite some speed. Arman thought that Harat would want to question him about all the facts regarding the case but instead Harat went right to the front of the boat and sat cross legged bolt upright with his eyes closed. To begin with he seemed to breathe quite heavily. He breathed in through his nose and then exhaled through his mouth, with lips that formed a tight circle. Soon the breathing stopped and Harat seemed to be sleeping quite upright. The reflection of the sun off the sea highlighted his large face. The waters lapped a rhythmic sound against the hull as the boat cut through the glass like waters. Arman didn't quite know what to do with himself, so he sat in silence staring at the horizon.

* * *

Suddenly Harat stirred, turned, and asked Arman if he wanted to play a game of Backgammon.

'Backgammon is a true reflection of life and has lots to teach us about the art of risk taking. Come I'll show you some of the finer points of the game. Have you played much before?' enquired Harat opening up what Arman thought was his attaché case. The board was set up even before Arman could answer.

'Yes, I have played but only as a child,' said Arman.

'Did you use the doubling dice?' asked Harat.

'Not really but I'm keen to learn,' replied Arman with enthusiasm.

'The doubling dice is an essential part of the game. Without it, it is like going to the races and not putting a bet on a horse,' explained Harat. 'The doubling dice is like the spices added to a stew to turn it into a flaming curry. It adds the element of risk and it's all to do with timing. Let's get started.'

Together they played through three trial games and Harat explained some of the strategies as they went along. Arman was slow, counting out the moves while Harat played without hesitation moving his counters with alacrity and precision.

'Like in life and especially before making any business decisions, there are many critical elements to be considered. This game is not just about the dice, although the dice play an important part of the outcome,' explained Harat to the attentive Arman.

The boat made steady progress as the two became absorbed in numerous games. The master taught his pupil well, calling out what would be the better option and why.

'Firstly, you must understand your opponent and their propensity to take risk. You must be always aware of the position of the board and that the dynamics of the game can be completely changed by one unexpected throw of the dice. You must be prepared to change your strategy quickly and efficiently. The game is fluid, and the outcome will depend on the skill of each player. Sometimes I will play a running game and go all out to reach the goal at full speed. Sometimes a more defensive game is called for. I will purposely lay traps, so I get some of my front counters taken and then returned to the start to build up a defensive wall. Slowly from a position of defence I will expand out but not too fast. You can't afford to leave any gaps for the opposition to get through.' Harat explained his moves as he made them. Normally he wouldn't have given anything away, but Arman was somewhat of a novice to the game and perhaps life in general.

'So, explain to me when I should use the doubling dice,' asked Arman.

'Yes, the doubling dice is the critical element. As I said, you must understand your opponent. It's all to do with timing. You must learn to double the stakes but always allow your opponent a glimmer of hope. Otherwise, he won't accept the challenge and will fold. If you have missed the opportunity to double, you might decide not to double and play for a back gammon gaining double the points that way,' explained Harat. 'When to double and when to accept a double can best be learnt by playing the game for points rather than money.' Harat laughed as he introduced the notion of money.

'Over the years I have earned a lot of money from playing back-gammon, but I would have also lost a lot. Overall, I may be up, or I may be down but what is essential is that I have learnt about life and how to play the game. I have learnt that one shouldn't give up until the game is over and once it is over, there will be another game with new opportunities.' Harat smiled and he said in English 'It's not what you earn, it's what you learn.' They both laughed.

They played game after game and were oblivious to their surroundings. A couple of hours had gone by when Vaz called out. 'I'll drop the anchor here and we can take the small rowing boat to shore.'

Harat called out 'That's fine. We'll just finish this game. It won't take long.'

* * *

They had entered a small horseshoe cove and were heading towards a golden desolate beach with green hills behind. It was in no time at all that Vaz was rowing the three of them ashore. His wife Yeva stayed on the boat and put out a line and a couple of nets to see what was lurking below. They had brought sufficient supplies to feed an army but fresh was always considered the best.

They beached the small rowing craft on the glistening white sand.

Harat took off his shoes and rolled up his trousers so Arman followed suit. Harat jumped into the shallow water and waded ashore. The beach was so pristine that it felt as if they had arrived at a desert island to look for buried treasure. Arman's house was some 100 yards along the beach nestled in the trees. What an idyllic spot thought Harat but made no mention of it. They approached the house that was just a two-storey shell. Harat could see that the roof was on, but the windows and doors were yet to be installed.

'So, what is the extent of the land that you own with this Syrian fellow?' asked Harat.

'The house is positioned near the southern most boundary of the property and I have had the five house sites marked out,' replied Arman. 'Each block of land has a thirty-metre-wide beach frontage and is fifty metres deep from the water's edge. Enough to have a house, a vegetable garden, a goat or two, and some chickens. From the front of the house, you get a wonderful view along the beach and to the rear you can see the wooded hills,' explained Arman with a broad smile.

'You have done very well young man,' said Harat.

'Would you like to see inside?' asked Arman as they got to the front entrance of the house.

'Yes, I would but actually I'm dying for a pee,' said Harat. 'I will nip around the back and into the woods. I won't be a minute.'

Harat went around the house and disappeared into the scrub which led to the woods. Although he did need to pee, his primary objective was to ensure that there was an escape route should it be needed.

Meanwhile, Arman went into the house and looked around. No progress had been made since his last visit. Suddenly, Arman became aware that Harat had been gone for quite some time, so he went to the back door and shouted out. 'Harat, Harat are you alright?'

'Yes, I'm fine' shouted back Harat as he appeared from the woods still adjusting his trousers.

'Come on,' he said to Arman. 'We had better get going before the winds turn the wrong way. Best to catch that afternoon breeze so we can have a clear run all the way home. We can set a sail to broad reach most of the way.'

'But don't you want to come and have a look at the house?' asked Arman in amazement.

'No, I've seen what I wanted to see. There's no time to waste,' replied Harat as he strode off back down the beach towards the waiting Vaz.

Arman thought this very strange that Harat had come all this way to see the house but hadn't even gone inside. He caught up to Harat who was striding at a marching pace.

Vaz rowed them back to the moored boat where Yeva said to them, 'This is a great place for fishing, plenty of crabs,' as she held a couple of a decent size crabs above her head. 'I've enough for one each, so I'll put them in the pot, and they should be ready soon.'

Vaz pulled up anchor and set the sail. Once they got out of the sheltered cove it was plain sailing all the way home.

Lunch was served and Harat made a real mess of his fine waist coat as the juice from the crab tricked down his face. He was in heaven.

* * *

After lunch Harat had his usual twenty-minute snooze. He said that it helped with the digestion. Awakening, he stretched out his arms with his mouth wide open in a hippopotamus like yawn. Turning to Arman, who was sitting on the side of the boat with his feet dangling over the edge, Harat said, 'Arman I have some matters I want to discuss with you.'

Harat went over to his attaché case and from an exterior pocket pulled out some papers but then put them back.

'I've got something I want to show you but before I do, I need to explain what has transpired. Come, pull up a cushion, sit with me and I will tell you everything.'

Arman moved closer to Harat and made himself comfortable.

'So, tell me how long it would take before the house could be completed,' asked Harat.

'I could most probably finish it before Christmas,' replied Arman.

'Do you think it could be completed by early December if you got a move on with it?' asked Harat.

'Well at a pinch it would be possible but why do you ask? I don't own all the land outright and I don't have the money to complete it.' Arman suspected that Harat was scheming something.

'Well, you see,' said Harat. 'After we had coffee yesterday afternoon, I thought a bit about your problem with this Syrian. I quickly came to the realisation that the real issue was that he owned half the land and that you are dependent on his part of the funds to complete the project. I thought to myself 'if this wasn't the case then there wouldn't be a problem. Is this correct?' he asked Arman in an interrogating manner.

'Yes, but he wouldn't want to sell his half of the land and anyway I don't have the money to buy it,' Arman mumbled as his response faded away to nothing.

'Ah well, this is what has happened,' said Harat with a broad grin on his face. 'You see I have many friends in Constantinople. I know a man within the Syrian community who owes me a favour or two. He used to be a police officer back in Damascus and when I mentioned your friend's name, he said he knew all about him. As it happens, your Syrian so called friend has been an extremely bad boy. He has cheated numerous people out of their livelihoods back in Damascus and has subsequently served time in prison. He then got mixed up with a criminal gang who turned on him for cheating them. They threatened him but somehow it ended up in a fight in which your friend killed a senior member of the gang. He was forced to leave Damascus in a hurry and has been hiding under a new name, petrified that one day he would be found by the gang. My police officer friend told me the original name of your friend, but I had to promise not to tell anyone of his true identity.' Harat sighed and then continued. 'Later in the evening I went to see a colleague of mine who is high up in the Titles Office. Even though it was late, he could get into the office and got hold of the original title and transaction documents relating to this bit of land of yours. It seems that your friend originally bought the land for considerably less than what he has told you, and that in fact, you should own at least 80% of the land.' Harat was grinning from ear to ear as he continued.

'This friend of mine in the Titles Office also got me a blank form for the change of ownership to the deeds. And thus, the scene has been set. We now have your so-called friend exactly where we want him. It has all fallen into place. The sting will be simple, quick, and effective.'

'What do you mean? I don't understand,' said Arman.

'Well, later last night at around 8:30pm a couple of my associates went round to your Syrian friend's house and knocked on his door very loudly. They are both exceptionally large, heavily built characters. In fact they wouldn't hurt a fly, but they can put on an act that certainly is intimidating. Even I get frightened,' giggled Harat. 'They called out and said they wanted to have a chat with him. Impersonation of the law comes naturally to them as they both had been police officers for many years. Once they got inside the house they set to work. No violence or anything like that, they didn't need to resort to it. All they had to do, was call him by his previous name. He visibly reeled backwards and asked his wife to leave the room. She knew nothing of his past. He immediately thought that they would be part of the gang from Damascus that had finally caught up with him. He was a dead man or soon to be, he thought. My rather large associates explained that they were not part of the gang but would be happy to spill the beans to them if he didn't cooperate. 'Then, what do you want from me?' he asked, trembling.

'All we want is for you to sign this release form handing back your portion of the land to Mr Arman Galutian and for that we will pay you the equivalent of 20% of the purchase price that you originally bought the land for. Just sign here and here.' To their surprise he signed the form immediately without even reading it. He was even more surprised when they counted out the 20% in cash.

'You see I don't like to cheat people,' said Harat pulling out a form from his attaché case. 'This deed in my hand, shows that the land is now 100% in your name,' said Harat with glee.

'Yes, but I now owe you the money that you paid, and I can't get hold of any more funds,' said Arman with a saddened face.

'Well, that's where I come into the picture,' replied Harat.

'What do you mean?' asked Arman.

'However, there are certain conditions that must be met,' replied Harat. 'Firstly, I want to buy the completed house and land that it sits on for the final agreed development cost, minus the 20% land costs that my colleagues paid on my behalf to your friend in cash last night. Secondly, the house is to be completed by the 1st of December this year. Thirdly, I will act as your agent and find a buyer for the remaining parcels of land, and you will get the full proceeds minus my 5% fee. And finally, I suggest that you give up the building game and return to work with your father and brothers in the family carpet business. This last item is a bit of free advice rather than a condition to our agreement.'

With that Harat held the deed papers out over the side of the boat and said, 'Of course the choice is ultimately yours. I can always drop this signed deed into the water, and we can forget the whole business.'

'No, no don't drop it,' called out Arman. 'I agree to all your conditions, and you are right about me returning to my family business. This building business isn't for me. There are too many sharks in the water,' This last statement was in hindsight, a rather apt thing to have said.

Harat laughed and pulled back the deed, putting it back into his attaché case. 'Good I'm so pleased you agree. I have brought along a written agreement form and contract between the two of us that I need you to sign and then all will be taken care of without any cost to you.'

They both put their signatures against all three of the conditions and Vaz witnessed the signing. All three shook hands profusely and Harat called out to Yeva 'Do you have any apricot brandy on board? I think this calls for a celebration.'

The brandy was extremely good.

'Tell me something' said Arman to Harat. 'Would you really have dropped that deed into the water? What if I had not agreed to the deal?'

'Well, the answer is both yes and no,' replied Harat. 'You see the piece of paper I held out over the water wasn't the actual deed signed by your scurrilous previous partner. It was just a piece of paper with lots of official writing on it. The real deed was still in my attaché case, and I had made sure that your so-called friend had signed over the land to an unnamed new owner. The name had been left blank for me to fill in later. As you had agreed to my terms and conditions, I will fill in your name onto the deed. If you hadn't agreed, I would have dropped the false paper into the water and then later put my own name at the appropriate place into the deed. I will now fill in your name.' And with that he produced the real land deed and with a flourish filled in Arman's name and told him to keep it in a safe place.

'How about another game of backgammon?' asked Harat as he opened his attaché case to lock away the signed agreement.

They sailed with a light breeze behind them playing backgammon and drinking brandy all the way home. They sang Armenian folk songs as Vaz accompanied them on his Armenian flute called a Shvi.

* * *

The house was dutifully completed by December 1st and Harat and his family spent numerous wonderful holidays there, swimming, eating, drinking by day, and playing cards and backgammon with their invited friends till the early hours of the morning.

Harat never told anyone of his ulterior motives for owning the house at this remote beach and how he had foreseen the turbulent times that lay ahead.

4

The Escape to Freedom

Harat and his family enjoyed the peace and serenity of the beach house at Turan, so much so, that Harat made an offer to buy the remaining four blocks of land that were technically owned by Arman. They negotiated a fair price and both parties were happy with the deal. Harat didn't need the money, which allowed him to take risks. Privately, he thought to himself, 'I can always sell a plot or two if things go bad. It will be a bit of insurance.' On the other hand, Arman needed the money as he had a young family and a rather high maintenance wife to satisfy. But of course, that's another story.

* * *

When Harat had to go away on business, he would be happy knowing that his family were safe in their house by the beach. Having completed his business trip, he would make his way down to the docks to find Vaz and ask to be ferried to the beach house at Turan. Vaz was going out fishing each day, so taking a passenger or two, wasn't a problem. When Harat asked Vaz to take him to Turan, Yeva, Vaz's wife would go with them. She always liked a day out on the water and appreciated Harat's jovial company. She enjoyed his wonderful stories, that were always stretched out to fill the length of the trip. She would be cooking up a meal on automatic as she delighted in Harat's intricate weaving of a familiar web. His stories were based on traditional themes but with hilarious variations. Harat on boarding the boat would immediately ask, 'Now what about a story? What haven't we had for a long time? What about the Money Story, or perhaps the Saucepan Story?' There were about eight different stories in total, but they were never told in the same way. They started off the same and finished the same but, in the middle, it was open to Harat's wild imagination. Sometimes the stories would get cleverly interwoven and would start as one story and finish as another. Somehow Samson always finished up crushing the columns with his bare arms but how it got to that state of affairs, was never quite the same. The stories and the way in which they were told, were altered to accommodate the listener. Harat loved an audience and was a master at holding their attention.

At the first Christmas, they had a big party and christened the house 'La Sirène', the French for 'The Mermaid'. Harat had once said that he had seen a beautiful mermaid frolicking in the shallow waters near the rocks at the eastern side of the bay. Everyone knew that it was just his imagination. 'Was she pretty?' someone asked. 'Oh yes she was very pretty but not as pretty as my darling Nanar,' he replied without hesitation as he put his arm around his wife, giving her a big squeeze.

Harat spent much of the day sitting on the upper rooftop balcony reading, writing, and doodling with watercolours or sometimes just simply staring out to sea. He liked to draw from his imagination rather than from life. 'Who wants to paint reality?' he would say. 'It is there in front of you and should be enjoyed at that moment. No, I want to paint from my imagination. It's a world that is alive and has the potential of being, rather than a frozen moment in time.' He was a mediocre painter, and his argument was used to camouflage any inadequacies. He didn't want to be judged as not able to get a good likeness. 'I prefer the 'Abstract' school of painting. I enjoy the added element of time.'

* * *

Those days on his balcony looking out to the golden sand below, hearing the gentle rhythm of the waves and observing through his binoculars the distant seas beyond, allowed Harat to think and plan. He was fearful of the unstable political situation that was developing around him, but happy with the safety and beauty that 'La Sirène' brought into his life.

It was on one of those many happy occasions on his private balcony that Harat looked down at the beach below and saw his wife Nanar lying in the sand reading a book, while Sevan the boy's nanny, played in the water with the twins – Davit and Vahan. Laughter and splashing could be heard above the rhythmic sound of the gentle waves. The sky was blue and cloudless.

Harat's mind drifted back to his childhood. He had grown up as a privileged only child, aware that he would inherit a considerable fortune from his wealthy parents. Seeing Sevan cavorting in the sea with his two sons reminded him of what had happened in the past and what she had once said.

Sevan's mother had been Harat's nanny, and the two families had always been close. Harat's family had been the dominant partners in the relationship, with Sevan's family playing the humble role of service. Their positions were perfectly clear, and it was a simple case of master and servant, but with the utmost of respect from both sides. Sevan's parents lived in a small house a few minutes' walk away but Sevan's mother, Nareh would always be at the big house from breakfast through to the evening meal. Nareh would often sit at the table with Harat's parents at lunch time but would serve and clear away the evening meal before going home to look after her husband.

Harat had been born in early September, just three months before Sevan. Times were extremely difficult for Sevan's mother Nareh, as her husband had died suddenly of a heart attack, just two months before she gave birth to her beautiful little daughter. After her husband's funeral, Harat's parents insisted that the heavily pregnant Nareh should come and live in the big house with them. They cleared a room for her, and Sevan was born in the big house on Christmas day. Nareh became the live-in nanny to both Harat and Sevan who grew up together like brother and sister, but just three months apart. After a year or so, Nareh decided to return to her little house nearby. Early each morning, Nareh would take Sevan to the big house to be part of the family and play with Harat. Nareh and subsequently her daughter Sevan, retained the use of the room in the big house. Often, after lunch, they would sleep there for an hour or so, especially during the hot summer months. The room was referred to as 'Nareh's room'. When Nareh became ill, she was cared for in that room and eventually died there, peacefully in her sleep. It then became Sevan's room even though she lived in her own house some six minutes' walk away.

* * *

As children, Harat and Sevan shared a personal tutor. They had all their lessons in the big house together. Harat's mother thought that the local schools were well below standard. Sevan was far more diligent than Harat who just wanted to go outside and play. Harat was by no means stupid and picked up things very quickly, but he lacked the concentration that came naturally to Sevan. They learnt to read and write together. As youngsters they behaved just like brother and sister. Fighting, squabbling and being competitive. They shared secrets together and Harat's parents were at pains to ensure that there would be no outward favouritism. However, between the parents, there was an unspoken awareness of their status in life; the thought of status never entered the children's heads. Harat and Sevan saw themselves as equals but different. One was a handsome, spirited young boy and the other an attractive, vivacious young girl.

At the age of thirteen, Harat was sent off to an all-boys boarding school in the English Cotswolds. There, he learnt to become a gentleman and from the other boys he learnt about the birds and bees. Harat was busy with sports and fighting with all the other boys at school, so didn't have time to feel homesick. Sevan, on the other hand, had really missed Harat's company, as she had no other school friends to play with. At the end of the first term, Harat returned home for two weeks holiday. His voice had started to break, and he noticed quite a change in Sevan both physically and hormonally. He felt rather attracted to her lithe form and found himself peeking at her when she bathed or slept during the middle of the day. She was aware of his behaviour and she even subtlety glanced at him without him knowing. Nothing happened physically between them even though they were young teenagers living under the same roof.

At the end of the first holidays, both families came to see Harat off. First a boat to Venice from where he would catch the train to London. He was dressed in his school uniform and looked most dapper. When it came to his turn to say goodbye to Sevan, it was quite natural that they

30

would give each other a warm embrace. As he gave her a hug, he felt a tinge of excitement as he smelt her hair brushing his face. She innocently whispered in his ear so no one else could hear 'Come back soon. I'm going to miss you.' These words played on his mind the whole journey back to school but were quickly forgotten as he became involved with the rough and tumble of boarding school life.

A great deal had happened since Sevan had spoken these words, but they had never completely been left behind. He often thought about what might have been, had he followed his dreams.

From his balcony, Harat delighted at the sight of his wife Nanar sitting on the sand reading, while Sevan played in the water with the twins.

* * *

The twins, Davit and Vahan were soon to be fourteen years old, when early one morning, Sevan arrived at the house with two coy Armenian sisters in tow. As agreed with Harat and Nanar, Sevan had brought them along to help with the daily chores around the big house. Hripsime fifteen and her younger sister Sara, who had just turned twelve, were Sevan's nieces.

The two peasant sisters had managed to escape from the horrific massacres of Armenians that had taken place some eight months prior in Diyarbakir, a town in south-eastern Turkey near the Syrian border. The girls had witnessed the massacre firsthand but had managed to escape through the woods. Their parents and baby sister had been killed but somehow, they had managed to flee with only the clothes that they were wearing. By the cover of night, they had made their way cautiously through treacherous pathways, making sure to avoid the Turkish rebel soldiers and marauding guerrillas who inhabited the dense forests. They reached the relative safety of the Syrian border via a town called Mardin. With the help of a Kurdish family, they had managed to cross into Syria at the border town of Ad Darbasiyah. 'Here, wear this black niqab,' the Kurdish woman told Hripsime. 'As you are now fifteen years old, you will need to pose as a Muslim woman, with only your eyes exposed. Best if you Sara, wear a head scarf and make sure you hide the cross around your neck.' The girls spoke an Armenian dialect and a bit of Kurdish which served them well until they had reached the Syrian border. Once they crossed the border it was hand signals only. They kept close together and avoided people as much as possible. In small villages the people took pity on them and gave them scraps of food. They lived rough and totally on their wits, killing wild fowl and rodents for protein.

They made their way to Aleppo where they stayed for a couple of weeks near the riverbanks. Although they were peasant girls who had never been to school, they found security and anonymity by wearing the black niqab and head scarf given to them by the Kurdish woman in Mardin. Tired, hungry and with no money they arrived in the coastal town of Latakia. They knew that they had an aunt called Sevan who lived in Constantinople. Sevan had been to visit her sister Kohar in Diyarbakir about ten months before and had spoken about life in Constantinople. She had desperately pleaded with her sister Kohar to come with her husband and their three daughters to Constantinople. Although Kohar had been keen to go, her husband was not as his brother and parents lived in Diyarbakir. 'At least send the two older girls to me' Sevan had pleaded to her sister. 'Sara is too young, and Hripsime won't go by herself. Perhaps next year if God is willing,' replied Kohar. Little was Kohar to know that fate would bring the girls to Sevan in Constantinople but in the most desperate of circumstances.

From Latakia in Syria, the sisters managed to bargain with a fisherman to take them to Cyprus. They cooked and cleaned for the Greek crew. By this time, the girls had removed their Muslim dress and became Christians again. The crew knew them as the two little Armenians and somehow treated them with the utmost respect. Mind you, the girls were street smart, and knew how to defend themselves. Sara only ever reached four feet eleven inches in height and could neither read nor write in any language. It was her feisty character shining through those penetrating eyes that would hold her in good stead throughout her life. One night, a young fisherman tried to rape Hripsime pushing her to the ground. Sara heard her screams for help and from behind, hit the young man on the head with a saucepan. The young man was knocked out cold and didn't move. He woke up the next morning with a severe headache. The captain of the boat and the rest of the crew took the side of the two young, spirited girls and were very sad to see them depart Cyprus.

Next, a boat took the young sisters through the Aegean Sea all the way to Constantinople.

* * *

The two young girls were hungry, dirty, and dishevelled as they knocked on Sevan's door. They didn't know her address but by continually asking for her by name, they eventually found her. They had slept rough in the shadows of Constantinople for a couple of weeks, avoiding the police and strange men.

Sevan immediately recognizing the two girls, ushered them into her house, letting them sleep for three days before bathing and feeding them. They then talked for two nights about all that had happened. They described the brutality of the massacre at Diyarbakir and how they had hidden in a chicken coup. They spoke of their mother and father and how they had been tortured before being burnt alive in their own home. They told her of their journey walking through the back roads of Syria and catching fishing boats to Constantinople via Cyprus.

Sevan told them that even though she had a small house they could stay with her. She told them about the Kaspar household and how she would introduce them to Harat, Nanar and the twins. She suggested that they might like to make themselves useful around the property and with the cooking.

While the girls slept, Sevan darned and washed their clothes. She bathed the girls, brushed their hair and bandaged Sara's ankle.

Finally, they were ready to be introduced to the Kaspar household.

5

Vahan's Departure

When Sevan arrived at the Kaspar residence, she took her two nieces through the imposing front doors, into the impressive circular entrance hall. The girls were amazed at the glittering chandelier that hung from the domed ceiling. The clerestory windows above allowed the filtered light to dance on the crystal prisms and pendalogues. The hall was large and used for soirées for up to eighty people. Under the magnificent chandelier was a highly polished, circular pedestal mahogany table with centrally placed, a large crystal vase of freshly cut flowers. The inlaid marble floor created an air of opulence that the girls had only dreamt about. Around one side of the circular hall, the marble stair spiralled up towards a second-floor ornate wrought iron balcony and three sets of double doors placed symmetrically opposite the main entrance door. On the ground floor opposite the marble stair was an antique French chaise longue. This stunning oversized and very elaborate chaise longue was of solid mahogany construction, upholstered in white leather with diamond tufted buttoning. The chaise longue was surrounded by large Kentia palms as a backdrop, throughout the hallway were statues of Greek maidens and gods sculpted from the finest Carrara marble.

Sevan pointed to the chaise longue and suggested that the girls sit there for a minute or two while she went to speak to Nanar. Sevan found Nanar in the small drawing room reading the morning paper and asked to have a word with her. She had previously explained what her two nieces had been through, and Nanar had agreed to help by giving the two peasant girls simple tasks around the house. Without hesitation, Nanar went to the hallway to formally greet the two girls. The girls were totally unaccustomed to formal greetings, so Nanar broke the ice by giving each girl a big hug and a kiss on each cheek. The girls were startled as they came from a peasant background where a kiss was reserved for amorous and flirtatious behaviour rather than a casual greeting.

'You are both most welcome to come and be part of our family,' said Nanar. 'Any family of Sevan's is part of our family too. We will find you some work to do and I'm sure that both Davit and Vahan will be delighted to have you around. Today you must go with Sevan to get some more clothes as I understand that you couldn't bring anything with you.' This was Nanar's way of telling the two girls that Sevan had fully explained the situation and that no more need be said. Thus started a new chapter in all of their lives.

* * *

When the twins first met Sevan's two nieces there was an instant spark between Sara and the two boys. Hripsime was rather circumspect, while the younger Sara was more natural and feistier. Each day Sevan set both girls simple tasks around the house while the boys were being home tutored. Sara couldn't wait for the boys to be set free from their lessons so they could all play games in the extensive grounds. They climbed trees and swam in the lake. They caught frogs and made-up plays together. Hripsime would stay with her aunt while the others played. The boys vied for Sara's attention; she enjoyed every moment of it. She soon left behind the memories of the horrific massacres of Diyarbakir and the terrifying journey to freedom, though the nightmares continued for some years to come. Hripsime being that much older and of a more sensitive nature, carried her burden with sadness. At the end of each evening after Sevan and Hripsime had cleared away the evening meal, they called out for Sara and went back to Sevan's house to sleep.

The years went by, and life was good. The two boys matured into fine young men with lean handsome bodies. They regarded Sara as a sister whilst Hripsime stayed distant. Unlike their father who had been sent away to boarding school in England, the boys had private tutors who came to the house. Although Sara was intelligent and smart, she never learnt to read or write as she lacked concentration. The boys taught her simple maths and how to use an abacus. Her brain was quick, agile, and very matter of fact. What she lacked in emotion and matters of the heart, she more than made up in terms of common sense and simple logic.

Davit, who was the outward going one of the twins demanded more of her attention. She liked his strong personality and charisma but tried to hide her favouritism. Although she admired Vahan's sensitivity and the way he presented her with headbands made from daisy chains or reading his poetry to her, she couldn't help showing her attraction towards Davit. Vahan became aware of the attraction between Sara and Davit, becoming despondent and distant from them. They played mean games towards him like hiding his clothes when they went swimming in the lake. It became obvious to all that Sara and Davit were becoming closer and that Vahan was on the outer.

Summer holidays were spent as a family at the beach house at Turan. Harat went there whenever business permitted. He loved being with his family, regarding Sevan as a sister and the two girls as his nieces. Standing on his balcony he looked down at the beach and saw Sevan taking the sun or talking with Nanar while Davit and Sara played water games in the sea. Often, he could see Vahan sitting on the sand with his head buried in a book. Vahan had become an avid reader, reading everything that he could get his hands on. He read the classics, enjoying Shakespeare and Dickens, or the Russian authors such as Gogol, Tolstoy and in particular, Dostoyevsky. Harat had accepted that Vahan was quite different to his brother Davit or himself. Vahan was studious and Harat could see him becoming a teacher or perhaps a librarian. Literature would be Vahan's life.

* * *

It was something of a surprise to Harat that early one evening, while the others had gone for a walk along the sand to explore the rocks at the other end of the beach, Vahan took the opportunity to approach his father, telling him of his intentions to study theology at the Armenian Catholic monastery off the coast of Venice.

'The monastery at San Lazzaro is a small island in the Venetian lagoon, and has been home to the monastery of the Mekhitarists, an Armenian Catholic congregation since 1717,' explained Vahan. It came as somewhat of a bombshell to Harat, but he could see that Vahan had totally made up his mind on the matter and, as long as he did it to the best of his ability, he knew it would all work out for the best. Harat quite liked the idea that one of his sons might become an archbishop. Harat always set his sights as high as possible.

'When do you think you will be going,' asked Harat in a matter-of-fact tone.

'I would like to get going in the next week or so,' replied Vahan. 'I have had an invitation from the Abbot, Artoush Sarkissian, to join his new intake of novices this September. I would like to get there a couple weeks earlier to settle in.'

Harat said, 'Then I will tell the others over dinner this evening and I'm sure that they will be happy for you.' Harat tried hard not to show his disappointment, but Vahan assured him that it was what he wanted to do.

That evening over dinner, Harat told the others of Vahan's intentions and that they should be happy for him. Of course, it came as a big surprise. Nanar couldn't keep away the tears at the thought of her son going away and perhaps never coming back. 'I may not be suited to be a religious person, but I must go and find out,' consoled Vahan. 'After the first three years I will be sent home to make the decision as to whether I will join the order or whether I will leave altogether. I will have plenty of time to think carefully about it.' He showed remarkable maturity for a young man that had just turned nineteen.

* * *

That night, as Vahan lay on his bed thinking about his decision, he heard the door handle being slowly turned. It was Sara who quietly entered his room and silently came to lie down beside him. She snuggled up to him and softly whispered, 'I don't want you to go. You will come back, won't you?'

'I will have to see what happens,' said Vahan. 'Look after Davit won't you.'

She kissed him gently on the cheek and vanished back into the night. He knew he would miss that warmth of her body and the scent of her cotton night dress.

* * *

All was quiet at the beach house as the laughter had gone on holidays. Harat could stand it no longer and desperately wanted to go home. The days appeared much longer as time went slowly. Finally, Vaz came with his fishing boat at the arranged time to take the family back home. Even the calmness of the waters and the length of the mast's shadow seemed to exaggerate the sadness that was felt by everyone. Suddenly, Harat decided to break the ice, reaching for his mouth organ to play some happy tunes. They all sang some lively sea shanties while drinking rather too much apricot brandy as time seemed to gather pace. They arrived back at the dock happy and a bit tipsy just as the sun was setting.

The next week went slowly for all of them except Vahan who was busy organising his trip. There was so much to do and little time to do it in. The house was quiet as they waited for the imminent departure of one of their company. Sevan and her nieces went back to the cottage every evening rather than staying at the big house.

Harat came and went frequently on business trips, but everyone was used to that. He seemed to have a bag permanently packed but it was understood by all, that he would be away for only a matter of days. The house would be quiet without him. However, the family knew that he would return shortly, showering gifts and much laughter. It was not knowing when or perhaps if, Vahan would be returning that put the household into disarray.

* * *

For Vahan's last evening, Harat and Nanar organised a farewell soirée. Sevan and the girls prepared the main circular entrance hall for the reception of the fifty-five invited guests. With family, close friends and senior staff, there would be a total of seventy-four people. The dress code was to be semi-formal. A small dance band was hired for loosening up the occasion. The Champagne flowed as exotic finger food arrived and was consumed with alacrity. Harat would be the master of ceremonies and of course tell his jokes and stories to the delight of his audience. The party spilt out onto the garden where some tables and chairs had been placed. Harat informed them that the party would have to end at 9:30pm as Vahan's boat was to sail from the dock at 7:30am the next morning. 'He hasn't even started packing,' said Harat, 'but knowing Vahan, it will take him all of thirty-five seconds.' They all laughed except for Vahan who didn't like being the centre of attention.

Like his father, Davit excelled at parties, circulating among the guests, and making them all feel special. 'So good of you to come. It wouldn't be a proper sending off if you hadn't been able to make it.'

Vahan, on the other hand, didn't have a clue on how to make small talk. Luckily Hripsime had similar problems at parties. Often, they would spend much of the time conversing with each other, rather than circulating the throng of partygoers. Although Hripsime didn't have the intellect of Vahan, they shared a sense of safety in each other's company. Davit and Sara flitted from guest to guest.

At precisely 9:30pm on the dot Harat called the party together to jointly wish Vahan a safe journey and then thanked them all for coming.

'Well that all went off rather well,' said Harat after the last guest had left. 'We had all better get off to bed as there's a boat sailing to Venice early tomorrow morning. We wouldn't want to miss the boat as they say in English.'

For Vahan that last night seemed to last for ever. He couldn't sleep for excitement of venturing into the unknown. The moon was full and the sound of a nightingale filled the air. Finally, Vahan managed to sleep for a few hours but was awoken at 5:30am by one of the servants.

* * *

The whole family came down to the docks to see Vahan off. Harat was telling jokes while Sevan consoled Nanar. One by one they hugged Vahan and wished him a safe journey. When Sara hugged him and kissed him on both cheeks, she whispered softly 'Please come back. It won't be the same without you.' Those simple words confused him and were to haunt him for the rest of his life.

Eventually Vahan walked up the gang plank and looked back to see his family huddled together on the dock. Sara was arm in arm with Davit and Sevan and Hripsime consoled each other. His father had his arm around his tearful mother. Little did he know that he would never see either of his parents again.

Finally, they all seemed to disappear into the distance as he realised that he was on his way to his new life.

6

Venezia

The small boat headed west as Vahan sat on the deck with the sun on his back. The waters were calm, but with the wind behind them, they made steady progress without the sensation of any effort.

* * *

Vahan got out a book to read but his thoughts got in the way. He wondered if he had made the right decision. He had an enquiring mind that needed to be exercised. Being at home with his family, he found no challenge to his thoughts. He was going to where he would encounter people who questioned life. He was an explorer of the intellect, but only in specific areas. Physicians explore the workings of the body; scientists ask questions about the laws of the universe and how things work, but Vahan wanted to know why. Sir Isaac Newton described the Laws of Gravity, but Vahan would ask, 'Why do we have gravity?' He looked forward to examining philosophical and theological questions. He may not come to any conclusions, but in some small way, he might progress the examination to uncover new insights. He was keen to enter the realm of serious debate.

He likened his path to that of an athlete who trained to maintain fitness, rather than run in a competitive race. The race would be run and there would be one winner and a number of losers. Winners may bathe in the glory of winning but eventually they too would become old and infirm. Vahan was in training to keep his mind agile and fit. He intended this to be a way of life for the rest of his time on the planet.

Vahan bathed in the soft sunlight and managed to read just two books throughout the trip. The first he read was *The Birth of Tragedy* by the German philosopher Friedrich Nietzsche. He read the later edition which had only recently been published. Sailing through the Greek islands to Crete, he could sense Nietzsche's discussion of the history of the tragic form and the introduction of an intellectual dichotomy between the Dionysian and the Apollonian.

Then Vahan read a novel called *The Idiot* by Fyodor Dostoyevsky. It had been first published between 1868–9, as a serial in the *The Russian Messenger* journal. The main character, Prince Myshkin, was portrayed as a most honourable man, full of goodness and kindness. Vahan felt empathetic to the prince and wanted to emulate him.

After a most peaceful sail through the Aegean Sea, they stopped for a few days to pick up supplies and change crew, before making their way through the Ionian Sea to the Adriatic coast of Italy. They hugged the Italian coast, being escorted all the way by a pod of dolphins. Vahan expected that it wasn't the same pod as their numbers fluctuated from just three, to around twenty-three.

* * *

The boat finally made its way into the Venice lagoon and docked near to Piazza San Marco. There, Vahan disembarked and thanked each member of the crew with a warm embrace. They had all become fond of this gentle soul and wished him well with his studies. One of the crew, a Pietro Caminiti, gave Vahan his address in Venice. 'You come and visit me,' he said in pidgin English, adding in his staccato accent. 'My mama, she cook good. She like cook for you. One day, you come see family. I know plenty people. I get boat for you.'

Vahan made his way into the square and was amazed at the splendour of its fine architecture. Abbot, Artoush Sarkissian had sent detailed instructions on what to do when he arrived in Venice. In those days, it wasn't possible to know an exact time or even date of arrival. Much depended on the wind. The Abbot explained in his instructions

that he would send a gondolier to pick up Vahan at midday each day.
This gondolier would wait for fifteen minutes at the entrance of the
Basilica di San Marco but if Vahan wasn't there, the gondolier would
return the next day. He told Vahan that he would be able to recognise
this particular gondolier as he would be wearing a red beret and that
Vahan should wear a knotted white handkerchief around his left wrist.
Abbot Artoush had drawn a little map with detailed notes describing
nearby items that Vahan might like to see. The map highlighted churches
and bridges as well as items like the Bibloteca National Marciana, all
with copious notes. Abbot Artoush also explained that once Vahan had
joined the order as a Novice, he would not be allowed to leave the island.
He suggested that perhaps Vahan would like to appear at the rendezvous
once he had completed his excursions around the City of Venice.
If he didn't make the rendezvous for a matter of fourteen days from the
11th of May onwards, it would mean that he, Vahan, had decided not to
join the Order.

* * *

Vahan took full advantage of the Abbot's suggestion and was impressed
by the magnificent buildings, the network of canals and bridges, as well
as the many pieces of fine sculpture in the piazzas. The spaces and forms
spoke to him of music. They spoke of Antonio Vivaldi. He could hear
the contrapuntal scales as he ascended and then descended the canal
bridges.

Of special interest to him was the Basilica of San Giorgio Maggiore,
designed by Andrea Palladio, an important 16th century Italian
architect who had written four volumes, setting out systematic rules for
architecture and construction. First published in 1570, they remain as a
set of rules, valued by architects around the world. Vahan appreciated
their simplicity and sense of order.

Vahan understood the difference between simplicity and naivety.
Simplicity is something that one strives for; it encompasses condensed
complex agendas. Sometimes a simple design will be arrived at by having
gone full circle; first adding and then eliminating the superfluous. Vahan
experienced first-hand the many fine edifices, and appreciated how they
addressed their contextual magnificence with confidence.

By day, Vahan visited most of the main places of worship, the galleries, and the libraries of Venice. By night, he observed the bars and other bawdy establishments. He found the churches, their history with their splendid ornate architecture, more impressive than the bars. In truth he felt uncomfortable in the bars but having walked all day he needed to rest. He was frequently propositioned by young ladies, and some not so young. He didn't take up their offers even though some said that seeing he was so handsome they would offer their services at half price. 'What's a fine young man like you doing in a place like this?' he was asked by a strange looking female with black lips, a white painted face and a shock of red hair that made her look even taller than she really was. She wore a green velvet sleeveless full-length dress, black lace gloves up to her elbows and tattoos of serpents swirling up the rest of her arms then twisting around her neck as if to throttle her.

'I'm just here to look at the fine buildings and art,' replied Vahan innocently.

'Well come back to my place and I'll show you something rather special,' said the woman.

Vahan declined the offer but wondered what it was that she wanted to show him. He never did find out that she was in fact a man, who acted as the bait for a group of rather debauched individuals, coming from the darker side of Venice. After nightfall, many of the nobility and wealthier merchants frequented this area in search of depravity and vice.

* * *

On the sixth day, Vahan found the gondolier with the red beret and together they climbed into his gondola to take him to the monastery at San Lazzaro degli Armeni. The gondolier was a large man with a barrel chest. Once he had met Vahan, he exchanged his beret for a black one, thus looking like all the other gondoliers. He introduced himself as Giacomo, saying that he was hired by the Abbot to transport people to and from the island. His bushy black eyebrows and full black beard together with his formidable stature made him appear a real force to be reconciled with. The island only housed the monastery and a few ancillary buildings. It was a fully fortified island with ramparts all the way round. The only way in was through a set of gates into a small docking station. Then, there were more locked gates that could only be unlocked from the inside. Giacomo was the only outside person that knew where the hidden bell was located. He removed a particular stone, took out a large handbell and rang it three times. After a minute or so, someone from inside, looked through a keyhole and recognizing the gondolier, opened the gates just enough to let Vahan through.

'Ah, master Kaspar' said the duty monk as he ushered Vahan into the compound. 'We thought that you might have changed your mind. Did you manage to have a good look around our beautiful city of Venezia? There is a lot to see, especially for a young man. Personally, the smell of the canals gets to me after three days. You must have a more tolerant nose than mine or perhaps not such a good sense of smell,' he chuckled and then continued 'Nonetheless, come this way and take a seat and I will let Abbot Sarkissian know that you are here.'

The monk led Vahan to a small austere office with a visitor's chair, a desk and much larger chair behind the desk. The monk indicated which seat he should sit in and told him to wait. Then from his pocket the monk got a large key to let himself into the inner monastery by way of a solid looking door at the side of the desk. Vahan waited. He had been half asleep when suddenly woken by the rattling of a key in the lock. A small, wizened man, in a black hooded habit and with the most vibrant eyes appeared from the door that the other monk had previously gone through.

'I'm Artoush Sarkissian, the abbot of this monastery,' said the diminutive man in a soft but clear voice. 'I'm sorry to have kept you waiting, but I had just started my hour of silent meditations.' He then explained that it was his task to make ready all novices, preparing them for the taking of vows to become fully-fledged members of the brotherhood. 'The instruction process takes the best part of three years and at the end of this period, you will need to decide if you want to take your vows or leave the Order all together. If you complete the preparations, you may decide to leave the Order for an agreed amount of time before taking your pledge. However, if you decide to leave before you complete the preparation then you may leave but you will not be allowed to return. The decisions are yours, but the consequences are set by us.'

The abbot explained the history, purpose, and secret nature of the brotherhood. He failed to mention the danger and negative forces coming from the outside world towards the brotherhood, and how the Order had originated from Christian Armenia, surrounded by Muslim communities, who threatened their Christian beliefs. The Armenians were seen as allies of the Crusaders but in truth they were overrun by the Crusaders and forced to assist them against the infidels. Prior to the Crusades, the Armenians got on well with their Muslim neighbours, with a relationship based on mutual trust and dependencies.

* * *

After about an hour of discussion, the abbot formally invited Vahan to step through the threshold of the door into the sacrosanct, saying 'Please call me Artoush'. The invitation was accepted and Artoush led the way.

7

San Lazzaro degli Armeni

Once they had passed through the doorway into the sanctum of the monastery, Artoush locked the door behind them with the key attached to a belt around his waist. Having locked the door, he put the key back into his pocket.

'Come this way,' said Artoush leading Vahan to a small, cavernous anti chamber. The first thing we must do is get you fixed up with the right vestments and unfortunately, we must cut off those golden curly locks. Please sit here and I will get a razor blade, scissors, and some water.'

Artoush came back shortly with a neatly folded brown habit, some clean undergarments and a cross for Vahan to wear.

'Now let's get started on those locks of yours,' said Artoush and proceeded to cut away at Vahan's hair. As Vahan's hair fell gently to the ground, Artoush chanted some prayers as if to ask for forgiveness. Suddenly Artoush let out a cry that Vahan thought was of anguish.

'What's the matter?' asked Vahan feeling that he hadn't done anything untoward.

'Nothing wrong,' replied Artoush as he continued to shave Vahan's head until he was completely bald. 'Put on this hooded robe and cross and we will go and find your room.'

Vahan followed Artoush down a wide corridor. The corridor was lined with locked doors that had a square, grilled viewing panel at a height to look into the room, but only when you got close to the door.

It reminded Vahan of a prison. He had never been to a prison but had read detailed descriptions in several books.

They arrived at a door without a symbol on it and Artoush told Vahan that this would be his room. He gave Vahan a large key and told him that it would be his responsibility to look after the key. He informed Vahan that personal possessions, although accepted, were usually frowned upon. He suggested that Vahan should go and meditate in the room for an hour before dinner, which would be served at 5pm in the room at the end of the corridor.

'Best to keep your door locked at all times, unless you are actually going through it,' said Artoush in his jocular tone. He then disappeared back down the corridor taking Vahan's old clothes and bags for safe keeping.

* * *

Vahan unlocked the door and entered his room. He relocked the door behind him and then closed his eyes to get a better feel of the space. The heavy sound of silence penetrated his consciousness. This was to be home for next three years.

The room was sparsely furnished with a writing table, a chair, and a bed with a small bedside locker. A square, high-level window allowed only a glimpse of the sky. At the foot of the bed were some neatly folded woollen blankets and on the wall above the head of a bed was an Armenian cross. On the table was a candle stick holder with a new candle. In the locker, were some thick woollen socks with hardened soles, to be worn as shoes. There was no cupboard for clothes as he was wearing all the clothes that he was going to have for the next three years.

During the interview, earlier that afternoon, Artoush had explained the daily routine. He had told Vahan that when he goes for dinner at 5pm, he should take the small candle with him. There in the dining room would be a flame for him to light his candle and to place it in front of him while he ate. At the end of the dinner, he could take the candle back to his room to read by before going to sleep. He would be woken by a series of bells at 4am and in silence, he would go to the washing and toilets areas. He would be expected to be back in his room for private meditation by 4:35am and a bell would be rung at 5:45am for morning breakfast starting at 5:47am and to be eaten in silence. Throughout breakfast, hymns and prayers would be sung by three monks. As Vahan was a novice, he wouldn't be expected to sing but would learn about the chanting during his noviciate.

After breakfast and washing his hands, Vahan would join the other two novices and Artoush for singing and joint intellectual pursuits. The Order was not a community that had taken strict vows of silence, but they tried to keep speech to a minimum, always considering carefully what needed and, more importantly, what didn't need to be conveyed.

In total there were twelve monks and three novices. The monks had specific roles and in the afternoons the novices were assigned particular tasks to assist the monks as required. The monastery was completely self-sufficient. The produce from the gardens together with freshly laid eggs and some goat's milk were sufficient to keep the Brotherhood well nourished. On odd occasions they gave their surplus of supplies to Giacomo the gondolier to distribute to the poor and needy of Venice. Giacomo was their only link with the outside world and even he never came past the outer gate. He was the only outsider that knew where the bell was hidden. The monks occasionally required items from the outside world. They could purchase such items with funds that had been invested in a Jewish bank in Venice. They offered a steady rate of interest, and the fund was continually growing from year to year. This had been the case for almost 180 years, so the monks weren't exactly short of a penny or two.

* * *

Each morning, the three novices would meet with Artoush and some of the monks. The monks wore black hooded habits while the novices wore brown. Each monk had an Armenian cross around his neck and a ring on their left little finger signifying their importance within the community. The novices had smaller crosses, with no rings on their fingers.

After another hour-long meditation, the novices would engage in their philosophical and theological dialogues, to be followed by training for skills that they could pursue once they had become ordained. Some would become scribes, while others translated ancient biblical manuscripts. The artistically talented, would progress to the restoration of sacred icons and manuscripts to their original glory. Some monks restored both ancient and classical sheet music, others made medieval instruments to perform on.

Although being predominately an Armenian Catholic community, they were encouraged to examine and compare other religions, doctrines, and philosophies. There was a very extensive library of ancient books, the learning of ancient languages was a prerequisite. Vahan was a very diligent student and keen to discover as much as possible. He learnt to read ancient Hebrew, Greek and Armenian within a very short space of time. This impressed Artoush, who recognised and was often astounded by Vahan's abilities. Artoush fought hard against showing any favouritism amongst the novices.

Sometimes, after the hour-long meditation, the three novices went with Artoush to the library for their studies. Artoush would guide them deeper into their chosen field of enquiry. Artoush with his fine, enquiring mind, would lead them into the unknown rather than teach them known facts. He was an educator in the true sense of the word. He told them, 'The word education comes from the Latin "eDucare". The Latin prefix "e" meaning "out of" while Ducare is from the verb "to lead". An educator leads out from the known into the unknown. We are exploring the unknown to expand the body of knowledge.'

As exercises in thinking, they would explore many philosophical and religious issues. They discussed issues such as 'Free Will' versus 'Determinism' or the social role of Catholicism. They investigated the role of the Confessional within the Catholic Church and tried to reconcile inconsistencies within the Church and Christ's teachings. If in truth, it is 'More difficult for a rich man to pass into the kingdom of heaven than for a camel to pass through an eye of a needle'; how can the Catholic Church and for that matter their own Order justify such wealth? They explored notions of love and forgiveness within society. They examined Truth, Beauty, and Love within art and poetry.

In the afternoon sessions the novices assisted the monks with their practical tasks. Some were taught the skills of gardening, cooking and the brewing of fortified wines, while others learnt and assisted with the scribing of ancient religious texts and the binding of books.

Vahan excelled at both the reproduction of iconography as well as the writing and playing of religious music from the past. There was so much to learn, and time went quickly.

* * *

It was about nine months into his noviciate that Artoush asked Vahan to come and see him in his room after evening prayers. 'I have an important matter to discuss with you. Don't be concerned, I am extremely pleased with your progress,' said Artoush. In fact, Artoush had never come across such an exemplary student, but he didn't feel comfortable telling Vahan such. 'I have some, what I think should be excellent, apricot brandy that needs tasting before we bottle it. I would like your opinion on it.'

After evening prayers Vahan made his way to the end of the long corridor to Artoush's room. He knew where the room was located but had never been inside it. Artoush kept the room always locked and did all his own cleaning. Vahan felt quite honoured to be invited to Artoush's sanctuary and as he gently knocked on the door, he had no notion of what was to come.

Artoush unlocked the door and opened it just enough for Vahan to step inside. The room was much the same as all the other rooms only considerably larger and stuffed with documents and antiquated books. Lit candles were spread around the room to create pools of light. There was a small alcove which housed a small table with two chairs. On the table Artoush had set the bottle of apricot brandy with two glasses.

'Come and sit. I have some questions to ask of you.' said Artoush.

Vahan sat down and Artoush poured him some brandy to taste. They agreed that it was exceptionally fine and then Artoush poured some more into both of their glasses.

'The question I have to ask of you is this,' said Artoush. Vahan waited with anticipation, wondering what such a fine brain would be asking of him.

'When you arrived at the monastery some nine months ago, while cutting your hair, I noticed that you have a birthmark behind your left ear lobe. My question to you is: Do you know of anyone else that has the same marking?'

Vahan explained that both he and his identical twin brother had been born with this imperfection and that the only other person that had it, was his father Harat. 'I'm not exactly sure if he was born with it but I understand that it is something that has been passed on through some of the males of our family.'

Artoush looked very concerned and said, 'Well if that is the case then we are all in a very dangerous position.'

'What do you mean?' asked Vahan. 'We have done nothing wrong so why are we in danger?'

Artoush sat back in his chair and started to explain the situation.

'You see I am also one of the males with such an imperfection as you call it. I too inherited it from my father. He passed away some twelve years ago, leaving behind me, my identical twin brother, who lives near Yerevan the capital of Armenia and our older sister Miriam, who lives in Venice. About five years ago, I decided to investigate this phenomenon about the birthmark and have come up with some startling information. Apart from my father and my twin brother, you are the first person that I have met that also has this marking.' Artoush pulled back the hood of his habit and exposed the mark behind his left ear. 'You see we may be related and there are forces out there that want to eliminate anyone with this birthmark. I suspect that there could be as few as a handful of males left with such markings and because most people have hair around their temples it is difficult for them to be identified. Not all males will pass on the markings to their sons, so the numbers are relatively small and more importantly unidentified.'

'So why are we in danger?' asked Vahan.

'My research has taken me back to biblical times and beyond,' replied Artoush. 'It appears that the first text that identifies a person with this marking was King David, the second king of Israel and Judah. King David, as you well know, is a central person in many holy doctrines and appears in the Islamic scripture as a link in the chain of prophets that preceded Muhammad. It is thought that Christ may well have also been linked to King David but so far this link has no certainty or proof. My readings suggest that Christ may have also had these markings behind his left ear but of course he, having no children, his marking died with him on the cross and not passed on. My theory but it still needs confirmation, is that Joseph the father of Christ had been previously married and had a son from his first marriage. In those days, getting remarried was not against the law but frowned upon even if the first wife had died.' Artoush sighed while taking a deep breath. He paused and then continued.

'I have discovered a secret Aramaic text that alludes to some ancient religious manuscripts that were once held in the city of Ani, a ruined medieval Armenian city, now situated in the Turkish province of Kars. The city was devastated by an earthquake in 1319 but it is thought that the manuscript had previously been faithfully copied by some scribes and that the facsimiles were deposited for safe keeping, in a vault in the Armenian Holy Church at Etchmiadzin, which is now considered the Vatican of the Armenian Church. In 1604 Etchmiadzin was plundered by the Safavids and that is when holy relics, scribed stones and manuscripts were taken out of the cathedral to be stored in New Julfa, now part of Iran. More recently and it is not known exactly when or where, these copies of the ancient manuscripts were taken from New Julfa to be hidden in a church not far from Yerevan. These documents are of paramount importance to both Christians and other religions. They are purported to show that Christ and other prophets are descendants of King David.'

'How exactly does this relate to us?' asked Vahan. 'Why would we be in danger?'

'Well, you see,' said Artoush with excitement in his voice, 'I have been reading some obscure texts from the holy library at Etchmiadzin, that make reference to the lineage of the prophets back to King David. They talk about the people who carry the lineage, can all be identified by a marking behind their left ear. It implies that Joseph, the earthly father of Christ had these markings.'

'So why would we be under some sort of threat?' asked Vahan. 'Surely, we would be revered by all mankind.'

'Not at all,' replied Artoush. 'If this knowledge gets out then all hell will break lose. The power of the Vatican in Rome would be greatly diminished if it was possible to prove that a person or people related to Christ currently walked upon this earth. It is in no one's best interest that the manuscript is found. They will all want the problem to go away, and you know what that means for us.'

'Wouldn't we be safer locked up in here? asked Vahan. 'Out there, we would be a lot more obvious.'

'I suspect that there is an informer amongst us that has already leaked your arrival and now lives amongst us. I have my suspicions of who might be the informer, but I can't be sure. Someone within the monastery has seen your markings and no doubt the word has got out.'

'How do you know that it has already been leaked?' asked Vahan.

'My sister Miriam who lives in the township of Venice, is the only one I have ever told. She is good friends of Giacomo our gondolier and is in fact his landlady. The other day Giacomo told her that he had been approached by some shady characters and asked if he had transported a man with such markings to this island? Of course, having only seen you with a full head of hair, he could quite honestly deny any transportations of such a marked person. These shady characters have managed to get it out of someone from within these walls that you are here. They have threatened Giacomo to help get some of the thugs into here to do their foul business. Once they are inside, they will not only find out about you but will see that I too have the markings. They will want to eliminate me and any of the research papers that I have gathered.'

'What are we going to do?' asked Vahan rather anxiously.

'I have had relatively little time to think about it and have purposely left it till the last minute to tell you what needs to be done,' replied Artoush. 'Now I want you to listen carefully to my instructions as I fear that later tonight is when our adversaries are likely to attack. My sister has sent word through Brother Marco that they have threatened Giacomo with his life unless he helps them get access to the hidden bell. When you hear the bell ring you are to immediately run to the northern ramparts. There, you will find a spiral stair carved in stone. At the bottom of the stair is a locked door that is just a metre above the sea level. I will give you a key that will open that door. Let yourself out onto the small landing and then as quietly as possible slip into the water. It may be best to take off your habit and drop it and the key into the water. You can swim, can't you?' asked Artoush.

'Yes, I can swim but how far is it to dry land?' asked Vahan.

'It's a good 1,500 metres so take it slowly and make as little noise as possible. The moon is waning, but you should be able to see the outer peninsula of the lagoon. Once you get to the land, you will find a small rowing boat tied to a mooring with a white and blue striped cover. When you untie the cover, you will find a towel and some dry clothes. I have put a large floppy hat for you to wear at all times. No one must see your ear markings. Now remember this address of my sister Miriam who lives in Venice. She has only a small apartment on the third floor and can hide you for a few days. You will be hunted down like vermin. Trust no one and try to get back to your father and brother to warn them of their danger. At this stage the thugs don't know what you look like or anything about your family but news travels fast as I fear that there is a traitor in our midst.'

Vahan nodded to show he understood and then asked 'What about you Artoush? How will you escape? Why don't you come with me?'

'I had thought of that, but I will have to take my chances,' replied Artoush. 'I feel I will have to stay to distract them from you escaping. With a bit of luck, they won't notice that I too have the markings and I will be able to escape later, when the coast has cleared. Wait three days at my sister's house and if I don't get there then make your way as quickly as possible to warn your father and brother of their danger. Don't say anything to anyone about it. Miriam will be expecting you. She knows the situation and will be able to help you.

Suddenly, loud ringing of warning bells could be heard throughout the monastery, with a lot of shouting coming from the entrance gate.

'Quick,' said Artoush. 'They have already come to get you. You must escape. Here is the key to the back gate.' He took a large key from his pocket and handed it to Vahan. 'Good luck my friend. Perhaps we will meet again, perhaps it will be in heaven.' With that Artoush put his fingers delicately on Vahan's forehead head and said 'Go now. Go in peace and go in strength young man.'

Vahan sprinted down the corridor to the door that led to the stone, spiral stair. He locked the door behind himself and ran down the spiral stair to the water's edge. He locked the outer door and stood on the small landing. He removed his heavy habit and with the key placed in the pocket he let go of the habit into the murky but still waters of the lagoon. In his undergarments he slipped into the cold water and quietly but with strength swam to the distant shore.

* * *

Vahan didn't look back but could hear the commotion happening behind him. The night was still but the disturbing sounds from the monastery carried across the black, smooth waters of the lagoon. Tired but safe, Vahan reached the pebble shore. He found the small rowing boat that Artoush had left for him and inside the canvas top he found a towel and some of his clothes that he had been wearing on his arrival at the monastery. Artoush had also left him some fruit and dates to give him energy. As he dried himself in the darkness, he looked back to see flames within many of the rooms of the monastery and then suddenly the sound of a large explosion. He watched helplessly while the fire raged, lighting up both the sky and the water surrounding the island. The sight would have been spectacular if it had not been for the destruction and total devastation that was taking place. Then the sound of another explosion as the fire took hold of the monastery and parts of the roof spiralled high up into the air before falling into the water. Vahan knew that although he had escaped to safety that no one could have possibly survived the heat of the inferno.

Dried and clothed, Vahan hid in a small copse of trees so as not to be visible. The fire had illuminated the whole area and Vahan feared being spotted. He couldn't sleep for fear but at the break of the morning light, he could smell the ash and the smouldering carcass of what had been the monastery. With stealth, he slowly rowed the small dingy away from the island monastery, making sure he hugged the land around the lagoon. He didn't care how long he took to get to his destination, the city of Venice; his first priority was not to be seen. Gradually the acidic smell of the cinders became distant, he started to breathe fresh sweet air again.

56

8

Miriam Sarkissian

The dawn light on the lagoon brought a serenity and calmness. All that could be heard was the gentle lapping of the waves against the small boat and oars gliding through the water. The early morning light highlighted the beautiful city of Venice in the distance and gave Vahan a sense of direction. It was early afternoon before Vahan was knocking gently on Miriam's door. He only hoped that he had remembered the address correctly. 'Who is it?' said Miriam in an anxious tone of voice. 'It's your brother Artoush's friend,' answered Vahan not wanting to say his actual name. Miriam opened the door just enough to let Vahan squeeze through.

* * *

'I am Artoush's sister Miriam,' she said as she ushered him into the small third floor apartment locking the substantial front door behind her. 'You must be Vahan, I was expecting you. You must be exhausted. Don't worry you will be safe here. You must rest for a few days. Take a seat and I will get you something to eat.' She pointed to the small table in the corner of the room that had two seats.

After eating a meal in silence, Vahan asked Miriam if he might have a quick nap as he hadn't slept for thirty-six hours and there seemed a lot to digest.

'Please wake me up in an hour or so otherwise I won't be able to go to sleep later tonight,' asked Vahan who was somewhat in a dazed stupor.

Miriam didn't obey Vahan's request and let him sleep. It was 7:30am the next morning when Vahan finally stirred. He had slept for sixteen hours straight and felt much better for it. Miriam was already awake and doing some household chores.

'Well, you certainly needed that sleep,' said Miriam in her broken Armenian.

'Yes, I must have,' replied Vahan in perfect Italian, 'I didn't realise how tired I was.'

'Come and have some breakfast, then we can talk about what has happened and what we should do next.'

* * *

Vahan had a breakfast of fruit and yogurt, followed by a slice of home-made bread that he dunked into some sweet, black coffee.

Miriam asked him to tell her what had happened.

He related in full detail the events of the previous day. Miriam listened intently but her face kept calm and pensive.

'So, are you sure there weren't any survivors from the blast?' asked Miriam.

'I can't say for certain but with the raging heat from the fire I don't imagine anyone could have possibly survived,' replied Vahan. 'Your brother was such a wonderful man. He cared so deeply for humanity. I will never forget his actions to help me survive this disaster.' Tears started to break through and then the floodgates opened as he couldn't control his emotional outcry and intense sobbing.

'Let it all out,' said Miriam but didn't put her arm around him. It wasn't that she didn't want to but knew that he would need to come to terms with his grief by himself.

Within a couple of minutes, the tears melted away and he asked her 'So why did this happen? Who would want to do such a thing?'

Miriam knew all about the situation and they talked openly. She knew that Vahan, his twin brother Davit and their father Harat all had the same marking behind their left ear, as had Artoush and their brother Haig Sarkissian in Yerevan. Artoush had told her about the danger that they were in and that they all needed to take every precaution.

'You see,' said Miriam 'You may be a living descendant of the most important prophets of the religious world. It means that no religious group can claim greater importance in the eyes of God than any other group. It puts them all on the same footing so to speak. The fear is that you may legitimately claim to be closer to God's earthly representatives than any of the current religious leaders.'

'But I don't have any thoughts of claiming anything of the sort,' said Vahan with a somewhat puzzled frown.

'Yes, but fear isn't always rational. It can twist the truth, and in their minds, it is easier to get rid of you rather than find the holy documents that would give you claim to be God's representative on earth. Artoush through his research has become very close to uncovering these documents and that is why they need to eliminate him. Artoush saw the birthmark behind your left ear and decided that he should become the fall guy letting you escape. At this stage, they don't know your whereabouts or even that you also have the birthmark. You will need to take great care to maintain your anonymity.'

'What and where is this research that Artoush has uncovered?' asked Vahan 'You speak of Artoush in the present. How can you be sure that Artoush survived the explosion at the monastery?'

'I can't be certain of anything. If Artoush did survive he won't be contacting me for quite some time,' said Miriam. 'He will need to keep his distance for fear of involving me or any other person that he contacts. If he has survived, he would have to be operating from the dark.'

They talked at length about what had happened, why it had happened and what they should do next. Vahan couldn't fully understand why the religious leaders should have anything to fear.

'You will need to stay here for a short while and then it is most important that you go back to Constantinople and inform your father and brother of their danger,' said Miriam. 'It is most important that you travel incognito and take this letter from Artoush to explain everything to them. You will need to grow a beard and a full head of hair. In the meantime, wear a hat to cover your marking.'

* * *

Vahan had remembered the name and address of Pietro Caminiti, the crew member of the fishing vessel that had brought him to Venice. He recalled his offer for Vahan to visit his mother's place and that Pietro might be able to assist with his travel back to Constantinople.

They decided that Miriam should accompany Vahan on his visit to see Pietro. As luck would have it, Pietro answered the door and immediately recognised Vahan and was pleasantly surprised that Vahan now spoke perfect Italian. He invited them in to meet his mother and Vahan introduced Miriam as his aunt. They went into the small apartment and were offered a drink of wine.

Pietro's mother kept bringing out nibbles that gradually became a full-blown antipasto. Pietro was keen to know what Vahan had been doing but Vahan avoided the subject, replying, 'Just a bit of this and a bit of that.'

Then Vahan broached the subject of needing to get back to Constantinople to see his family. Vahan and Miriam had agreed on the story that they had received news that Vahan's father Harat, had become seriously ill, so Vahan wanted to get back as quickly as possible. They also alluded to a recent robbery that had occurred, where the thieves had stolen Vahan's money and hit him on the head leaving a deep scar. This little white lie would explain the need for Vahan to wear his hat.

'Do you remember saying that if I needed help to return to Constantinople then you might be able to help with such a passage?' said Vahan. 'Unfortunately, I have little money, but I have a strong body and am not shy of hard work.'

'You might be in luck,' replied Pietro. 'Our boat sails to Crete next Tuesday and I'm sure I can put in a good word to our captain Orlando. I'm sure that from Crete you will be able to find another boat.'

'That would be wonderful,' said Vahan 'How can we confirm that it will be alright with captain Orlando?'

'I'm having a drink with him this evening around 8pm so come around to the bar and we can set it up then,' said Pietro.

'Don't worry,' said Vahan 'I'll be there.'

* * *

And so, Vahan found himself working his passage back to Constantinople with the letter from Artoush to warn his family of the danger. The fishing was hard as the catch was plentiful. They hugged the Adriatic coast of Italy as far as the port of Brindisi. Each night they would set sail out to sea and bring back their haul around 4:30am. Vahan would help wash, sort, and gut the fish. By 6am they would have set up their stall at the quay displaying their night's catch. By 8am they would be back on board and sleep in their hammocks till 4pm when they would set sail again and repeat the process. After a couple of catches they would set on further down the coast to the next port. The work was unforgiving. Vahan quickly tuned and toned his body to deal with the physical stress. One good thing was that the fish were bountiful and abundant. Each morning at the end of the quayside market, the captain would reward Vahan with some of the takings. There was no time to spend the money he received, although some of the crew bought alcohol and tobacco to comfort them during the cool nights. Vahan neither drank nor smoked tobacco, so pocketed his earnings.

They continued down the eastern coast of Italy towards to the port of Leuca. From there they made it across to the Island of Corfu and then on to Crete. Vahan was the youngest member of the crew and was given all the difficult tasks. Being on the open sea was good for Vahan. He became bronzed and extremely fit. His beard was thick, and his curly hair became bleached in the sun. His skin became rugged and tight as the salt air played its part. He became more confident and ready to face the world. He left behind the introverted, younger brother role that he had once assumed and was keen to return home to show his family, especially his father and brother, what he had become. Although he was stronger and more positive, he maintained the softer side of his personality.

One of the crew members, a man called Vincenzo, wanted to take him ashore to get drunk and visit the whore houses during the middle of the day. 'The girls are best after lunch,' he told Vahan. 'Yes, but I need to sleep during the day, or I wouldn't be able to work at night,' Vahan would reply. 'Maybe I will come with you at the next port.' Both knew that Vahan would say the same thing at every port, but the hollow words had to be said.

Arriving at the island of Crete was the extent of the trip for the Italians, they would stay there a couple of days before returning to Venice. The Italian crew were well known on the Island and were treated as brothers amongst the fellow fishermen. They tried hard to persuade Vahan to go back to Venice with them, but he was resolute in his mission. The captain tried offering more money but soon realised that money wasn't the issue. The fishermen knew nothing of Vahan's circumstances, but liked his kind and considerate manner, always ready to help. The captain knew all the fishermen in Crete, and it didn't take long for him to find a Greek boat that was going on to Constantinople that needed an extra hand.

'You won't regret taking on Vahan,' said the Italian captain to the Greek captain. 'He's a hard worker and gets on well with the other men. He is a steadying influence and not only takes a bit of ribbing but can give some too. I'm sorry he won't be coming back to Venice with us.' It was with this recommendation that Vahan set off home to Constantinople.

Vahan's beard and hair grew as he worked tirelessly hauling in the fish. He no longer needed to wear a hat but wore a headband to keep his hair from falling in his eyes. Vahan had left Constantinople as an insecure youth but was returning as a confident, physical young man, with a strong muscular, tanned body. His glinting eyes and shining white teeth against his dark windswept face bore no resemblance to the man that had left home just over a year ago. In his mind he was preparing for the impending battle for acceptance from his brother Davit and especially from his father Harat. He was ready for his rite of passage in which it is said that a boy must defeat his father to become a man. He was ready for the fight; he was ready for round one. He hadn't forgotten his mission to warn both Davit and Harat of the danger and what he assumed had happened to Artoush back at the monastery. He thought often of the strength of mind that Artoush had spoken about, and how his calm and considerate intellect had given him purpose and direction. Vahan owed his life to Artoush and his sister Miriam.

The Greek fishing boat finally arrived at their destination, Constantinople. They docked early one crisp morning at the fisherman's quay and prepared their market stall. The buyers came from far and wide to buy the fresh fish. By 9:30am all the fish were sold, and it was time for Vahan to bid his farewells to his Greek friends and make his way home to his family. The captain gave him a big hug and told him that he would always be welcome to go out fishing with them. He was tired and exhausted but somehow found the energy to walk the familiar streets and laneways.

* * *

It took him an hour and a half of solid walking before he turned the corner into the street where he lived. Nothing could have prepared him for the horror that he was about to encounter.

9

Sevan Davidian

As Vahan rounded the corner into the street where he grew up, he saw that their house was surrounded by barricades. Turkish soldiers with rifles were positioned to stop anyone getting into the property. As he got closer, Vahan could see that the house had been totally gutted by fire and was still smouldering. He knew at once that he was too late and feared for the worst. There was a crowd of onlookers, who like ghouls, were bathing in other people's misery. No one recognised him. One of the bystanders explained that around 8am that morning, there had been a large explosion followed by a raging fire that had engulfed the whole property. All that remained, were the smouldering embers, the bitter smell of ash and steam from the blackened cinders. The fire brigade had done their best but because of the intensity of the heat, nothing had been saved. Vahan cautiously backed away and couldn't believe what he was seeing. He didn't ask too many questions but let others tell him what had happened. There was nothing that he could do, and his immediate instinct was to run away as fast as he could. He kept his head and resisted absconding, as it would have only brought attention to him. Slowly he recoiled and felt completely lost. First the explosion at San Lazzaro, and now this second devastation.

* * *

Scared and bewildered he decided to seek refuge with his old nanny, Sevan. In a daze, he found his way to Sevan's little cottage where he knocked on the solid front door. A faint voice from behind the door asked, 'Who is it?' He was relieved to hear Sevan's voice, which he recognised immediately. 'It's Vahan,' he whispered in a low voice that was only just audible through the solid door. As he heard the key turning inside, he couldn't hold back his tears. The door was opened just enough for Vahan to slip through into the darkened house. The timber window shutters were closed to protect any form of intrusion or light penetrating into the rooms.

'Come sit down,' said Sevan. 'By the state of you, you must have seen what has happened.'

'Yes, I have just come from the house, and I'm too late to warn anyone. Do you know who is responsible for this? What has happened to my family? Has anyone survived?' came a flurry of questions, one after another.

'We don't know who is responsible, but we suspect that there are no survivors.' Sevan appeared very matter of fact and controlled. 'You mustn't go anywhere near the place as it is obvious that they intended to wipe out the whole family.'

'They did a pretty good job of it,' said Vahan through his tears. 'Are there any survivors? What has happened to mama and papa? What has happened to Davit?' he whimpered.

'It only happened early this morning and they are still identifying the charred bodies. Apparently, they have removed your parents who were asleep in their bed but there were a lot of staff that have also suffered. I don't think that Davit has been identified yet but we suspect that he hasn't survived,' replied Sevan. Her voice quivered but she managed to control herself from breaking down.

'What has happened to Sara and Hripsime?' asked Vahan. 'Were they in the house?'

'Sara and Hripsime are both away,' replied Sevan. 'They left by train last week to go to Yerevan to see if they could find an uncle from their father's side of the family. Sara has written to me to say that they think their uncle is on his way to India and that Hripsime wants to stay in Yerevan a bit longer. Sara wants to come back to Constantinople.

I think she is missing Davit. You know that those two had become very close but had had a lover's tiff. She says that she will be arriving back in Constantinople tomorrow morning and asked if I could go and meet her at the station. I think she wanted to surprise Davit. Davit was young and needed to experience life, but she is of the nesting kind, wanting to start a family. She doesn't know about the explosion yet and I just don't know how I will be able to meet her at the station and tell her the sad news.'

'I could come with you if it would be of any help,' said Vahan.

'Would you? That would be such a comfort to both Sara and me. Having someone else there to share the burden would be most supportive and welcome,' replied Sevan as she couldn't hold back the tears.

Vahan held her in his arms while she sobbed and for once he felt strong. Sevan was like his alter mother and it was a measure of how much he had grown. He now took the emotionally supportive role rather than being the young boy that needed to be supported. His arms were strong and protective. Night came slowly and they talked by candlelight into the early hours of the morning.

Eventually, Vahan said, 'We must try and get some sleep before we go to meet Sara. She will need all the support that we can give her.' He felt that he was the one that needed to stay strong.

Both Vahan and Sevan knew, that although Sara projected herself as a feisty young woman, she also carried a vulnerable side that she worked hard to conceal. They feared that unless handled sensitively, Sara could spiral down into the depths of depression. They would need to tread carefully, to shield and protect her from having to expose her fragility.

That night Vahan slept in Sara's bed, and in the morning at first light he was woken by the cockerel. He pondered whether he should tell Sevan why he had returned to Constantinople but decided that it would be better to delay telling her about it. It would only have made Sevan more anxious.

Neither Sevan nor Vahan slept more than a couple of hours as they both couldn't stop questioning what needed to be done. What could they do? Sevan prepared breakfast while Vahan did his morning meditations to try and clear his mind but found that all sorts of emotions surfaced. Anger, sorrow, confusion all crowded his thoughts. He knew that he needed to stay strong. He couldn't believe that both his parents and his twin brother had gone forever. Perhaps it was just a bad dream, and he would soon wake up to find that they had survived. Then reality returned to crush his hopes, with the realisation that he was now all alone.

* * *

Sevan and Vahan ate breakfast together in silence. Finally, Sevan broke the silence to tell Vahan that they should wait till they had brought Sara back home before they mentioned anything of what had happened. They feared that Sara wouldn't be able to contain her feelings, breaking down in public. Neither of them was good at handling outbursts. Each person reacts to trauma in their own way. Sevan could contain her feelings to an appropriate time and place, while Vahan was the kind of person who harboured his emotions, sometimes taking years for them to surface. Often his buried feelings would start to fester. Through his meditations, he could only scrape the surface of his mind, never knowing what was lurking beneath and the effects on his subconscious. Sara didn't hold back; her sudden outbursts cleared her air, allowing the healing to begin. This was fine for Sara, but her eruptions were sometimes directed as anger towards the people around her. Once her wrath had dissipated, she would become profusely apologetic.

For some recipients, intense fury leaves permanent scars. It is a force open to interpretation by the receiver. Some will reel backwards but others will retaliate. However, rage needs to be expunged – if trapped, it becomes septic.

* * *

Sevan and Vahan got to the station, some twenty minutes earlier than required, only to find that the train had been delayed. No one could tell them exactly when it would arrive. 'It could be soon,' was the only answer that they were given. The wait was intolerable. Sevan thanked Vahan many times for coming with her. Finally, three and a half hours late, Sara's train arrived. She was one of the first to alight and came running down the platform towards them. She was surprised to see them as she had expected Davit to come to greet her. Initially she mistook Vahan for Davit but when she got within three metres, she realised that it was

Vahan on the platform and not her beloved Davit. Davit had proposed marriage to her from the platform just before she had left for Yerevan. She had told him that she would give him her answer when she returned. It was customary, in the Middle East, that a woman would respond to her initial offer of marriage by saying that she would have to consider it a bit longer and would politely ask him to enquire again later. Usually, this was simply a flirtatious game that went on at least three times before the woman capitulated. Of course, Sara had instantly known what her final decision would be but wanted to play the game. She planned that on her return, she would accept Davit's proposal, on the very same platform from which he had made it.

'Where is Davit?' Sara asked, immediately followed by, 'What are you doing here Vahan, I thought you were in Venice for at least another couple of years.'

Vahan didn't want to be confronted by the first question, so he simply answered the second question with a simple 'It's nice to see you, Sara. Did you have a good trip to Yerevan?'

Sara talked with excitement all the way home about her visit to Yerevan and how she wanted to go back there with Davit as soon as possible. Both Sevan and Vahan didn't have to say anything as Sara bubbled over with enthusiasm. She talked at her aunt Sevan, rather than with her, while Vahan carried her suitcase a couple of paces behind.

Sara didn't question any further why Vahan was there to meet her and didn't even question that his physical appearance had totally transformed from a stooped recluse to a sun-soaked bronzed young man with bleached hair and suntanned arms. She was used to Vahan being the meeker brother and only subliminally registered his transformation. She was so excited at being back home that she hardly noticed his penetrating blue eyes and how they sparkled in her infectious presence.

* * *

When they got back to Sevan's little cottage, Vahan put the small suitcase into Sara's room that had been cleared for her homecoming.

'Let's have a cup of tea,' said Sevan 'We have something we need to tell you.'

'Yes, I will put on the water,' replied Sara excitedly. 'I have lots to tell you about too.'

The water seemed to take forever to boil but eventually they were all seated at the little table with a glass of black tea in their hands. Sevan had made some sweets that went down a treat.

Finally, Sevan started to relate to Sara the events that had happened. Sara couldn't believe what she was hearing. Sevan couldn't hold back the tears as she told Sara of the tragedy that had befallen them. Sara let out a scream as she heard the words that Davit had been engulfed by flames. Both women sobbed as Vahan encompassed them with his powerful arms. The three of them didn't move for what would have been a good half an hour. Finally, Sara's shaking seemed to slow down and Vahan released his comforting arms asking if they wanted another cup of tea.

That night, Sara cried herself to sleep. She woke early, still stunned by the news. She didn't know if it was a nightmare or reality. Vahan was asleep on the floor beside her bed. She closed her eyes for a good ten minutes and then instinctively got out of bed and snuggled up close to Vahan on the cushions. She imagined that he was Davit and felt the warmth of his body close to hers. Vahan woke to find Sara lying peacefully with him and started to gently stroke her hair. They were like brother and sister in a trance. Sara could feel his gentle touch and imagined that Davit was still with her. Vahan recalled the warm aroma of her cotton nightdress. It was the same warmth that he had felt the night that he had told his family that he would be going to Venice. The night that she had climbed into his bed and had softly whispered 'I don't want you to go. You will come back, won't you?' That phrase and, that scent, had entered his subconscious in the way that fragrances do.

* * *

The next morning after a small breakfast, Vahan decided that he should tell them what had happened in Venice and why his family in Constantinople had been so violently eliminated. He felt that they deserved to know. He told them that he had returned home to warn his parents of the danger, but he was too late. It was all his fault. He felt entirely to blame. He told them about the abbot called Artoush and how he had died having planned Vahan's escape from the monastery.

Then he showed them the birthmark behind his left ear. He explained to them the significance of this birthmark and how it had been carried down through the ages, from ancient times. The markings could only be passed on from father to son and in some cases didn't get passed on at all. He explained that Artoush also had the same marking and that he had become aware of some secret documents, hidden in a remote church somewhere in Armenia. These documents would prove that Christ and his older half-brother also had the same markings, with possible links to other prophets. The religious authorities would seek to destroy the lineage, as it threatened their influence.

Both Sevan and Sara were dumbfounded as they listened, in mesmerised silence, to Vahan's explanation. Finally, Sara asked in a meek tone, 'Does this mean you are related to Christ?'

'Nothing can be proved until the secret documents are found,' explained Vahan. 'You see the religious fanatics are searching for these documents so they can destroy them before the world finds out about them. In fact, the documents are safer not found. Their secrets are hidden by their obscurity.'

'But you are in danger,' said Sevan 'If the religious authorities eliminate all the young men with the markings, they will eliminate the evidence. The documents are the key, but you are the evidence.'

'Yes, you are quite right,' replied Vahan. 'Not only am I in danger but also anyone connected to me is in danger too. I must go into hiding and not be found. At this stage the religious authorities, as you call them, will be thinking that I died in the fire at San Lazzaro monastery. I have a bit of time but mustn't delay my escape.'

'Where will you go?' asked Sara. 'Nowhere will be safe.'

'I think I will go to the beach house at Turan,' replied Vahan, 'it will be safer than here.'

'Then I will come with you,' replied Sara looking at Sevan for her approval. 'You will need someone to help you and I don't think I can be of much use here.'

'Go with Vahan as I can manage by myself,' Sevan reassured Sara. 'Anyway, I might go to see my sister in Yerevan but will stay here until things settle down a bit.'

That evening Sara put on a head scarf and went to see Vaz the fisherman, asking him when he might be able to take them to Turan. 'Not till Tuesday,' was his reply. He had heard all about the explosion and fire at Harat and Nanar's house and wondered what was going on. Sara played dumb, saying that she didn't know much about it as she had been away and had only recently returned from Yerevan.

'Can you be at the dock by 7am on Tuesday morning,' asked Vaz. 'How long will you be staying there?'

'We're not sure at this stage,' said Sara. 'It may be just me as Sevan will be staying here till things get sorted out. I know I can trust you.' Sara didn't let on to Vaz that Vahan was still alive.

As Sara left, Vaz gave her a hug which was most unusual. He felt so sorry for the young woman and could sense her anxiety. 'We will be alright,' said Sara. 'We can look after each other.' Vaz released her from the hug and gave her a wry smile. He assumed that Sara was talking about Sevan and herself. 'Don't worry, you have God to look after both of you,' he said reassuringly.

Sara and Vahan made their way down to the dock at 7am the following Tuesday. Vaz was much surprised that it was Vahan and not Sevan who removed the hood of his cloak and revealed his golden hair. Vaz knew not to say anything as he immediately understood the need for secrecy. They set sail ten minutes later. Sitting on the edge of the small boat Vahan and Sara held hands in silence. Both knew that they would never see Constantinople or Sevan again.

* * *

Once the small boat had got out of sight, Vahan removed his cloak and shook his blonde curly hair. Vaz was surprised to see the new fit and healthy looking Vahan, who moved with agility around the boat. Sailing had become second nature to him. He was like a fish in water.

Vaz dropped them off on the beach at Turan and told them that he would be back around the same time the following week. They would recognise his boat by the yellow and green flag. He wished them well and said he would bring them some supplies.

That evening Vahan made a fire on the desolate beach while Sara cooked some vegetables and spiced rice. The next day, they would go fishing off the rocks and would feast on fresh fish on a platter of rice. When the fire had eventually burnt itself out, they made their way back to the house and it seemed quite normal that they should curl up in bed together. Somehow, Sara found the transition of being with Vahan only natural. She had been brought up as a peasant girl from Diyarbakir where warmth and tenderness flowed without restriction. Vahan hadn't been with a woman before, so Sara led him gently into a world of adulthood.

They fell asleep and woke late the next morning. The sun was already quite high in the sky. They lived on the isolated beach, falling into the rhythm of the summer sun and the sound of lapping waves. Each day melted into the next. They talked incessantly but Sara wasn't at all interested in hearing about the books that Vahan was reading. She found Harat's backgammon boards and together they played game after game, until the early hours of the morning. Sara was much more skilful than Vahan at playing games that required strategy, so had to let him win from time to time. He was the so so-called intelligent one, but she was shrewd and extremely cunning. She was street smart and read the game well. She could also read Vahan.

Life slipped by and as arranged on Tuesday afternoons, Vaz would sail into the bay and come ashore with supplies and a note from Sevan. Sometimes there would be a letter for Sara from her sister Hripsime who had heard all about the devastating blast and the death of Davit and his parents from Sevan. As Sara had never learnt how to write, she dictated to Vahan a reply to her sister. Vaz would deliver the reply to Sevan who would then forward it to Hripsime in Yerevan.

The new century dawned and letters from Sevan described the turmoil that surrounded her in Constantinople. She told them that they should go far away to be safe. She told them that her sister in Yerevan was taking Hripsime to Calcutta in India, to join a growing Armenian community. There, they would be able to get help to settle in a new country. Calcutta was a city with great potential and a thriving economy. She described the troubled times of people with Armenian heritage in full detail. She wrote that she was too old to travel and that she would see her life out the best way she could. No one knows what happened to Sevan but after six weeks, the letters stopped coming. Vaz told them that all the doors and windows to her cottage were locked and that no one knew of her whereabouts. They suspected the worst.

Sara and Vahan soon realised that they would have to leave this idyllic place and seek refuge in another country. Safety was everything. Their anxiety intensified by the day.

Then one day Sara announced to Vahan that she thought that she might be pregnant but didn't know exactly for how long. It had been about eight weeks since she had been back from her trip to Yerevan, and she couldn't work out how many cycles she had missed. 'It could be just two months, but it could be three,' she told Vahan 'I just don't know.'

'If it is two months,' replied Vahan, 'then I must be the father. But if it is three months or more, then you must be carrying someone else's child.'

Sara started to sob uncontrollably. 'Perhaps this child belongs to Davit,' she wept. 'He's dead and the child will be born without a father.'

Vahan eventually managed to console her by telling her that it didn't really matter who the father was, as he and Davit were identical twins. 'Harat and Nanar would have become grandparents and that is all that matters,' he said to Sara reassuringly. 'Anyway, the child will have me as a father, and no one will know otherwise.' Once again, the shadow of Davit hovered over Vahan as he receded back to his childhood and that perhaps he had been born ten minutes after his brother. Vahan always assumed the worst, never considering that he might have been born first.

That night, Sara and Vahan talked till 4am in the morning. They resolved that they should leave as soon as possible for Smyrna, now Izmir, before deciding where to go from there. 'We are a family now and we must find a safe place for our child to flourish,' said Vahan with the emphasis on "our child".

Sara was comforted by the words 'our child' and vowed never to tell anyone anything to the contrary. She began to love Vahan for whom he was. For her, Davit soon dissolved into the distant past.

The next day, they packed their meagre belongings, ready for Vaz to come to take them on the first step of the arduous and often dangerous journey that lay ahead.

* * *

Their eldest son Zaven was born in the Persian city of Isfahan on the way overland to Calcutta. Zaven didn't have the hereditary birthmark behind his left ear. Not all sons had such a birthmark. It seemed without reason, as to who did, and who didn't.

Vahan got a teaching job in a high school in Isfahan, teaching mathematics and comparative religious studies. The students adored Vahan and appreciated his kind and gentle ways. Sara became an excellent mother and created a bountiful vegetable garden adjacent to their small, rented house on the outskirts of the town.

Some years later, a letter arrived from Hripsime urging them to come to Calcutta. She told them that there was a large Armenian community and plenty of work for those who wanted it. Sara was keen to go and to be with her sister. Vahan just wanted to please Sara.

* * *

They stayed in Isfahan for a good three years until Zaven was running around on his own two feet. Then one autumn morning, the three of them with their paltry savings, set off in almost biblical fashion along the Silk Road to a new continent, in search for a new life of peace and prosperity. Little did they know of the perils that would lie ahead.

10

Davit's Escape

The journey that Vahan, Sara and their three-year-old son Zaven made to Calcutta, was far more arduous than they had expected. Once they reached the Indian sub-continent, they were hit by disease and difficult terrain. Vahan was struck by a virulent form of dysentery that would keep re-emerging for the rest of his life. This severely limited his capacity to hold down any kind of work, consequentially the family suffered great setbacks.

* * *

Little did they know that Davit, Vahan's twin brother, had managed to escape the devastating blast that had engulfed their parents and the family home. One of the grossly charred bodies, reported as one of the twins, was in fact the terrorist who had ignited the bomb. Whether he had been a suicide bomber or just caught up in the blast wasn't ever known.

The wise and cautious Abbot Artoush had not only helped Vahan to escape from the inferno of the Monastery at San Lazzaro degli Armeni, but as a double security, he had also given his sister Miriam two sealed packages. The accompanying note requested, that should anything happen to either Vahan or himself, Miriam should send both packages to Harat in Constantinople. One package contained a small, locked metal box with a lengthy letter explaining everything in a secret code. The second package contained a key to open the box of the first package, as well as a code to decipher the letter of explanation inside the box. Artoush had verbally explained his plans to his sister Miriam and told her that it would be important to send the packages to Harat separately. In this way the first package would be dependent on the arrival of the second package and the second package meant nothing without the arrival of the first package. Artoush had written the coded letter to be decoded into Latin. He had assumed that Harat would be able to understand the Latin text.

When Harat received the two packages, he was able to decipher the message that Artoush had sent to him. The letter started from the beginning and explained everything in clear and logical order. It warned Harat of the imminent danger and strongly suggested steps that should be taken to protect himself and his family. The letter concluded that if he was reading this letter, it meant that he Artoush had been captured or killed.

* * *

That evening Harat invited his wife Nanar and his son Davit to his study, to explain the solemn situation. He told Davit to make his way to Europe, while he, Nanar and Sevan would wait for Vahan, before setting off to Yerevan. Harat told Davit that they would be able to keep in touch but would need to maintain their exact locations secret. Then Harat ceremoniously burnt the letter and the translated copy in the metal box. 'We don't want anyone to get hold of this letter, do we?' he said. 'Come, let us say a prayer for God to keep us safe and may we all be united as a family again sometime soon. Sleep well my son,' he said turning to Davit. 'You will need all God's strength and wisdom to carry you forward.' Nanar who had held her emotions back suddenly burst into tears. Harat put his arms around his wife and Davit took this as a cue to embrace both of his parents. Then Davit went to pack his belongings, in readiness for the morning. Davit would always remember the last image that he had of his father holding his mother and gently saying to her, 'No need for tears, we are in safe hands. God will look after us.'

This last image of his parents would haunt Davit for the rest of his life. It would become the subject of a painting that he would paint many years later. It is now held in a private collection in Montevideo and shows a man consoling a seated woman. A small dog is curled up at the woman's feet oblivious to what is going on. Nearby on a round side table, is a small metal box with the lid open. Flames indicate that something is burning in the box but also in the corner of the room, an open fire burns profusely giving a glow to the room and the strained face of a large man. The seated woman appears very distraught. The meaning of the small fire in the box and the large fire in the corner of the room isn't evident unless you know their particular significance.

* * *

Davit had always wanted to go to Paris as he spoke French to quite a high level. He wrote a letter to Sara telling her that he was going to Paris and that he hoped that she would come and be with him. He left the letter for his parents to give to Sara on her return from Yerevan and hoped that his proposal for marriage would be accepted. Harat and Nanar were aware that Davit had intended to propose marriage again to Sara on her return from Yerevan. They were in full approval of the union and hoped she would accept. They were pleased that Davit had made his own choice rather than it being an arranged marriage as was the custom in those days. As progressive parents they believed that love should be the basis for a good marriage, rather than marrying for pecuniary gain. Besides, they had more than sufficient funds and only looked for their sons' happiness.

Early in the morning mist, well before his parents had woken, Davit with a small shoulder bag, left for the main railway station. As he boarded the early train from Constantinople towards the Bulgarian border he wondered if he would see his family again.

At 8:15am that morning, the size and more so the timing of the devastating bomb completely changed the Kaspar family for ever. It was a pivotal turning point for what had been a happy and supportive household. If only the bombing had been just one day later. Vahan would have been back from Venice and would have accompanied his parents to Yerevan. Sara would have returned from Yerevan and presumably accepted Davit's second proposal of marriage and they would have made their way to Europe together. Life for the Kaspar family was shattered.

Thus, the brothers were separated. Davit went west to Europe while Vahan went east to Asia. Both considered the other brother had died and it was now their sole objective to create a new family and preserve the secret of their heritage and birth right. Some years later, Vahan would marry Sara, but Davit only carried an embroidered linen handkerchief that she had given him as a token of her love. This was the only item that he had of hers and he would treasure it for the rest of his life. Sara Davidian had been his first love; she would always hold a special place in his heart.

* * *

Davit had a friend named Sargis, who lived in a town called Kirklareli, some two hundred and twenty kilometres west of Constantinople. Sargis, who had studied medicine at the medical school in Constantinople, now had his first job as a doctor. Davit knew that he could stay with his friend for a few days, before deciding where he would go next. Sargis was pleased to see Davit, telling him that he had a spare bed so he could stay as long as he liked.

Around midday the next day, Davit went out to look for a newspaper and some Turkish coffee. Sargis had left for work at the hospital and wouldn't be back till much later that evening. When Davit sat down to read the paper, he saw a headline *"Explosion and fire at a large mansion in Uskadar."* The article went on to describe the explosion and the subsequent fire at around 8:15am in the morning. *"The fire totally gutted the mansion that belonged to Mr Harat Kaspar, a prominent Armenian businessman."* It stated that there were no survivors from the incident and that it wasn't known exactly why the bombing had taken place. It ventured that it was probably due to a debt that Mr Kaspar was owed by an aggrieved debtor. It then went on to say, *"Mr Kaspar, his wife and one of their sons has been killed in the explosion. The exact whereabouts of the other son isn't yet known."*

Davit quickly folded his newspaper, finished his coffee, and left in haste. He left a note for Sargis saying, 'I must apologise for my sudden departure, but I must take the train to Çorlu.' He had written this note to throw anyone off his tracks, as in reality, he took the train in the opposite direction towards Tsarevo, a small Bulgarian town on the shores of the Black Sea.

78

Davit was stunned to find out the details of the tragic incident in a newspaper article. It was one thing to receive a letter from Artoush articulating the imminent danger but quite another thing to read about it as a matter of fact in a newspaper. The letter from Artoush didn't have the finality that the newspaper had. Although it spelt out the danger, the letter gave a sense of challenge and almost adventure. The newspaper article left no hope. His world closed in on him, as he found it difficult to breathe.

Davit was understandably scared for his life and felt that he should lie low. He felt very confused and alone.

* * *

From Tsarevo Davit made his way on foot towards a hidden monastery, St Petka, up in the hills. He decided it would be safer not to stay at the monastery, but to camp in the nearby woods, adjacent to a fast-flowing stream that wound its way down to the Black Sea.

He needed to maintain his distance in order to fully digest what was happening in his mind and to his body. He spent his time fishing and hunting in the woods and wrote a letter to Sevan but never got a reply.

It took quite some time for Davit's demons to subside. Not having anyone he could talk to, his recurring nightmares, started to fester.

Camping wasn't easy but after three months, he felt it was time for him to move on. Western Europe was his target. London, Paris, Vienna, or Rome? Perhaps a smaller town such as Florence, Oxford, Prague, or Barcelona might suit him better. Anyway, there was no returning now, fear supplanted his curiosity to look back. He organised his trip overland and decided to head for Austria. He knew that trying to plan too much wasn't the way he operated but that he would instinctively know what felt right. There was no rush, as nothing would bring back his family. If death destroyed hope, then only time could be his healer.

* * *

It was with a sad heart that Davit packed his little tent and started out on his long trek to a new life in Western Europe.

11

La Belle Époque

It took almost a year from when Davit left his camp site in Bulgaria, to when he reached Paris. Not speaking fluently, the languages of the countries that he had passed through, he had been forced to work in a variety of menial jobs; in restaurants, picking fruit and even as a grave digger in Zagreb. He would work for a while, just enough to earn some funds to be able to move on to the next place. He was trying to get to London where he knew his father had friends, who might help him.

* * *

Along the way he spoke with very few people but did numerous drawings, filling up a total of four sketch books that have been passed down the generations. Each sketch was dated and usually the location was noted. The drawings varied from landscapes to internal scenes. Some were sketches of faces and some of built forms or streetscapes. They are a visual diary with no written notes. The sketch books tell the route that Davit took and the speed of his travels. In some cases, there were numerous drawings in the same location indicating that Davit stayed some time there, either earning money or perhaps the cold weather hampered his travels. He seemed to have stayed for quite some time, around the lakes of the Salzkammergut, not far from Salzburg in Austria. Not only are there numerous drawings of the small towns perched on the edge of the beautiful lakes but also many drawings of a young woman called Margareta. Who Margareta was is somewhat of a mystery but by the number of sketches he made of her, Davit must have become completely besotted.

From his drawings, we can track Davit's journey from Tsarevo through to Paris. Belgrade – Zagreb – Ljubljana – Salzburg – Innsbruck – Zurich – Basel – Paris. When he got to Paris, satiated by travelling rough, Davit decided that Paris was where he would stay for a while. Paris was truly alive, and Davit revelled in it. He soon found himself in the artist quarter of Montmartre. He befriended artists like Picasso and Matisse and the rest of the *'Les Fauves'*. He would often visit Picasso in his studio in the ramshackle building known as the 'Bateau-Lavoir'. Davit was referred to as 'Le petit Armenien' and seen as rather exotic. Constantinople was little known about and considered at the other end of the world. Davit soon became totally fluent in French, and it didn't take long for him to feel part of the scene.

Like his father, Davit could tell a good story and could hold the attention of a large crowd. To earn money, he busked in the streets of Montmartre, telling colourful stories and playing the haunting sounds of an Armenian reeded instrument called a Duduk. This street busking soon turned into impromptu street theatre. The crowds paid good money to come and see the burlesque turns that thrilled them night after night. A small troupe of actors acted out topical skits, that like his father's stories, had a theme that varied slightly at each performance. Usually, the story would conclude with a moral, but this wasn't revealed until the end. The crowds loved it and came back regularly demanding more.

* * *

Typical of the stories was one that his father had told, and which was always referred to as "The Money Story":

> *There was in a far-off foreign land, a wealthy farmer who had an idle son. When the farmer's wife died, the son was late for her funeral and generally didn't care about anyone except himself and his work-shy friends. The father tolerated his only son and realised that it was his fault for having totally spoilt him.*
>
> *One day the elderly farmer had a bad accident falling off his horse.*

The father was taken up to the smallest room in the house and laid on a bed, slowly dying with no one to visit him except a young land girl that had helped him in the fields. Before he died, he asked her to call for his son. The son reluctantly came to see his dying father but showed no pity or kindness towards him. The son only wanted his inheritance. The father asked for one last dying wish from his son, saying:

'Son, I know that all your life I have spoilt you and that you have never had to work. When I die, you will become a wealthy man with lots of money to spend on your so-called friends. One day when all your money has been frittered away, you will ask your friends for help, but they will reject you. Realising the follies of your ways, you will become very depressed and have no one to turn to. You will become suicidal and will think of doing away with yourself. But when this happens, I ask that you listen to my dying request.'

'Well get on with it, I haven't got all day,' interrupted the son in a gruff tone 'What is your request?'

'Son,' sighed the father with a heavy heart. 'When you are about to kill yourself, I ask that you come to this room and hang yourself from the cord that supports that ceiling light fitting.' He pointed to the cord that dangled from the centre of the ceiling.

'Yes, yes I'll do whatever you want.' said the son in a surly tone of voice. 'Can you hurry it up a bit as I've got to go and meet some of my friends at the bar for a drink.'

The next day the father died, and the son celebrated by taking out all his idle friends to get totally drunk. He said he wanted to celebrate his father's life, not feel sad about it. The son paid for everything, and his friends pretended to like him. In truth they all despised him.

A year went by and soon all his father's money had been spent. Never mind he thought, my friends will help me out. I have been good to them, and they owe me some favours. He went round to see his best friend Elijah and asked for a loan. Elijah just laughed and thought he was joking. The next day he went to Bertha and knocked on her door. She opened her upstairs window and emptied a bucket of dirty water onto him. One by one they sent him packing laughing and ridiculing him. Eventually he realised that his father was right, and a deep depression set in. He was about to do away with himself but remembered his father's dying wish. Slowly he made his way up to the little room at the top of the farmhouse, stood on a small stool and tied a rope to the ceiling hook. He put the noose around his neck. He took a deep breath and kicked away the stool. To his amazement the whole ceiling gave way and he fell to the floor with a bump. As the ceiling caved in, lots of money fell to the ground with a note that said 'Son, I knew that one day this would happen, so I left you only half of my wealth and the other half I hid in this false ceiling. Please use this money wisely and work hard to keep the farm. Have a good healthy life and help those in need rather than waste your money on those that only like you for your money.'

The son took heed of his father's words and worked hard to make the farm very successful. He married the young land girl that had helped his father and they had lots of healthy children.

Harat had told both of his sons this story many times but still they would ask for it time and time again. Often, he would drastically change and expand the methods in which the so-called friends showed their disdain towards the son and thus embellish the storyline to suit the audience. The telling of these stories was all to do with the timing and facial expression. These stories were handed down from father to child who copied the timing and expressions to a tee.

Soon, Davit found that to make more money he needed a confined space and preferably with shelter from the elements. He found an old shed where he could charge people a small amount to listen to his stories. Then he found a couple of mime artists that would act out the scenes in the background. The stories took on a bizarre vaudeville bent but always with an underlying message. Much laughter and merriment were had, and the crowds couldn't wait for the next session.

Whilst Davit was becoming well known for his exotic little productions, he thought of them as simply making a living. He kept his life as a painter quite separate. He had grown up in an aristocratic household and felt uncomfortable living like a bohemian artist, in a dark and dingy garret. He painted with passion but saw his plays less about art but more about a fun way to make money. He had many friends from all walks of life including the Russian, Jewish painter, Marc Chagall.

Davit appreciated his humour and dreamlike quality in his paintings and drawings.

* * *

Davit had been in Paris for a couple of years when he met a young and attractive law student called Jacqueline Dubois. Jacqueline was tall and graceful. She had a mass of jet-black wavy hair that framed her pre-Raphaelite facial features. She wore her clothes with elegance and style. The two met in a very crowded bar. Jaqueline while taking a tray of drinks to her friends at a corner table accidentally spilt the drinks all over Davit. The whole tray of drinks not just one. Davit was soaked. He was stunned not only because of the drinks but because of her beauty. It was love at first sight. Jacqueline apologised profusely but Davit claimed it was his fault and rebought the round of drinks for her friends. They spent the rest of the evening talking to each other and then went back to his little apartment. They emerged some three days later only because Davit had a performance of a new story to present, and Jacqueline had lectures to attend. She moved into his little apartment, never taking a backward step.

Jacqueline finished her legal studies while working for a small legal firm as a junior clerk. Davit worked on his performances, and they saved just sufficient money for their modest way of life.

Marriage did not seem important to them, just as long as they were together. However, simply to appease her mother, they did get married before their first child was born. Jacqueline's father had died when she was a child, and she had no siblings. 'If your mother would prefer that we are married, then married we shall be,' said Davit.

The formal ceremony was followed by a lavish party for all their friends at the bar in which the couple had originally met. Jacqueline, dressed in a flowing full length white dress and colourful flowers in her jet-black hair, clasped Davit's hand as he related the story of how they met at that very bar. Then suddenly, but with purpose, he proceeded to pour his drink all over Jacqueline. 'There now we are square,' he said as Jacqueline looked astonished. Everyone burst into laughter and then the dancing began.

* * *

Marriage and subsequent parenthood were the best things that could have happened for them. They had not realised the emotional tension that each had been living under. Jacqueline finally received full acceptance from her mother Lucette. Jacqueline had grown up in Switzerland as a single child to a single mother. Mother and daughter had been close, so much so that at times, Jacqueline had felt rather suffocated. She had left Lucerne for Paris to follow her career as a lawyer, leaving behind an over dependant mother who felt helpless and continually worried about what might happen to her rather naïve daughter in the wild and sleazy districts of Paris. Would her daughter ever come back to look after her when she became elderly and infirm? So, the invitation to come to Paris for the wedding was such a relief. It meant contact with her child again. Jacqueline had been busy and in the four years away, had only written to her mother for Christmas and birthdays. Even then the letters had been short, making little mention of Davit. When Lucette arrived in Paris, she felt greatly relieved to find that her daughter had settled down with a charming, handsome young man. She admired Davit and saw that he was kind and loving towards Jacqueline. She felt that she had gained a son who would replace her husband as head of the family and that she would soon inherit a grandchild that would bring happiness back into the family. She so much wanted to be surrounded by the sense of family.

Jacqueline was pleased that her mother and Davit got on so well, and that her mother would be around to help with the up bringing of their child when it arrived. She had suppressed her mixed feelings of anger and guilt towards her mother. She had left her mother behind in Lucerne as she wanted to be free to live her life fully and not bound to her. She needed to explore but felt her mother's demands holding her back. She realised that it wasn't her mother's fault that her father had died and saw how tenderly she had nursed her father to no avail. Would this be her role towards her mother when she got older? The marriage to Davit and becoming pregnant offered her a new role. She would become a dedicated wife and mother and her own mother would also have a part to play. This resolved so much for both women, giving both a purpose.

For Davit marriage and becoming a father was full of responsibilities. He would need to become the provider and less self-indulgent. He was tired of the free and easy life and looked forward to a settled family life. The theatre was so unpredictable and did not offer a steady source of income. He wouldn't be able to rely on any form of income coming from Jacqueline as she had become committed to looking after the baby. Davit discussed the matter with Jacqueline and together they came to the decision that they would invest in a small bistro. They had heard about a rather run-down café that was for sale. They had saved the money for a deposit and with a loan from the bank were able to buy the café. Davit together with some friends set about decorating the premises. He wanted to personalise the space and make it feel a creative environment for both the theatre and the Arts. It had a very exotic décor that was greatly influenced by some of the cafés that he had experienced in his youth in Constantinople. In one corner he prepared a little stage that could be used for simple impromptu theatre or music. The café could also be used as a gallery by some of his painter friends. Davit was in his element. He would call the café L'Armenien.

It was a highly creative time for both of them. Davit wanted to open the café with an exhibition of his own paintings. Jacqueline decided that the "Law" wasn't for her and that motherhood and running the café would be her life. She could always go back to "Law" if she ever felt like it. At that point in time the café became everything. Lucette, her mother also got swept up in the buzz. She decided to stay in Paris to help her daughter with running the café and the raising of her grandchild.

Davit had some paintings that he wanted to exhibit but thought that a few more would not go amiss. One morning he awoke early from a dream and couldn't go back to sleep. The dream was very strong and explored depths that he had resisted plunging into. He had been dreaming of his twin brother and felt that Vahan was trying to contact him. In the dream his brother had appeared from behind a mirror. Davit had heard that his painter friend, Victor also had a twin brother but who had died at birth. Many of Victor's paintings could be interpreted not as self-portraits but as his search for his brother whose soul he inhabited. Davit's painting would be of himself looking into a mirror and seeing a reflection that was just slightly different. In the painting, Davit had a full scruffy beard whilst the reflection's beard had been trimmed. On close examination, there were numerous other inconsistencies that had been purposefully incorporated to give a ghostlike, almost spiritual dimension. In the painting Davit had his fore finger of his left hand pressing against the glass touching the reflections fore finger of the mirror image. The image was reminiscent of the touch from God in Michelangelo's *Creation of Adam*. In Davit's dream, he had been able to speak with Vahan through the mirror though the conversation was muffled and not at all clear.

This painting was well received and later, Davit would paint a number more on the same theme exploring the mysteries of his subconscious mind and parallel universe.

* * *

The café was opened just two weeks after the birth of Davit's and Jacqueline's son, Emile. The café was a great success, and the opening was enjoyed by all and was spoken about for many years to come. The tables were cleared away at around 9pm and everyone danced to a gypsy band that Davit had hired for the night. Davit had met the leader of the band, Dimitar, near Vidin on his travels through Bulgaria. They had met again by chance in a café in Paris and had remained friends ever since. Dimitar would bring his tight knit band to play at L'Armenien a couple of times a month and each time they performed they proved to be a roaring success. People would make bookings for a table well in advance, sometimes three months in advance.

Young Emile Kaspar had the most striking appearance. He had the dark features of his father with the strong piercing blue eyes of his mother. As soon as he was born Davit questioned whether Emile had inherited the family birthmark behind his left ear. Sure enough, Emile had the same marking as many other male members of his family. The same marking that Harat, Vahan and he, Davit had inherited from countless previous generations. Davit was so proud and wished his own mother and father had survived to see their grandson. He often felt the emptiness that his parents and brother Vahan had left behind, but soon after Emile's birth, he decided to write a final letter to his beloved nanny

Sevan, telling her about Emile. He had written regularly but had never got a reply.

* * *

The uncertainty about his parents, his brother Vahan, his nanny Sevan and her nieces, Sara and Hripsime, left Davit confused and suspended in no man's land. No one came to tell him that hope was no longer an option. The logical explanation was that they had all suffered in the fire or captured soon after. He tried hard to forget what had happened and to let it all dwell in the past. Somehow the subconscious mind wouldn't let them die nor let him forget about them completely. Time heals much but the subconscious doesn't have a temporal dimension.

<h1 style="text-align:center">12</h1>

<h2 style="text-align:center">The Futility of War</h2>

Davit's son Emile Kaspar, was just two and a couple of months old when war broke out. Davit and Jacqueline's café, L'Armenien, struggled as many young men were called to the front. Davit was enlisted into the French army in early 1915. The café closed to a bit of a whimper. The staff just left after a couple of drinks and never came back. The tables and chairs were left in position, but the tablecloths were removed. A handwritten sign on the window, said that the café was closed until further notice.

The next morning Davit reported for military duty, while Jacqueline packed her suitcase and together with young Emile went to the station in the hope of catching the next train to Switzerland. She had retained her Swiss national documents, enabling her a safe passage to the border. From there she would have to walk across the check point into Switzerland carrying both her suitcase and her young son. Women, the elderly and disabled huddled in groups trying to cross but without the correct papers they waited in vain. Some tried to tag along with a Swiss national but failed. It was too dangerous to try and help the unfortunate people as your own passage could be put in jeopardy if the guards found out. It was each person for themself.

Jacqueline's mother Lucette came to the Swiss French border to meet her daughter and grandson and together they travelled back home to Lucerne and safety. Tired and exhausted Jacqueline was only too happy to arrive at her mother's house but couldn't stop thinking about her beloved Davit. She wrote letters every day to his battalion; but nothing came back. Jacqueline with Emile strapped to her front, would help her mother manage the small holding they had on the outskirts of Lucerne.

* * *

They had a couple of dairy cows, some chickens, fruit trees and a large vegetable plot. They were sheltered from the war that waged fiercely in other parts of Europe but if they didn't listen to the radio or read the papers, they lived in an eerie silence. Having risen around 4:30am each morning she would head off to milk the cows and then return to make breakfast for her mother and son. After her breakfast and before heading back to tend to the vegetable patch, Jacqueline would write a letter to Davit, asking her mother to post it. This was her way of coping. She heard nothing back but at least she poured out her feelings each time she wrote.

Then completely out of the blue, she was out in the garden, when her mother came running out with a letter for her. It had a French stamp and a typed address. It came from the French Army hospital in Rouen, Normandy. Jacqueline rushed inside to the kitchen and found a knife in one of the drawers. Fearful of the worst, she took a deep breath as she opened the letter. Reading in silence, her mother waited with anticipation. When Jacqueline got to the end of the letter, she raised her head up to the heavens and closed her eyes. A small tear, that escaped from her left eye, rolled down her cheek.

'What does it say,' snapped her mother. Jacqueline, having forgotten about her mother's presence, abruptly came back to earth exclaiming, 'He is still alive. He is still alive.'

Slowly, Jacqueline read the letter to her mother. It explained that Davit had been fighting at the front, showing extreme bravery and leadership. He had been promoted up the ranks, becoming a captain. During the fighting at the Battle of The Somme, he had been severely injured but had been rescued and taken to the Army Hospital near Rouen. He had regained consciousness but had lost his left leg below the knee as well as the use of his left arm, which might need to be amputated to prevent the spread of gangrene. He had given his wife's name and address, asking that she be contacted. The letter went on to explain that due to the number of casualties, hospital beds were at a premium, making it necessary for him to be moved to allow for other cases. It was requested that relatives should contact the Hospital as soon as possible, to arrange for the transportation of their loved ones. The letter was signed by a Dr Vincent Belvedere.

Jacqueline turned to her mother saying repeatedly, 'I must go immediately and get him. I must go and get him.' Her mother agreed but told her of the dangers. Jaqueline wrote a letter back to the hospital, telling them she would come and collect her husband as soon as she could get a train. She went into Lucerne, to post the letter and then to the railway station to enquire about trains to Paris and Rouen.

There was a train that she could take the next morning at 7:15am. It was a train coming from Milan and it would take her all the way to Paris. There she would have to make her own way across the city from Gare de Lyon to Gare Saint Lazare. From there she would be able to catch a train to Rouen, but would need to stay the night in Paris before making her connection. After posting the letter, Jacqueline went back to see her mother and young Emile. She couldn't stop her beaming smile, with the knowledge that Davit was still alive and that she would soon bring him back home to safety. She didn't picture the broken man with missing limbs, but only thought of the beautiful man that she had known and loved.

'Daddy is coming home,' she said to the young Emile who didn't know what to expect. The notion of having a father hadn't really registered in his life but he hoped it would be someone nice to play with. He was only used to his mother and grandmother as adults but another male in the family was yet to be absorbed.

* * *

That night she put young Emile to bed and told him that he would have to be well behaved when his Daddy came and that if he was especially good, Daddy would tell him a story every night.

'Can Daddy sleep with me in my bed?' asked Emile.

'No Daddy will sleep with me in my bed,' replied Jacqueline.

'But I want Daddy to sleep with me,' said Emile.

'Well perhaps we can all sleep in the same bed,' said Jacqueline.

'We will have to ask Daddy what he wants.' She blew out the candle and just looked in wonder at her beautiful little boy as the moonlight of the full moon lit up his cherub like face. Soon they would be a complete family again.

* * *

She hardly slept that night, waking at 4:15am, she decided to get up and have a cup of tea. Before she knew it, it was 6:30am. The daylight broke as the birds started their morning song. She made herself ready to make that journey to fetch her husband. She kissed her mother, then told Emile to be a good boy and that she would bring back his Daddy. Emile was nonchalant about it, but as she stepped out of the door, he wanted to go with her. 'No, you must stay here to look after Nana,' she told Emile, who then felt most important.

The train arrived on time, she found herself a window seat, to view the pristine Swiss countryside as it passed by. She must have fallen asleep as she was awoken by an official asking for her passport, as they were about to enter France. The scenery changed and France looked like a tired war-torn country, suffering under the horrors of conflict. The small towns seemed shabby, the people at the stations appeared lean and hungry. This wasn't the same country that she had left some fifteen months ago. The closer they got to Paris the worse it became. The war was taking its toll.

They got to Paris as the dusk set in. The gas lamps only served to highlight the people's sallow faces. The gay Paris that she had once known, seemed to have morphed into a dilapidated Dickensian slum. *A Tale of Two Cities.* She remembered how the book started …

> *It was the best of times, it was the worst of times, it was the age of wisdom, it was the age of foolishness, it was the epoch of belief, it was the epoch of incredulity, it was the season of Light, it was the season of Darkness, it was the spring of hope, it was the winter of despair, we had everything before us …*

She fully understood the comparisons that Dickens was alluding to. Life's ups and downs compressed into a city within such a short period of time.

It was twilight as the train pulled into the station. Within the turmoil and the squalor, Jacqueline carrying her little valise, made her way on foot from the Gare de Lyon station to the Gare Saint Lazare. Along the way, unkempt men would ask her where she was going or if she needed a strong man to carry her suitcase. She walked fast looking neither left nor right but straight ahead with purpose. She decided to walk along the northern bank of the Seine. The river gave her breathing space but some of the pungent smells were less than desirable. Her feet ached as she was wearing her best shoes. The big heavy coat that encompassed her diminutive frame, gave her a layer of protection.

From time to time, she stopped and took in the splendid sights of yesteryear. She marvelled at the Cathedrale Notre-Dame de Paris and hobbled along by the side of the Musee du Louvre, along the Quai des Tuileries to the Place de la Concorde. There she stopped for a while and sat on a bench watching the hustle and bustle of Parisian life. Her thoughts were confused. Her mind went back to the Paris she knew with Davit, and then to Emile and the tranquillity of Lac Lucerne. She thought of how wonderful it would be to have her little family back together again. She realised that she hadn't eaten since breakfast, and it had been a long and exhausting day. She didn't realise that she was nodding off to sleep on the bench and woke some hours later to pitch darkness. Slowly she made her way up the Rue de Royale to the Place de Madeleine. She went around the L'eglise de la Madeleine and along Rue Tronchet towards the station. There she found a small café and decided to get something to eat. She sat at a small table in the corner of a café, deciding to wait there till they closed then make her way up to the station. To her surprise a young teenage waitress, came up to her and said, 'Madame Kaspar it's you, isn't it?'

'Yes, but how do you know me?' replied Jaqueline.

'My father is called Dimitar and he used to perform at your café, L'Armenien some years ago. He loved playing there and used to speak so warmly of those days. How is Davit? It is such a pity you had to close that café. My mother often took me to watch my father play. The music was so alive. Anyway, what are you doing in this part of Paris?'

Jaqueline took a deep breath and replied, 'And what did you say your name is?'

'Oh, I'm so sorry,' replied the enthusiastic young woman. 'My name is Chloe and I work here every Tuesday and Thursday evening for Madame Breton. That's her behind the Bar, she's the proprietor. I'm sure she would love to meet you.' With that the young Chloe called out excitedly. 'Madame Breton, Madame Breton, I want you to meet Madame Kaspar. She's the most superb person and she used to have a wonderful café called L'Armenien. My father played there lots and lots.'

The café wasn't busy, so Madame Breton came over to speak with Jacqueline. 'I'm Sophie Breton' she said extending her hand to be shaken. 'It's so nice to meet you. I knew your husband Davit soon after he came to Paris. He started that troupe that mimed while he told the most wonderful stories. Such energy, such charm. What is he doing now?' she enquired.

Jacqueline explained the whole story and that Davit had been seriously injured and how she was on her way to the military hospital at Rouen to pick him up and take him back to Switzerland. Both Sophie and the young Chloe listened intently.

'What horror is this war. What a waste of human life,' said Madame Breton with a tremble in her voice. 'You are lucky that your husband is still alive. Where there is life, there is still hope. My husband was killed in the trenches. Death is so final.' Madame Breton closed her eyes but couldn't hold back the tears.

This sorrowful scene of death and misery, drifted through mutual compassion to its inevitable conclusion and a stillness of reflection. Sophie Breton finally broke the silence by saying 'Well no use in feeling sorry for oneself, there's work to do, mouths to be fed. Can I get you another coffee Madame Kaspar or perhaps something a bit stronger?'

'No, no,' said Jacqueline. 'Just a glass of water would be wonderful and by the way please call me Jacqueline.' It seemed that contrary to French custom even though they had only just met, they used their Christian names rather than the more formal surnames. After all they had just shared their emotional and physical losses and had trusted each other with a depth of sorrows.

'A glass of water for Jacqueline,' said Madame Breton to the young Chloe. 'Come on we can't stand around looking gormless, can we?' she barked.

That night Jacqueline slept on a couch upstairs in Madame Breton's apartment. She was so tired that she would have slept through a hurricane. The next morning Madame Breton woke up Jacqueline saying, 'You must have some breakfast before you catch that train to Rouen.' The two women seemed to share a common sadness except Jacqueline still had her husband and a little boy with hope for a brighter future.

* * *

Jacqueline gave Madame Breton her address in Switzerland saying, 'When this war is over and when normality has returned, you must visit us in Lucerne.' It was said in politeness, and never did she think that it would happen. In turn, Madame Breton said 'Please give my best wishes to your husband Davit and let him know that my husband Charles thought very highly of him. Just tell him that Charles and Sophie are with him.'

13

The Rescue

By the time Jaqueline got to the station, the train to Rouen was waiting on the platform. Once again, she found herself a window seat as the train eased out of the station. Thoughts of her husband Davit, her mother Lucette, her son Emile, the kindness of Madame Breton, and the futility of war, all streamed through her mind. She hadn't realised that she had dozed off until she heard the squealing of the brakes as they pulled into Rouen station. The train slowly eased out of the station, leaving her deserted on the platform. She felt alone, not sure where she was meant to go. Eventually, she found a porter and asked the way to the military hospital. 'That's at Claire Mare about 12 kilometres along the road towards Le Havre. Just keep walking and you can't miss it,' said the porter, pointing in the direction that she should take.

* * *

She had walked for almost an hour when a van stopped and asked if she needed a lift. She explained that she was going to the military hospital. 'I'm going past it so hop in and I'll give you a lift,' replied the driver. He kept whistling a local tune and didn't want to say anything. She was fine with not having to talk.

About 25 minutes later he said, 'Here you are madame. The military hospital is just in there.' He was pointing to a small château. She thanked him, then walked up the gravelled path to the front entrance. She rang the bell, and a young nurse came to greet her, asking her to wait in the reception area. An older nurse came to tell her, 'Madam Kaspar, the director, Dr Korukian has said that he wants to talk with you before you see your husband. I will let him know you are here.'

Jacqueline waited for what seemed ages, but in fact was less than ten minutes. Finally, a thick set man with a white coat, a stethoscope around his neck, supporting a bushy black beard and heavy dark eyebrows came down the formal marble staircase, saying to Jacqueline in a deep formal voice, 'Madame Kaspar, my name is Victor Korukian, I'm the director here and I would just like to have a few words with you before I take you to see your husband, Davit.'

She followed him into a small office as he sat down behind an impressive desk. 'Nothing to worry about,' said the director, 'but I thought I should talk to you about Davit before you see him. You see he's not in the best of conditions and frankly very lucky to be alive. He took a massive blast on his left side and has lost his left leg and the use of his left arm. His face doesn't look too pretty either. You see I used to know Davit and his twin brother Vahan as young boys back in Constantinople. My father Takvor and his father Harat had become good friends. My father was a hard-working Armenian, who worked in the market trading in fruit. Harat was a big shot and lent my father some money that he was struggling to pay back.

So, my father went to see Harat hoping that they might come to an amicable agreement. Harat loved his fruit and certainly didn't want my father to go out of business. Together they decided that my father Takvor, would put together a box of his best fruit and deliver it to Harat every Friday evening. They worked out that the debt would be paid back in around thirty-three months. As a young boy, I helped my father, and it was my job to deliver the box of fruit to Harat every Friday. His face would always beam as he unpacked the surprise package. Harat was very shrewd as he knew that if you give someone a break, helping them in a time of need, they will do anything to repay the debt. Throughout the week my father would select his best usually exotic fruit, making an extra effort in quality and presentation.

By the time the thirty-three months of deliveries were completed, my father's business was going from strength to strength. I continued delivering the fruit for many years to come and my father only charged Harat the cost price. You see, even though the debt had been fully paid, the kindness that Harat showed my father has not been forgotten, and I feel that I need to help you in every way I can.' Victor Korukian paused, taking a deep sigh before he continued, 'Now enough about the past. You will want to see your husband. Leave your case here and follow me.'

* * *

Jacqueline, with some trepidation, followed the doctor up the stairs. He took two stairs at a time whereas she could only take one. He walked, with elongated strides, along a wide corridor with rooms either side. The doors were open so Jacqueline could see the wounded soldiers, four beds to a room. She was struck by how quiet it all seemed. Most of the patients seemed to be asleep or perhaps in a coma. She made eye contact with a few of the men who tried to smile back. There was a particular smell, mainly of ether or other medical potions. It was all exceptionally clean, but not clinical. Eventually they got to Davit's room. Davit smiled a coy smile at her as she entered the room. He seemed to recognise her as someone he knew but wasn't too sure who she was. Jacqueline was stunned. She had somehow expected a warm reception not a gentle smile without words or recognition.

'Well look who's come to see you,' said Dr Korukian. 'It's your wife Jacqueline. She's come a long way to see you and wants to take you home.' Jacqueline looked on in anticipation but soon realised that Davit wasn't recognizing her. His eyes were glazed as he grinned a meaningless, vacant smile.

'Well, I will leave you two together for no more than five minutes to say hello,' said Dr Korukian. He turned to Jacqueline and said, 'Perhaps when you have finished, you could come back downstairs to my office, so we can make some arrangements.'

Jacqueline held Davit's right hand in both of hers and started to speak gently to him. There was no big flood of emotion. There was nothing coming from Davit.

'I've been writing to you every day,' she said, 'but I don't suppose you would have received any of my letters.' She found it difficult to speak for both of them as she seemed to be the one, who not only asked the questions, but answered them too. 'Do you know how much longer they will want you to stay here?' she asked followed by, 'I suppose they will want to see how you recover.' It seemed Davit had lost the desire to speak. He just grinned.

Eventually, she said her goodbyes to Davit, promising to come back soon. She kissed him gently on his forehead and made her way downstairs to speak with Dr Korukian. Once again, she had to wait in the reception area, but it gave her time to regain her composure.

Dr Korukian was sitting behind his desk sucking on his pipe. 'Well, my dear,' he said with a pensive expression on his bearded face. 'We will need to keep Davit here for at least another couple of weeks before you can take him home. We need to monitor his wounds and ensure that they won't flare up again. Once we have ascertained that he is fit to travel, then and only then, we will ask you to take him as we need the bed space for others coming from the front. Do you have any immediate concerns or questions?'

'I have two immediate issues that concern me,' she replied.

'Yes, go on, fire away,' said Dr Korukian.

'Firstly, I would like to stay close by so I can visit him regularly. Is there some cheap accommodation around here?'

'Yes, I have thought about this,' interrupted Dr Korukian. 'I would like to make you an offer that I think might suit all three of us. You look like a fit, caring young woman, and we need all the help we can get around here. We would love you to stay for a couple of weeks and help us out wherever you can. Many of the soldiers don't have any visitors and someone to come and give them a bit of attention would be so beneficial. Some need letters to be written to their loved ones and some need letters from their sweethearts to be read out to them. There are also numerous menial jobs such as, emptying bedpans, helping the invalids to walk or, pushing their wheelchairs out into the sunshine and not forgetting to rescue them from the rain. There are a million little jobs to be done. And I have a bed for you in the nurse's quarters but I'm afraid you would have to share a room with three other nurses. What do you say about my offer?'

'Yes, yes I would love that,' Jacqueline replied.

'So that's sorted,' interjected Dr Korukian. 'And the other concern?'

'I'm just worried how I will get Davit all the way back to Switzerland,' said Jacqueline.

'Don't you worry about that,' said Dr Korukian. 'I can arrange something for you. I'm not meant to, but I have friends in high positions in the Red Cross. I can write them a request for transportation all the way to the Swiss border. I will tell them that he needs a nurse to travel with him. You might need to borrow a nurse's uniform from one of the nurses. I am sure we can find a nurse your size that will be happy to lend you some of her uniform for the trip. No, you just relax and help where you can.' With that he got up and said, 'Nurse Candide will show you the ropes. Don't forget your valise,' he said handing her the petite case. 'Any problems come and see me.'

'Thank you so much how can I thank you enough,' said Jacqueline.

'Not a problem, it's a pleasure for me to repay the kindness that old Harat gave my father. A friend in need is a friend indeed as the English would say.' He put his arm around her as he opened the door and said to the receptionist. 'Can you ask nurse Candide to look after this young woman please?'

Jacqueline was overawed. Not only did Dr Korukian sort out everything with such kindness but that he had the time to add the word *'please'* to each of his requests. This somehow changed the dynamic of him being the boss, giving out commands, to him being an equal, requesting rather than ordering his staff around.

Two weeks went quickly, and the nurses appreciated the help that Jacqueline could offer. They told her not to get too close to any of the wounded as it made it more difficult for them when she had to leave. They told her of the anger that some of the wounded felt towards their situation and how it made it worse when someone who seemed to understand left them. Many of the soldiers were just young men struck down in the prime of their lives.

* * *

Jacqueline visited her husband Davit each morning and would talk with him. She quickly tired of things to say and found her soliloquy exhausting. She would sit in silence just holding his right hand. Then suddenly out of the blue Davit mumbled something. It was the first time he had spoken.

'What did you say? What did you say?' she asked as she bent forward to put her ear close to his mouth.

'Can you tell me a story?' he said grinning from ear to ear.

'Ah, you are back with us,' she said as if nothing much had happened. Davit still had a grin on his face but said nothing more.

"Well, you see, there was a wealthy farmer that had an idle son," she started in the same tone of voice that Davit used when he told his stories. Davit closed his eyes and listened with contentment while she told the complete story about the 'farmer and his son', word for word.

Each morning she would ask Davit which story he wanted her to relate, but he always nodded his head when she mentioned the "Money story", about the farmer and his idle son. Then one day, as she was telling the story, she added a section of her own. She made up a part where the destitute son went to see his friend Ursula, asking her to lend him some money. Ursula replied:

> *Oh yes, I have plenty of money to give you but unfortunately it has fallen into a big vat of wine. If you take off your clothes and jump in, you will be able to retrieve the muslin bag with some gold coins in it.' The young man took off his clothes, jumped into the vat, but found no bag of gold, only a thick layer of mud at the bottom of the vat, and hungry fish swimming about, wanting to bite him. Covered in slimy mud up to his waist and bitten by the fish he managed to get out of the vat but without any gold coins. 'There wasn't any bag of gold coins,' said the young man as he got out of the vat covered in mud. 'Now I remember,' laughed Ursula 'My brother came last week with his fishing net and scooped out that bag of gold coins. But it was so funny seeing you covered in mud with no clothes on. Ha ha ha,' Ursula chortled.*

Davit let out a tittering laugh and it was from that time on, that his diction greatly improved. He was soon able to form individual words and quickly progressed to speaking complete sentences. It didn't take long before Jacqueline decided it was time to take her husband back to Switzerland.

All the nurses were sad to see her go, as she had lightened their workload with laughter and grace. A nurse of a similar size to Jacqueline, was happy to lend her a uniform for the journey. 'I will post it back to you as soon as I can,' said Jacqueline.

Finally, Dr Korukian wished Jaqueline and Davit a safe trip home, and turning to Davit, he jokingly chuckled, 'You've got a good one there, look after her. And don't forget to eat plenty of fruit!'

Davit with the help of a stick in his right hand and Jaqueline supporting his left side, managed to hobble to the waiting Red Cross van. The driver had been instructed to take them all the way to the Swiss border at Ferney-Voltaire. This was as far as he was permitted to go. Jacqueline and David would have to walk across the no man's land border, some three hundred metres to the Swiss side of the Geneva checkpoint. Together they hobbled across to the checkpoint and Jacqueline produced her Swiss passport and marriage certificate to Davit, who still travelled on a French passport. The Swiss officer was rather abrupt to begin with, but his tone softened once he learnt that they were going to Lucerne. Being originally from there, he had known Jacqueline's mother. He had been too young to know much about Jacqueline, who had left for Paris when he was still a child. The officer stamped their documents and with somewhat of a flourish said, 'Welcome to Switzerland. May you enjoy your stay, and travel in peace.' They started to hobble on down the road when the young officer came running after them saying, 'If you wait twenty minutes, I will be off duty and can give you a lift into Geneva. I will be going past the main railway station where you can catch a train to Lucerne.' Davit was amazed at the kindness of the Swiss and knew immediately that this would be his home for the rest of his days.

* * *

At the station, Jacqueline was able to get tickets to Lucerne for later that day. She had also been able to send a cable to her mother saying that they were on their way and an estimated time of arrival at Lucerne. There on the station platform were Jacqueline's mother Lucette, and young Emile, who was rather confused at seeing Davit as an old man with only one leg and a crushed arm. It didn't take long for Davit and Emile to form a very strong bond. Davit stayed at home and was there when Emile came back from school. Jacqueline trained as a nurse while her mother tended the cows and vegetable patch. Davit took up painting, mainly water colours and was to become a revered artist. His artwork expressed his exuberance for life and his journey through dreams to a better world. Davit noticed that his son had that special birthmark behind his left ear and spoke often to Emile of his family and his own childhood back in Constantinople. He related the stories that his father Harat had told him as a young boy and spoke with sadness of his own parents and his twin brother Vahan. How they had died in the devastating blast and subsequent fire. He would often say to Emile, 'One day we will go to Constantinople and then on to explore the exotic secrets of the orient.'

It was with great sadness that Davit would think of his twin brother Vahan, and how they might have shared their lives and grown old together. Little did he know that Vahan had survived the blast and was now living in India, married to Sara. Vahan also thought frequently of Davit and was under the impression that he had died in the inferno.

* * *

And thus, the brother's lives were scattered to distant lands. Their paths had been broken; with only memories to carry them forward, they went their separate ways.

PART 2

Never give up hope

West   East

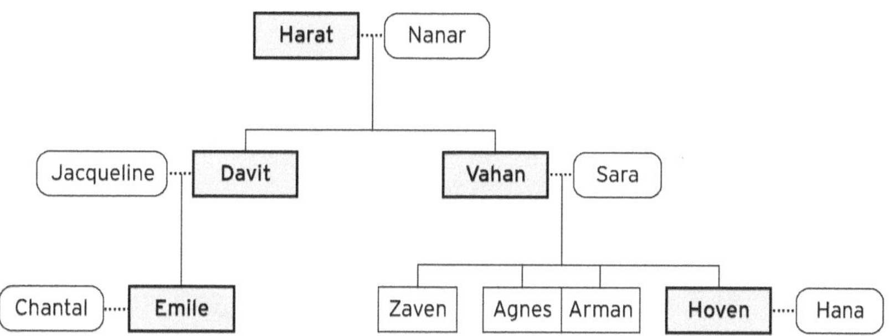

14

Sara Kaspar

The journey that Vahan, Sara and their three-year-old son, Zaven made to Calcutta was far more arduous than they had anticipated. Once they hit the Indian sub-continent they were confronted with disease and difficult terrain. Vahan was struck by a virulent form of dysentery that kept re-emerging for the rest of his life. This severely limited his capacity to hold down any kind of work and consequently, the family suffered great setbacks.

* * *

Vahan went inside himself. Gone were the days of the young, bronzed fisherman with a strong physique and abundant curly hair. His whole body seemed to collapse under the slightest pressure. He recoiled from life and felt removed. Once again, his mind floated towards esoteric issues of theosophy, and it was only through his meditations that he was able to find his solace.

Sara was forced to take up the reins and soon found herself resenting what she saw as her husband's indulgences. Sara had come from a peasant background up in the hills around Diyarbakir, a remote area of Turkey. She hadn't had the opportunity to learn to read or write nor had she the inclination to do so. She had learnt about riding horses bareback and fishing in mountain streams. Hers was a life of practicability and hardship. Their initial love for each other became strained and it was as much as they could do to remain civil towards each other.

An incident happened in a small village outside of Kabul, Afghanistan. Neither Vahan, nor Sara spoke about it, but in later years, Vahan related some sketchy details to Zaven, their eldest son.

According to Zaven, one night when Vahan couldn't sleep, he left their small tent and walked towards the nearby village. The night would have been bitterly cold, as the full moon illuminated the dirt pathway through the village. Suddenly from within one of the small mud houses, Vahan heard the screams of a woman and the shouting of a man. The screams of the woman ended abruptly, and the man's shouting turned to weeping. Vahan froze and was too afraid to enter the house, to see if he could help. He continued on his way. The next morning, the body of a woman was found by the river. She had been stabbed numerous times. News of the murder spread like wildfire and although the man was charged with the murder, he was set free. The local judge said that the man had admitted to the murder of his wife, he wasn't able to commit him to a prison sentence as it was alleged that the wife had committed the first offence, being an adulterer. The man was reprimanded for the murder of his wife, with the judge simply saying that he should have let the courts decide the fate of his adulterous wife.

When Sara found out that Vahan had heard the screams of the woman, she irrationally blamed Vahan for the murder. She scolded him, saying that he should have gone into the house and protected the woman. It didn't seem to matter to her that Vahan may have also been killed. What hurt Vahan the most was that she rebuked him saying, 'Davit would have been brave, he would have defended the woman.' This last comment really hurt Vahan badly as it brought back all his insecurities. Insecurities that he had fought so hard to put behind him. The comparison with Davit affected Vahan more than the illogical wrath that Sara projected towards him. Vahan felt isolated and his delicate pride had been belittled. The relationship between Vahan and Sara was broken and was never to be fully repaired.

* * *

By the time they arrived in Calcutta, they couldn't stand the sight of each other, deciding to separate before it turned nasty. In fact, this was the best thing that they could have done as reconciliation for them just wasn't possible. Sara took young Zaven and went to live with a half cousin, Rose. They were all desperately poor, and being poor in Calcutta in those days was by no means a good thing. They were surrounded by beggars and thieves that scoured the rich and middle-class suburbs for whatever they could plunder. Human dignity was discarded, and life was precarious. Survival was as much as could be hoped for.

Cousin Rose was just 19 years old. She was renting a small room and worked at a nearby restaurant. She was happy to share what little she had with Sara and Zaven but they both realised that this could only be a temporary arrangement.

* * *

Rose at the age of six had become separated from her parents. She had been at the local market with both parents, when mistakenly snatched by villains, who had hoped for a large ransom. The villains soon found out that her parents had little money, so dumped Rose in a small village, 80 miles further towards the foothills of the Himalayas. Some weeks later, Rose managed, with the help of the police, to find her way back to her parent's house in Naliapur, but by that time, the house had been abandoned and subsequently sold to new occupants. The police couldn't help Rose find her parents, and it was assumed that they had both been murdered. Rose was initially put into an orphanage but soon was taken in by some neighbours who felt sorry for her. Rose always believed that her parents had been abducted rather than murdered. On reaching the age of fifteen, Rose left the neighbour's household and made her way to Calcutta to find employment. She found work in a restaurant belonging to an elderly Armenian gentleman called Dikran Constantine. Dikran arriving in Calcutta at the age of twenty, had chosen to change his original surname of Kourokistian to Constantine. He wanted something that was more acceptable to the British but still reflected his heritage.

Dikran Constantine was a hardworking businessman. He had never married but had thrown himself fully into his many and various business ventures with mixed success. He ran a couple of restaurants as well as running a variety of food stalls in the markets. He owned a couple of rundown commercial properties and a residential property that he rented out. He was well organised but was a man who just couldn't resist a gamble. He won and he lost, but somehow had managed to make ends meet as he moved precariously through life. Mr Constantine had been a friend of Rose's adopting parents in Naliapur and had known about the disappearance of her real parents. He wanted to help young Rose by offering her a job at one of his restaurants. As part of the terms of employment, he allowed her to eat meals at the restaurant but stipulated that she could not take any food home. In this way he thought he would get a good many more hours of employment out of her.

It was one afternoon, soon after Sara and her son Zaven had moved into a small room at Rose's apartment, that Rose came back home brimming with excitement. Someone had come into the restaurant and had told her that her parents were still alive and were living in what was at that time called Bombay, now Mumbai. He had given Rose an address written on a scrunched-up piece of paper, telling her that she would find them there. She was so excited, she wanted to leave immediately to go and see them.

Rose asked Sara if she would look after the apartment and her belongings while she was away. They decided that they should both go and see Mr Constantine the next day to ask if Sara could take over Rose's position in the restaurant for a short while. Mr Constantine could sense Rose's excitement and gave his approval, as long as she worked with Sara for a couple of days to show her the ropes. Rose couldn't wait to take the train to Bombay and find her parents. Sara soon picked up the reins at the restaurant and a couple of days later, at 7:30am she took the young Rose to the main railway station. They embraced on the platform and Sara wished her cousin a safe trip and hoped that she would find her parents in good health. As the train pulled out of the station Sara held Zaven's little hand and wondered what life had in store. She didn't think too long as she knew she would shortly be expected at the restaurant and that there was work to be done.

* * *

Rose had told Sara that she would write as soon as she had found where her parents were living. No letter arrived and Rose never came back. She seemed to disappear into thin air.

Sara worked hard in the restaurant and her energy was noted. The regular clients loved her no nonsense manner, as she gave back the banter she received. She was able to take young Zaven to work with her and he played by himself outside in the back courtyard. The cook and other staff loved having him around and kept feeding him. Sara yelled at the staff that they weren't to feed him as he would grow so large and burst. Once told off by Sara, they didn't do it again. Soon, Sara became in charge of the restaurant and organised the staff. Dikran Constantine came regularly to his restaurant and admired the way Sara operated a very profitable and happy business.

Dikran told Sara that it was time for young Zaven to go to school and how important an education was for a young boy. She argued that she had done alright without an education and that it wouldn't be necessary. Dikran realised that in principle Sara wasn't averse to education but thought that perhaps she couldn't afford it. So, Dikran offered to pay for Zaven to go to school at which Sara was only too pleased, completely changing her tune and saying how important education was for a man to progress in life. This offer of payment by Dikran was twice blessed. Firstly, Zaven got an education but equally as important, it cemented the friendship between Sara and Dikran.

*　*　*

Dikran was some thirty-five years older than Sara, old enough to be her father. Missing out on having children and grandchildren of his own, he had buried himself in his work. Here was a young woman without a father figure to speak of and a young child without a grandfather. Although it was never spoken about, Dikran and Sara enjoyed a father and daughter relationship that over the years paid dividends to both parties. Sara soon became embroiled in some of Dikran's other ventures, trying to keep him in order. She never stopped his petty gambling as she realised that it was just part of him. She directed him towards a backgammon school for elderly men. This helped to provide companionship for him, as well as creating a distraction from his urge to buy and then try to resurrect failing businesses.

Sara became Dikran's right-hand woman who mingled confidently with people. She had a fiery temper when she needed it but was also kind when it was called for. Dikran focused on the accounting and administrative side of things while Sara attended to the daily running of the business. Their partnership worked well. Dikran didn't mind that Sara appeared to wear the pants as long as he made the final decisions on matters. In fact, he always agreed with whatever Sara suggested and would say 'Well if you think so, then so it shall be.' He just liked to have the last word.

Sara moved into a small apartment in a block of six flats that Dikran owned. He lived downstairs whilst she and her son Zaven lived on the second level. On many evenings, Dikran would babysit Zaven, so a small bed was installed in Dikran's downstairs flat. Sara would come home late from the restaurant, exhausted by working hard and the long hours. Dikran would help carry the young sleeping Zaven to Sara's flat upstairs. The arrangement worked for many years with more ups than downs. Dikran and Sara both realised that they needed each other. Sara was the 'doer' while Dikran thought of himself as the 'thinker'. The business improved but was still hampered by Dikran's insatiable desire to buy failed businesses that were well beyond resurrection. Backgammon could only resolve so much.

* * *

Then one day Sara came down to drop off Zaven, finding Dikran slumped at the table. It turned out that he had suffered a partial stroke. Sara was devastated. Dikran was taken to hospital and stayed there for two nights before he was sent home to recuperate. Recuperate he did but never fully recovered. The right side of his body was severely affected, his speech was slightly slurred, and his right arm and leg were limp. His mental capacities were eventually restored but because of his physical constraints, he couldn't carry out his administrative role. There were bills to be paid, tax receipts and numerous letters to be written.

Sara went to work at the restaurant in a state of shock. What would she do without Dikran? She had lunches to supervise and attending to the unruly staff was by no means an easy task. Then, out of the blue something happened that caused a new direction to her life.

She was serving lunch to a particularly grumpy and arrogant man who was making sexist and derogatory remarks towards her. Suddenly from behind her, she heard a deep stern voice say to the objectional customer, 'That's not an appropriate comment to say to my wife.'

Sara quickly turned around to see Vahan towering above her and staring at the customer.

'I think you should make an apology to her immediately,' he said and then bent forward and grabbed the customer's plate. Both Sara and the customer were stunned. The man made an apology to Vahan who then gave back the plate of food. The restaurant was silent for a moment or two and then returned to the normal barrage of sound. The grumpy man never returned to the restaurant.

'What are you doing here?' asked Sara of Vahan. 'I've come to have lunch,' replied Vahan. 'Isn't that's what people usually do at a restaurant. Anyway, what are you doing here?'

'I work here,' she replied. 'If you want some lunch, sit down over there,' she said, pointing to a small table in the corner. 'I will get you a menu or you can choose from the specials board. The Chicken Pulao is good today,' said Sara in her trained manageress patter.

Vahan sat at the small table and ate his lunch in silence. When the last of the lunch customers had left, Sara wiped down the tables, before going to sit opposite Vahan. 'It's nice to see you,' she said to Vahan with a smile. Life as a single mother didn't really suit Sara. Even though Dikran had been a steadying influence, she had missed having someone to blame when things didn't go quite right.

'It's nice to see you too,' replied Vahan, as he stretched out his hand to hold hers. 'How is Zaven?' He must be almost five by now. Would you mind if I came over to see him?'

'I'm sure he'd love to see you. Why don't you come over around 4:30pm this afternoon and perhaps you can play a game of football with him in the park. He loves kicking a ball, even though he is so totally uncoordinated.'

With that Sara gave Vahan her address and so started chapter two of their topsy-turvy marriage.

* * *

Vahan stayed the night, and the next day Sara took Vahan downstairs to meet Dikran. Both Vahan and Dikran hit it off immediately.

'Look what the wind brought in,' said Sara as she introduced Vahan to Dikran. 'He just happened to come to the restaurant for something to eat.' Vahan never told Sara that in fact he had known that she worked there, and that it was no accident that he had come to the restaurant. He had been missing Sara as well as wondering how his son Zaven was going.

Sara hadn't talked much about Vahan to Dikran, so Dikran hadn't felt comfortable about making too many enquiries on the matter. Before his stroke, Dikran had felt good about being the male influence on both Sara and Zaven, but was now only too happy to share the position with Vahan. After all, Vahan was the rightful heir to the position and besides, Dikran was getting on in years.

Vahan, with his gentle ways slipped back easily into Sara's life and to begin with it was as if nothing had ever happened. Vahan had a part-time job in a second-hand bookshop. He was in his element as he could read to his heart's content and was good at helping customers to choose a book they would enjoy. Dikran needed assistance with the paperwork and running his numerous businesses. Vahan could tell people 'Not only do I work in a bookshop, but I am also a bookkeeper for Mr Constantine.' Vahan loved books.

Vahan soon moved into the flat with Sara and for a while, all went well. Vahan helped Dikran two days a week, worked at the bookshop, played house husband for Sara and father to Zaven. He would pick up Zaven from kindergarten and take him to the park before giving him supper. He enjoyed putting his son to bed each night, telling him stories until he fell sound asleep. Then he would make dinner for Dikran, Sara, and himself. Sara would make clothes for all of them while Vahan read well into the night.

* * *

Life was fine for a couple of years; that was before Sara found herself to be pregnant again. This really put the spanner in the works. The larger she became, the more exasperated she was. Vahan did his best to keep her and her hormones from totally overboiling.

The twins were born on 15th April 1912, the same day that the *Titanic* sank on its maiden voyage across the Atlantic. When Vahan read the dramatic news of the sinking, he wanted to name the twins after a couple of the Greek mythological characters referred to as Titans. There were several male and female Titan names to choose from. After considerable deliberation, he suggested that his son should be named Cronus and his daughter should be called Phoebe. He put forward his suggestion to Sara who reacted vehemently, rejecting it out of court. After a week or so she agreed that Vahan could choose the middle names, but that she would choose their first names. She argued that they were her children, so she should choose their names. She refuted the fact that Vahan had anything to do with the birth of her children and that they were simply a gift from God.

'I'll have nothing to do with this "*Mitalogical*" Greek rubbish,' she raged, 'I want them to be Armenian.' And so it was that the twins got their middle names Cronus and Phoebe.

The girl was named Agnes and the boy Arman. Sara wasn't a natural mother and resented the fact that she had to stay at home albeit for less than two weeks. She couldn't get back to work fast enough. Looking after babies wasn't for her.

* * *

Vahan gave up his part-time job at the bookshop to help in the restaurant. It wasn't long before Vahan found himself back in the role of house husband. He was a born carer and enjoyed having the twins to look after. As soon as Sara had left for work, Vahan would feed Zaven, and the twins. Once fed, Vahan would take the twins downstairs to be looked after by Dikran so he could walk Zaven to school. Vahan would return home, clean the house and then go downstairs to see Dikran for a chat and put the world to right. Dikran would bring out a small bed that Zaven had used when staying with him, for the twins to sleep in. Vahan and Dikran would sit outside, drink tea and smoke revolting cigarettes. Then Vahan would make lunch for himself, Dikran, and the twins before going to fetch Zaven from school. Looking after the children, cleaning the house, shopping and cooking gave him little time to read. Money also became an issue so Vahan went to see if the bookshop would have

115

him back. They needed someone for Monday, Wednesday, and Friday from 11am through to 2:30pm, this suited him fine. He could take Agnes and Arman with him as they were well behaved.

* * *

Dikran missed Vahan's company and got a bit bored with his own company. He would go to play backgammon with some of his friends but missed the stimulating conversations that he had had with Vahan. It was at one of these backgammon sessions, that Dikran got duped into buying yet another fraudulent business. Dikran started playing backgammon most evenings. He played as if it was a game in which you just moved counters around a board. He never appreciated the skill and strategy that was required. They played for money, somehow Dikran seemed to be winning all the time. He played often against the same Persian gentleman who was always there and ready to play. Dikran kept a score of his winnings and one day the Persian gentleman said to Dikran 'You are such a good player I have lost count on how much you are winning.' 'It's 243,400 rupees' replied Dikran without any hesitation. 'Is it as much as that?' said the man. 'There's no way I can afford to pay you.' They discussed how the debt could be paid, and the man suggested that he would be happy to part with his thriving taxi business worth around 450,000 rupees. The deal was struck, Dikran could have the business if he wiped off the debt that he was owed and paid just 150,000 rupees. The next day Dikran went with the cash in a hessian bag and signed the papers, making the deal legal.

Dikran then went to the workshop where the taxi was housed. He met a local Hindu man who owned the workshop and once it was established that Dikran was now the proud owner of 'The Bengal Transport Company,' the man showed him out the back and pointed to a broken-down car that was the taxi. In fact, Dikran hadn't realised that not only did the so-called company comprise of an old car but also an old bus and an even older truck. None of these vehicles could be considered road worthy, even by Indian standards, and the registration on all three vehicles would soon be running out. The owner of the workshop explained to Dikran that the three vehicles had been brought to him for safe keeping a week ago, and that he would be charging 1400 rupees a month for looking after the vehicles. Dikran had been well and truly duped and he soon realised that he had bought a liability rather than a profitable business.

Dikran never saw the Persian man again. Looking at the state of the saloon car, the old bus and an even older truck, Dikran realised the mistake that he had made. He felt very silly and was too embarrassed to admit his mistake, especially to Sara. He could hear the chiding that would be dished out to him. 'I work hard and long in your restaurant and all you do is waste money,' he could hear her berate, but only in much stronger and more colourful language. Not only had he spent 150,000 rupees to buy a worthless company but what was he going to do with this pile of broken-down vehicles. He had to get them out of there fast, the rent would be exorbitant.

Dikran remembered that some fifteen years earlier, he had bought a warehouse full of flour from a Punjabi man. The flour would be worth a mint or so he thought. Unfortunately, Dikran procrastinated over the sale of the flour and wasn't at all happy with the offers he received. He felt if he just hung on a bit, he would be able to strike a much better deal. Finally, someone wanted to buy the flour at the right price but when he went to see what he would be purchasing he found the flour was riddled with weevils. No one would buy the flour and eventually he had to get the flour transported to a site way out of town and buried underground. One good thing was he kept the empty warehouse and although it was in a very rundown area, it was ideal to house his broken-down car, bus, and a small rusty truck.

* * *

The next day Dikran went with a Bengali man, and they used the truck to tow first the bus and then the car to the warehouse on the outskirts of town. He covered the three vehicles with several tarpaulins and padlocked the gates. Perhaps one day he could sell the lot to a scrap metal merchant. Perhaps it would be best to forget about the whole issue and pretend that they didn't exist. He put it down to one of those lessons in life. Dikran never returned to the Backgammon school, as he was too embarrassed to show his face.

15

Zaven and his Siblings

Vahan and Sara's fourth and last child named Hovhannes, was born on 23rd April 1916. There had been confusion concerning the exact date of his birth as the handwritten birth certificate wasn't at all clear. Some thought it could be 28th April, but Hovan, as he was always referred to, was just happy to have been born. Vahan had been quick to point out, that the 23rd was exactly three hundred years since the death of William Shakespeare. 'You missed him by a mere three hundred years, but he is still very much alive today,' Vahan would tell his son jokingly, but Hovan would scrunch up his nose, wondering what a three-hundred-year-old man might look like.

* * *

Hovan was born with piercing black eyes that followed you around the room. The first thing that Vahan noticed was the birthmark behind his left ear. Neither of his two older boys Zaven nor Arman had such a birthmark. Vahan was overjoyed on seeing the same birthmark that he, his father and his twin brother Davit had inherited. Vahan never mentioned the birthmark to Sara as he didn't want to raise the subject of his brother Davit, fearing it would only generate sad memories. It might also trigger the recollection of the incident in Afghanistan and her hurtful comparison to Davit. Vahan knew when to keep silent on such matters. Instead, he conveyed his joy to the elderly Dikran, who might have been foolish as far as business was concerned but was a good listener regarding matters of the heart. Dikran never offered any advice but simply made the right noises at the right time.

Vahan spoke at length to Dikran about his childhood and how his twin brother and parents had been killed by the explosion at their house in Constantinople. He talked about his time in Venice and how Artoush had helped him escape from the seminary. He told Dikran that Artoush also had this special birthmark and how he had feared for his own safety. Dikran swore that he would never tell anyone about the birthmark but suggested that one day, when the time was right, Vahan should speak to Hovan about it, but never to write anything down on paper. The secret was kept between the two men, the rest of the family would never find out about it. The truth was concealed; only Hovan, in the fullness of time, would become aware of it.

* * *

Dikran Constantine died of heart failure a couple of years after Hovan was born. Sara wept for three days solid, then suddenly decided that she had things to do and a family to feed. Sara blew hot and then cold in consecutive breaths. Her emotions were fluid but once put behind her, they never resurfaced. Vahan was totally devastated. He had admired Dikran and although he didn't consider him an intellectual equal, Dikran always tried to do the right thing. As Dikran had requested, they buried him in the grounds of Calcutta's Armenian Church. Only the Kaspar family attended the funeral. No one from the backgammon school showed up. Dikran had been an intensely private person, with his own family and any friends that he might have had before Sara and Vahan, simply fading away into the distant past.

The next day, Vahan, Sara and the four children, went to see the Public Trustees about Dikran's Will. The Executor, in a solemn tone, read out the formal Will that had been written in verbose, legalese language. It meant nothing to any of them. Then, the Executor explained in plain English, that in principle, Dikran had wanted to bestow his worldly possessions to Sara but had also stipulated a list of items to be given to particular members of the family, at specific times.

Sara was to hold the titles of the six apartments, but Vahan would be permitted to live in one of the flats. Sara was to choose first which apartment she wanted to live in and then Vahan could choose his apartment. Each of the four children on turning eighteen years of age, would inherit an apartment. Sara was to hold the titles of all the apartments until each child reached their age of entitlement.

Vahan would not be allowed to borrow against his apartment or to sublet it. It would be solely for his personal use and security, but upon his demise, his apartment should be sold, with the remaining funds, divided equally between the surviving family members. Dikran had noticed Vahan's growing propensity for gambling, and also thought, that if Vahan lived in the same block of flats as Sara, they might reconcile their differences. Dikran was right about not giving too much to Vahan, gambling had indeed taken a hold. However, trying to get Vahan and Sara back together was a dismal failure. In fact, living in the same block of flats drove them further apart.

'Who will get the first choice between Agnes and Arman?' asked Sara of the executor. 'Whoever was born first' replied the Executor, not understanding that Agnes and Arman were twins and that no one knew who had been born first. In fact, Sara did know that Agnes was the older by a matter of eight minutes but had pretended that she didn't. Vahan was silent as the subject was a bit too close to home.

'We could just spin a coin,' said Zaven whose common sense came to the fore.

'Yes, we could spin a coin,' agreed Vahan realising the simplicity of the resolution.

* * *

As for the rest of the Will, confusion reigned as some of the specific items seemed rather obscure. 'What is this about a workshop that houses a taxi, a bus and a truck? Why should they be held for Zaven until he turns sixteen years of age?' exclaimed Sara, demanding, 'Why didn't we know about this?' After the commotion had died down, it was decided that, as Zaven would be turning sixteen in three months time, that he should be given these items immediately to save any duplication of paperwork or transference fees.

There was a pittance in Dikran's bank account, but most of the other items including the restaurant were debt free. Many of the items would need a lot of effort and funds to make them viable and in some cases, they could be seen as a liability rather than an asset.

Sara set to and decided to sell off many of the non-profit making enterprises that Dikran had left her. She kept the restaurant going and of course honoured Dikran's Will putting Zaven's name as the sole owner of the warehouse that housed the broken-down vehicles. Sara chose a downstairs rather than upstairs apartment. She had three children that needed access to a garden space to play in. It was decided that Vahan would take an upstairs apartment and that Sara would move into what had been Dikran's downstairs apartment. It made sense for Zaven the eldest child to live upstairs with his father, and the other three children to live downstairs with Sara. Vahan agreed to the arrangements. He would have anyway chosen an upstairs flat but wanted to make Sara feel he was doing her a favour.

* * *

As soon as Zaven turned sixteen, he applied for an apprenticeship with the French Motor Car Company. Although he had been very bright at school, he wanted to do something that was mechanical. His decision met with approval from his mother, but his father expressed his disappointment that his eldest son would not become an academic. After he completed his two years of apprenticeship, Zaven was immediately given a job with the company that had trained him and soon took over as the chief mechanic of the Servicing and Repairs department.

In the evenings, Zaven would go to his warehouse and work on the broken-down vehicles that had been left to him. He invited another apprentice to come and help him in the workshop. Together they worked on the car, taking it apart and thoroughly cleaning all the parts. Some of the components needed replacing, but they didn't have the money to buy new ones. His friend Gupta said that they should get second-hand parts, but Zaven would have nothing of it.

'It's new or nothing,' he would say. 'I want these vehicles to last for forty years. I will find the money or will just have to work overtime.' Slowly they took the bus and the truck apart and laid them out systematically on the floor ready for reassembling, once he could afford to do so.

Zaven unlike his father was extremely hard working. He was out of the house by 7:30am each morning and didn't return until 10pm most nights. By day, he worked at the French Motor Car Company and by night, he worked on his own vehicles.

At the age of eighteen, Zaven became the proud owner of an apartment. He chose an upstairs apartment, deciding to keep the existing tenant, while continuing to live with his father. He used the rent he received to buy new parts for the vehicles that lay in pieces on the floor of his workshop. He was not only smart but was also hard-working and determined. He was his mother's son. He was going to succeed.

Within two years Zaven had managed to get all three vehicles up and running, painting them with a red, white and blue theme. He admired the French influence of his employers and would be faithful to them for many years to come.

* * *

Meanwhile Sara worked hard at the restaurant. She had mixed success, as other restaurants came and went. Her business was steady and would prove to last the test of time. Her main source of income was from the apartments she held and rented out for the children. She realised the need to learn to read and write but didn't have the time or inclination to do so. She hated the fact that she would have to go and seek Vahan's help and was determined to give her children the best education that she could afford. Arman and later Hovan were sent to a nearby all-boys school called St Josephs. The school wasn't cheap, but it had a good reputation. Arman was more interested in sport and girls, whilst Hovan excelled in Maths and Science. Arman represented the school in both cricket and hockey, he enjoyed team sports with their camaraderie and the element of competition. Hovan preferred individual sports and was a mean squash player. Vahan took great interest in his children's education, while Sara just saw schooling as a necessary evil and a financial drain. Both boys enjoyed the school's debating society and on one occasion paired up to represent the school at the State's finals. Arman played the fool while Hovan took the considered well-argued pathway. Arman's summing up became legendary, with the audience from both for and against the motion, splitting their sides with laughter. Arman did eventually become a barrister but with only medium success. He found he couldn't sway the judge by simply mocking the opposition. Arman became a larger-than-life character and a big scotch drinker. He once said that he only married Jessica because her father owned a boutique distillery in Perthshire, Scotland. Jessica had in her youth, been a model and Arman enjoyed her looks as well as her vivacity. He admitted to Hovan that he had learnt to laugh at the appropriate times even though he couldn't always fully understand her broad Scottish brogue. Their marriage lasted less than a year.

* * *

At the age of eleven, Agnes was sent away to a Catholic convent. The convent was up country, in a town called Allahabad, Uttar Pradesh. Like her father, she was a studious scholar who excelled in arts subjects with only a meagre pass in technical matters. She was a talented musician and loved playing Chopin's nocturnes. Later, Agnes would go on to University in Delhi to study literature and the history of art. Eventually, she went to do research at the Sorbonne in Paris, specialising in classical French art and literature.

During the first school holidays, Agnes returned home feeling rather at a loss. Her three brothers neglected her, and her father, who lived upstairs, found it difficult relating to her. Agnes felt distant from her domineering, hard working mother Sara, who in turn didn't have much time for her studious daughter. Sara once said of her daughter, 'What's the use of a B.A. if you haven't got any common sense.' Agnes missed the friendship of her school friends and could not wait to get back.

One girl at school, soon became Agnes' best friend. Victoria wasn't the brightest of girls but was a very good hockey player, who would represent India in the under sixteen schoolgirl's team. Victoria was an orphan who had been abandoned by her mother. Although Anglo Indian, she could pass as a European. It is thought that her mother had been quite light in complexion and that her father was an upper-class Englishman who never knew about her birth. Poor Victoria had been taken in by the nuns but didn't have anywhere to go to during the school holidays.

When the girls returned to school after the first school holidays, they were asked by the English teacher to write an essay about what they did during their holidays. 'I want you to write about your feelings rather than a list of what you did,' said the teacher. Victoria struggled to write more than six lines and it wasn't at all complimentary. In true Agnes style, she wrote a lengthy poem in the form of a lament. She bemoaned the lack of any close friendship and the pleasure of returning to school with its structure and companionship.

The English teacher, a nun called Sister Claire, spoke about the essays at the next staff meeting and asked what could be done. The next day, the mother superior called both Agnes and Victoria into her office. Sister Claire was there too. The mother superior said to the girls who were standing in front of her, wondering what they might have done wrong, 'It has come to my attention, that your school holidays have not been what they might be. Holidays are meant to be a relaxed interlude to contemplate and consolidate the previous term and to prepare for the term ahead. However, they should also be a time to grow and develop friendships outside of the collegiate experience.' Then she dropped a bombshell. 'We think that it would be good if you Victoria could go to visit Agnes for a few days next holidays. We can put aside a few meagre funds for your train trip with a small stipend for food and lodging expenses. What do you think girls?' They both looked at each other and beamed with approval.

'We would love it, it would be simply wonderful, wouldn't it Vicki,' said Agnes ardently.

'Unfortunately, that is only the first step,' said the mother superior 'Next we will need to ask Mr and Mrs Kaspar for their consent and then I would have to pass it through the school's board of governors.'

All was agreed and the next holidays, Vahan took Agnes and her two younger brothers Arman and Hovan, to the main railway station to meet Victoria. Both Sara and Zaven were at work.

'There she is,' called out Agnes as she ran down the platform to help her friend with her bags. The two girls came slowly back to be formally introduced to Vahan and the boys. Vahan put out his hand to shake hands with Victoria saying in a very formal way 'Welcome Victoria, I hope you have a pleasant stay with us.' Victoria ignored his hand and instead gave him a big hug saying. 'I'm sure I will have a wonderful time Mr Kaspar and by the way everyone calls me Vicki.' Turning to Agnes, Victoria said 'These handsome young men must be your two brothers.' And then she proceeded to give both Arman and Hovan a hug. The boys were somewhat surprised at the show of affection especially on the platform, but they soon got used to it and quite liked it, especially from such an attractive young girl.

Vicki was shown where she would be sleeping. 'We have to share a bed,' said Agnes. 'Would you prefer the left or right side?'

'It makes no difference to me,' said Vicki, 'I'm just so happy to be here.'

That evening Sara and Zaven came home from their respective work. Zaven was more than taken by the young Vicki. The whole evening, he kept glancing at her hoping that no one would notice. Of course, it was obvious to all of them except young Hovan who wanted her to play with him. Zaven hadn't seen such a beautiful girl in real life before and to think that she would be living in the same block of apartments. He was almost six years older than Vicki but then love doesn't take such matters into account.

Vicki soon came to stay for the full duration of the school holidays. Agnes was no longer craving to go back to school, but instead wanted the holidays to last for ever. Agnes was intelligent, studious and reserved, while Vicki was sporty and gregarious. Although totally different personalities, they formed a close bond of acceptance and understanding.

* * *

Vicki, with her charm, beauty, and inner presence, became part of the Kaspar household. Agnes wanted her to be the sister that she never had, and little did she know that her wish was soon to be granted.

16

Emile and Chantal

Davit, never fully recovered from the serious injuries, suffered on the battle fields of northern France. He remained indebted to his wife Jacqueline who had risked her life to come to care for him and take him back home. Home was a timber chalet on the outskirts of Lucerne in southern Switzerland. His son Emile, only ever knew him as a broken old man with stories that flowed like a gentle stream. Although Emile grew up in a monetarily poor household, it was the abundance of spirit and wealth of kindness, that would shape his life.

Each morning Jacqueline would make sure that her husband was comfortably seated in his wheelchair at the breakfast table, with everything ready for him to prepare lunch. She would then walk Emile to school by 8:15am and on the way, they would pick up young Konrad Gottlieb who was in the same class as Emile. After dropping off both boys at school, Jacqueline would continue to her work at the local hospital. Her friend Heide Gottlieb, Konrad's mother, would pick up both boys from school, taking them home for lunch, that had been lovingly prepared by Davit.

Emile and Konrad, grew up together, delighting in Davit's stories. His soft gentle voice would often send them off to sleep. At a suitable age, Davit got the boys to take it in turn to read out loud. Both boys copied Davit's reading style.

Jacqueline became a senior nurse at the local hospital in Lucerne. She was too old to become a doctor as this would have required many years of fulltime study. Besides, Jacqueline had her work cut out with her aging mother, her invalid husband, and her growing son. Emile was a great help around the house, quickly growing into a fine and intelligent young man. Jacqueline was concerned that Emile wasn't getting sufficient physical exercise. His father had been forced to lead a sedentary life and so couldn't take his son out hiking, sailing, or fishing. The boys, Emile and his friend Konrad, needed adventures outside of books and chess. She expressed her concerns to her colleague Dr Boshard who said, 'I think I might have a solution. Can you give me a week or so as I need to write a letter to my cousin who runs a special school up in the mountains?' Dr Boshard wrote to his cousin Dr Schriver and the response came back saying that the boys would be welcome to come for a month to participate in their school summer programme.

Dr Schriver and his wife had set up a school for children with special needs. The school was in the foothills of the lush Swiss countryside at a small village called Unterägeri in the canton of Zug. Dr Schriver and his wife were specialist paediatricians, researching problems relating to children with learning difficulties. They ran a special school during the normal three school semesters, but during the summer holidays, they would run a school camp for children of all different nationalities. Many of the participants were the children of diplomats or military personnel living in remote or volatile situations. The children usually went to boarding schools but during the long vacation, they were sent to an organised summer camp in Switzerland. The children were aged between eight and fourteen years old and the camp was run specifically with a theme that when literally translated became the expression 'Learning through Fun.' It wasn't easy to get a place at the camp and certainly wasn't cheap. Dr Boshard had asked his cousin Dr Schriver for a special concession, and it had been granted.

* * *

The boys had just turned ten years of age when they first went to the summer school at Unterägeri. Konrad's father drove them to the school and the boys although excited were somewhat apprehensive. The boys revelled in it and wanted to stay there forever. The children came from around the globe speaking a variety of languages and practiced a diversity of faiths. There were in total about sixty children and some twelve 'leaders' as they were called. These leaders were often students themselves who had completed their high school education and were awaiting their examination results and acceptance to university. It was like one big, coordinated party where fun was the central theme. There were water activities on the nearby lake which was less than ten minutes' walk away. Rowing, canoeing, fishing, and learning to swim. There were also activities like hiking in the hills and many orienteering games. In wet weather they played board games, painted, and made clay pots. In the evenings there were singalongs as well as a sort of miming charades that were particularly popular due to the different languages.

At first Emile and Konrad stayed close together but they soon found their own friends. Emile grew close to a similar aged French girl from Lyon called Chantal. Emile's parents had taught him some basic French expressions, but with Chantal, his language skills significantly improved. They chose the same activities so they could spend time together. They sat next to each other at mealtimes and were inseparable except for sleeping in separate dormitories. At the end of the month, they kissed a gentle departing kiss and promised to write to each other. Konrad had a variety of companions and made good friends with an American called Roger Freiberg who came from New York. Konrad learnt a lot of English expressions that he spoke with a strong Bronx twang. Konrad remained lifelong friends with Roger, who later became a renowned Avant Guard artist.

* * *

At the end of the summer camp, Chantal and Emile wrote to each other as pen pals. The thrill of getting letters meant so much to both of them. They vowed to keep their contact a secret from everyone else. Of course, both sets of parents knew about the monthly letters but neither set of parents suspected anything more than a special friendship but as the years went on this special friendship became much more than special. At their second summer camp they were inseparable. They tried to keep their friendship a secret, but it was obvious for all to see. The staff at the camp played along with this young love. Little did they know that the young Emile and Chantal were laying the foundations for a future romance, that would culminate with marriage and a life together. The other children at the camp teased both Emile and Chantal, but they shrugged off their comments with a smile. The two youngsters whispered sweet nothings to each other in private and at the end of the second summer camp, they promised to write every week. They didn't want to let their parents know and receiving letters every week would have been too obvious and besides, their affections would be heightened by the cloud of secrecy.

It was Emile who devised a plan to use the facilities provided by the Post Office. He had once been in the post office on the way back from school, when he observed a man asking for his mail. Poste Restante was generally available at the bigger post offices, and they soon learnt how to communicate in secret. Telephoning was too public and would only be used on birthdays and at Christmas. Letters were the way to go. All through their teens, the two young romantics wrote to each other at least twice a week. After receiving a letter from Chantal, Emile would write a response that evening, and post his letter on the way to school the next day. The staff in both post offices began to know them and would just hand over the letters without asking for a signature. Then one day Chantal's mother went to the post office and the lady there asked if she had come in for her daughter's mail. Their cover had been blown. At first, it was seen as a disaster by both Chantal and Emile, but, in fact, both sets of parents had known about their close friendship but not about the letters. Chantal's parents decided that they would pay a visit to Lucerne and meet Emile's parents. They took Chantal with them, and all went smoothly. Both sets of parents became friends and were delighted that their respective offspring had found their perfect match. Theirs was a union made in heaven.

* * *

The letters continued but were now sent directly to their respective homes. The staff at the Post Office only saw them when they needed a new supply of stamps. By the age of fifteen Chantal and Emile had become support staff at the summer camps at Unterägeri. Chantal was a good swimmer and taught many of the younger children how to swim in the lake. Emile took the younger boys on hiking expeditions. He knew the mountains well and made sure the boys were safe. In the evening they would sit around the campfires and sing songs with the children. Emile played a small squeeze box and a harmonica while Chantal would lead the children to sing verses of songs from around the world. Waltzing Matilda was a favourite, although some of the words didn't make sense. The children liked it when Emile and Chantal broke into yodelling which they both did remarkably well.

* * *

Emile and Chantal were gifted children and academically towered above the other children in their respective schools. Emile would help Konrad with his maths homework and couldn't understand why Konrad found it so difficult. Emile specialised in the scientific realm while Chantal was well-rounded in both the sciences and the arts. Emile had seen how his mother had been appreciated in the hospital and already from the age of sixteen, had decided to study medicine. This made-up Chantal's mind, for although she had seen herself as a pure scientist and perhaps working as a biologist or perhaps a research chemist, she decided to also study medicine. She wanted to be near Emile and besides she could always branch out into research once she had a medical degree. They did their medical training together at a renowned medical school, attached to the hospital in Zurich.

Both shone brightly in their studies but early on it was decided that Emile would concentrate on being a general physician while Chantal, after completing her medical studies, was invited to work as an assistant to the professor of microbiology and immunology at Basel medical school. They spent their years of study living together, but not married. Everyone thought of them as husband and wife and neither let on otherwise. At the end of their final medical exams, they decided that they would get married. Living in sin as it was thought of in those days, might hinder their careers, so they decided to get married in a private chapel with the minimum of fuss. Konrad was the best man and Chantal's cousin was her only bridesmaid.

Emile decided that he might like to work as a paediatrician but before embarking on specialist studies he thought it would be a good idea to spend a year or so doing fieldwork. It was an obvious choice as he was very much welcomed to work with Dr Schriver at the special needs Kinderheim at Unterägeri. Dr Schriver and his wife were at the forefront of research for children with a wide variety of needs. They were somewhat experimental in their approach, researching the effects of hot baths with certain herbs and added minerals. They wanted to see whether the baths affected the children's nervous systems and to document the results.

* * *

Chantal would often visit Emile at Unterageri. She loved the clean mountain air and spending time with the children. She loved taking them for long walks by the side of the lake.

17

Hovan Kaspar

Soon after her benefactor Dikran died, Sara decided she wanted nothing more to do with her husband, Vahan, the father of her four children. Vahan's small apartment at the northern end of the block of flats, had a separate set of external stairs. Sara lived in a three-bedroom ground floor flat at the southern end of the block, their paths never had to cross. No one was allowed to talk to Sara about Vahan, not even to mention his name. She would have thrown Vahan out onto the street, but her benefactor Dikran had made a stipulation in his Will that one of the apartments should be made available for Vahan to live in rent free for the remainder of his life.

Having her husband living in a flat above her did nothing for Sara's stability. She felt trapped but also needed to express her frustrations from time to time. The birth of Hovan had brought complete closure to a long-suffering relationship that had started in turmoil and ended in disdain. Vahan felt there was nothing that he could do to resolve the broken marriage. When Hovan innocently asked his father to come downstairs and make up with his mother, Vahan replied, 'You know, when the crockery has been broken, it is better to accept that it has been shattered and throw it all away. Sometimes, it is better to buy a completely new set of crockery, but in my case, I have decided to eat off paper plates.'

* * *

Hovan was much loved by his three older siblings. Agnes, who had just turned seven years old, had maternal instincts, loving Hovan as she might have loved a doll. She bathed him and fed him as if she was a surrogate mother. She taught him how to read and write and later tried without success to teach him how to play the piano. She became a talented musician with a wonderful ear and perfect pitch. Once she had heard a tune, she could play it without hesitation.

On the other hand, Agnes's twin brother Arman was a bit of an oaf, who only wanted to play sport. Good at both cricket and tennis, Arman tried to coach his younger brother Hovan, but without success. Arman became somewhat of a philanderer, expending copious amounts of time in the cinema, imagining he was a Hollywood star. He liked Gary Cooper and Clark Gable, but his favourite was Cary Grant, spending time in front of a mirror mimicking that lyrical stutter. At the tennis club, Arman tried to play like Fred Perry, but had only seen him playing on film at the cinema. Arman thought he was god's gift to woman but was baffled as to why they didn't respond to him in the way he thought they might. He even asked his twin sister to try and find out why girls didn't like him. His vanity knew no bounds.

* * *

Sara was a workaholic and just wanted to make money. She felt it was her duty to the late Dikran that she should expand the empire that he had left to her. Not that it was much of an empire but the bequeathed block of six flats in Little Russell Street gave the family a good deal of security.

Zaven, the oldest of the three brothers, left school to work as a mechanic. The truth is that Zaven held everything together despite the tantrums of his unpredictable mother. He would console her when she flew off the handle at the slightest thing, he brought in hard earned cash to feed the family, and he made sure that his father, who lived upstairs, was catered for by bringing grocery supplies and a bundle of newspapers for him to digest each day. Soon after Hovan was born, Zaven moved upstairs to live with his father. He sometimes went downstairs to eat meals with his mother and siblings but was only too pleased to excuse himself to get away from his erratic mother and squabbling siblings.

He much preferred just chatting peacefully with his father about esoteric matters and loved listening to his stories from the past.

To avoid any meetings between his parents, Zaven rigged up an elaborate set of pulleys, cords, and bells, much in the manner that the Victorian English households had for the landed gentry to call for a maid. Each morning before Sara went off to work at her restaurant, she would pull a cord that would ring a bell in Vahan's apartment, letting him know that she was leaving. Vahan would wait a few minutes and then go downstairs to pick up Hovan his youngest son. He would then take Hovan upstairs to look after him, until his mother returned in the evening. When she had prepared a supper for the family she would once again ring the bell letting Vahan know it was time for young Hovan to be returned. Hovan grew up thinking that this bell ringing was completely normal and quite happily flowed from one parent to the other. He accepted that his parents didn't want to speak to each other and wanted to avoid any direct contact. Luckily for the siblings, both parents had agreed never to speak badly of the other, in front of their children. Hovan grew up thinking that all mothers must be erratic and that all fathers would be full of wonderful stories.

* * *

The grounds around the block of flats were extensive, allowing space for the young Hovan to kick a ball or practice tennis against a wall. On rainy days, Hovan would stay upstairs with his father who would read books to him, till he fell asleep. Hovan especially loved the Rudyard Kipling Jungle books, asking Vahan to read them over and over again. Vahan told him the stories that his father Harat had related and told him of the wonderful times he had had as a child in Constantinople. Vahan spoke about his travels to Venice and about the Monastery in the lagoon. He spoke extensively about Hovan's grandparents Harat and Nana and about his own twin brother Davit but never about his wife Sara and their arduous journey overland to Calcutta. Hovan fully accepted that his mother lived downstairs and his father upstairs. His world was divided; it was only the rickety external stairs that transported him from one world into another.

* * *

At an early age, Vahan introduced the subject of Hovan's birthmark behind his ear. He showed him his own birthmark and then used a mirror to show Hovan that he had one too. He explained that his grandfather Harat and his uncle Davit both carried the same markings, but that his brothers Zaven and Arman didn't.

'How come they don't have what we have got?' asked the young Hovan. 'Well, we have been chosen to be special,' replied Vahan wanting to be positive about it. He explained that his friend, the abbot of the monastery, had the same marking, but he didn't elaborate about what had happened to him. 'You must not let anyone know about the marking or you will be in great danger,' said Vahan. 'It's our secret. You mustn't even speak with your brothers about it.'

'I suppose they will want one too, won't they?' replied Hovan showing that he was too young to understand the implications, or the danger involved. Vahan realising that Hovan was too young to be told about such things, didn't bring up the subject again for a good many years.

* * *

Every time Vahan saw the young Hovan he could imagine his own father Harat as a child. The same self-confidence and congenial manner that people were drawn to. He not only resembled his grandfather but also had that cheeky smile. Hovan was smart and had an easy, pleasant way with people of all ages. At school, every child wanted to be his best friend. He was friends with everyone but didn't have favourites. He had a natural ability to charm and entertain a crowd. He did this by being very centred within himself but not in any self-absorbed way. He appeared genuinely interested in what people had to say, asked questions, and listened carefully to their responses. When his mind was made up, he stuck to it.

Even at an early age, it seemed that one could hear Hovan's mind ticking over as he pondered a complex problem. Then suddenly out of the blue he would come to the resolution of the dilemma. His explanation for his decision would be precise and cut through to the heart of the matter. Often, he asked what appeared to be stupid questions, but it was just his way of buying time while he thought through the issues. Hovan had the same incisive thought processes as Harat his grandfather. It was this astute quality of summing up a situation, that laid the foundations for them to be successful businessmen. Hovan's mother Sara not only recognised but greatly admired this gift of being decisive. She often told the young Hovan that it was such a pity that he would never get to meet his grandfather and thought how proud Harat would have been with his youngest grandchild.

When Hovan was nine years old, his eldest brother Zaven got married to his fiancé Victoria and exercised his right for them to occupy one of the flats that their benefactor Dikran had left to each of the Kaspar family.

Hovan moved upstairs to live with his father but still ate meals downstairs with his mother. He grew up being independent and relating to both of his parents separately. His easy manner smoothed his path as he glided from one parent to the other.

* * *

Zaven completed his apprenticeship at the French Car Company with honours, and they offered him a good, secure job. Zaven was at a quandary as to whether he should take the offer or whether he should set up his own bus company. He had fully restored his bus and was ready to take passengers. Zaven asked everyone what he should do hoping someone else would make the decision for him. He spoke with his mother Sara, his sister Agnes and his wife Victoria but only got a similar response from all three of them. 'You must do what you feel is right,' they said to him. 'But I don't know what is right,' he would reply. He even asked his brother Arman what he thought he should do. Arman just grunted as if to say he couldn't care less. He hadn't really expected anything more from Arman.

That evening, after dinner Zaven went to see his father and ask him what he thought. Should he take up the offer of a managerial job with the French Car Company or should he take a risk and start up his own bus company. As Zaven spoke about the pros and cons of either case Hovan listened quietly in the background. Then suddenly Vahan turned to Hovan asking his youngest son for his opinion.

'I think he should have a go with setting up his bus company,' said Hovan but not offering any reasoning to support his opinion.

'Why do you think that?' said Zaven taking his much younger brother's comment seriously.

'You say that there is a rival bus company about to start on the same route,' replied Hovan. 'Once they get a foot in the door, you won't get a chance to set up a viable opposition bus company. If you keep in favour with the French Car Company, you can always go back to them if your bus business doesn't work out; but if you continue working for them, you will never know if your bus company would have been successful. Besides, I can come after school and all day on a Saturday and Sunday to assist you if it would be of any help.'

Hovan's forthright logic made complete sense and Zaven returned to his flat declaring to his wife Victoria 'I think I have to give the bus company a go and if it doesn't work out then I can always go back to the French Car Company and ask them for my job back.' He said it with such conviction that Victoria thought he had made the decision himself.

And so it was, that Zaven started the first of his many successful businesses. He handed in his notice to the French Car Company and the director there wished him well, telling him that if things didn't work out as planned, there would always be a job waiting for him. As it happened, Zaven did eventually also set up his own car workshop and had a lucrative contract to service and repair all the French Car Company's private cars.

After school, Hovan would wait at the bus stop for the bus that was being driven by Zaven. Hovan would take up a position at the back of the bus with the task of looking out for the rival company's bus. As soon as he sighted a competitor, he would let Zaven know by blowing on a shrill whistle. Zaven would normally drive along at a snail's pace so more people would be waiting at each bus stop, but on hearing Hovan's whistle, Zaven would slam his foot down on the accelerator. The bus would lurch forward starting a mad race to get to the next bus stop and the waiting potential passengers. He would straddle across the middle of the road to block the passage of the rival bus. Sometimes if there was no one waiting at a bus stop, Zaven would sail on past not stopping to let passengers off. There was much shouting and sometimes the rival bus company would in frustration bump into the back of Zaven's bus. Zaven decided to attach some heavy-duty bumper bars onto the back of his bus so if they did try ramming, they would come off second best. It was a like a chariot race through the streets of Calcutta. No one got hurt but that was more a matter of good fortune rather than design. Most of the passengers enjoyed the excitement of the battle and were disappointed when the rival bus company went out of business. Zaven made a successful offer for their bus and painted it up in gaudy colours to be the second of the 'Bengal Tigers fleet of Superior Buses'.

* * *

Sara could neither read nor write but none the less had successfully run her own affairs. On one occasion Sara needed a letter to be written and was forced to ask Zaven if he would write the letter for her. Zaven equipped with pen and paper took the dictation. Sara wanted to write a letter of complaint to the Minister of Health and Hygiene. She felt she had been unfairly dealt with by an inspector who had written a scathing report on her restaurant. In fact, the inspector had been bribed by a competing restaurant proprietor. Sara started off the dictation as if she were talking to the Minister standing in front of her. Very soon her expletives became somewhat inflammatory and potentially slanderous. Zaven repeatedly told his mother that such words were not appropriate and made numerous suggestions, all of which were rejected.

'I don't care what you think,' yelled Sara. 'I just want you to write what I am telling you to write, or I will get someone else to write it for me. Anyway, what would you know about writing a letter.'

Zaven obeyed his mother and took a fresh piece of paper. As she dictated her erratic obscenities about the Inspector in question, Zaven knowing that his mother couldn't read or write, verbally repeated her words as he pretended to write them down but instead wrote the words, he thought were more suitable.

'Thank you,' said Sara, 'you have been a very good son.' Zaven had brought along a blank stamped envelope upon which he then wrote down the address. 'I can post the letter for you' said Zaven but Sara snatched the letter saying she would post it herself. Zaven left pleased with his deception and went upstairs to his apartment, thinking nothing more about it. The next day Sara discretely showed the letter to her youngest son Hovan and asked him to read to her the letter that Zaven had written on her behalf. 'No, no, no,' cried out Sara as she realised that Zaven had written the words that he had thought more appropriate. 'I didn't want anything like that you idiot. What I said was "%*@#*!!".' Then she made the young Hovan write out the letter she wanted but this time asked him to read it back again. Hovan had written the obscenities that she dictated word for word. She smiled her cheeky smile as he read the letter with all the obscenities back to her. She promptly asked for the letter that Hovan had just written.

Somehow, Hovan cleverly dropped both his and Zaven's polite letters on the floor, making it look like an accident. With a slight of hand, he passed Zaven's polite letter to her as if it were the one that he had just written and then proceeded to tear up his own letter with the obscenities in front of her. She seemed not to realise the subtle exchange of letters that Hovan had performed in front of her. Sara still beaming placed the letter into the envelope, saying that she would post the letter the next day. It was a couple of weeks later, that she got a lengthy and loquacious response from the Minister. Hovan read the response to her:

After a comprehensive investigation of most irregular behaviour, the Inspector in question has fully admitted to accepting a bribe made by an opposition restaurant proprietor.

On further examination of a competitor's restaurant, it has failed to meet the required hygiene standards and to make the necessary alterations within the given timeframe and as such, their licence had been suspended. Furthermore, the original Inspector has now been expelled from the Department for accepting bribes …

And it is thanks to your well written and precise letter clearly pointing out the criminal activities of the Inspector involved that we have now been able to ensure that true justice prevails.

As Hovan read out the response from the Minister, he substituted the words "Well written and Precise" with the words "Direct and Articulate".

Sara smiled from ear to ear saying, 'You see, you have to say what you mean in this life.' "Direct and Articulate". She repeated over and over again.

No one ever told Sara that Hovan had switched the letters and it had been thought that she went to her grave believing that she had posted the abusive letter as dictated to Hovan. 'All's well that ends well' quoted Hovan to his brother Zaven. 'Let mum think that it was her letter that got the results she wanted.'

In years to come the Minister for Health and Hygiene was also found out for accepting bribes and was stood down. No one ever asked Sara if she had bribed the Minister concerned but her restaurant went from strength to strength, and she never had any problems from any of the inspectors. For many years all four inspectors had a table reserved at her restaurant for lunch every Friday.

Soon after Sara had died, at the age of eighty-six, her daughter Agnes was going through her mother's personal effects and found the polite letter that Hovan had written to the Minister still in the sealed envelope. Perhaps she had been aware that Hovan had exchanged the letters and instead of posting it, had presented her case directly in person to the Minister for Health.

Sara had outwitted both of her sons and in the process had learnt a lot about each of them.

* * *

Hovan completed his HSC and at the age of sixteen, decided to leave school to work with his brother Zaven in his workshop. By that time, Zaven had also started a trucking service and taxi business as well expanding his fleet of buses. When Hovan joined him, they bought a garage which became the headquarters for the Kaspar Empire. Hovan soon became the head mechanic repairing all the vehicles as well as servicing cars for the French Car Company. Hovan had met a young girl called Marianne. She came from an extremely wealthy family that had been part of the founding members of the East India Company. Marianne's mother Paula was from a wealthy Armenian family, but her father, Sir Anthony Graham was as British as they come. With a mixture of British and Armenian, Hovan found this high-spirited young girl most beguiling. Marianne not needing to work for a living, chose to do some charity work. 'It's just a drop in the ocean,' she would say adding, 'but of course the ocean is just made up of lots of little droplets.'

* * *

Hovan and Marianne became inseparable and made a most handsome pair. Marianne brought out the best in the hard-working Hovan who also liked to play hard. Each Saturday they enjoyed going to the Calcutta races. As Marianne would say, 'To have a flutter on the nags.'

Hovan started placing quite heavy bets. Sometimes he would win substantially, and they would then go out to dinner before dancing the night away. On the times he had lost heavily, they would go to a café and then to the cinema. Money came and money went. Gambling was in his blood and losing at the horses never seemed to worry him. He saw it as just part of the day out.

Then one day disaster struck that was to completely alter both of their lives. Marianne contracted Polio and was paralysed from the waist down. Her parents, looking for a cure for their only child, took her to America but that was to no avail. Hovan was devastated and fell into a deep depression. Marianne, knowing that she would be in a wheelchair for the rest of her life, insisted that Hovan should forget her and find a fulfilling life for himself. Through letters, their friendship flourished.

* * *

Hovan spoke often with his eldest brother Zaven, and it was Zaven who suggested there was a six-month engineering apprenticeship in a place called Sheffield in England. Hovan knew that he needed to get away from Calcutta for a while and what better place than Sheffield. Hovan spoke with his father who told him that Sheffield was in the north of England and encouraged him to give it a go. He told his mother of his intentions but added that he would be back within a year. Sara thought it was a stupid idea, besides it was winter there and would be freezing.

Hovan booked a one-way passage to Southampton and then wrote a letter to the company in Sheffield asking them to consider him for the apprenticeship. Such was his confidence or perhaps complete naivety, that just notifying them of his interest, would be sufficient. He told them the date that he would be arriving and that they would find him to be a "hardworking and conscientious young man".

He wrote to Marianne, who replied that she was really pleased for Hovan and suggested that there would be plenty of other fish in the sea. Then added, 'If you don't like fish, then try oysters instead.'

The night before his departure the family enjoyed a splendid meal prepared by Sara and Agnes. They all wished Hovan well, telling him to write and tell them everything. At the end of the meal, Zaven gave a little speech wishing Hovan 'Bon Voyage' and then said that Sara had a present for Hovan. She went into her bedroom and came out with a badly wrapped bundle.

'It's very cold in England so I thought you might find this useful' she said gleefully as she handed him the parcel.

Hovan opened the present and was surprised to find a big army trench coat. 'You can wrap up nice and warm or even use it as a blanket if you want,' said Sara. 'You must keep it with you at all times.'

The next day, Hovan kissed them all as they stood on the quay to wave him goodbye. 'Do write,' said Agnes. 'Have a good time,' said Zaven. Sara just said, 'Hang onto the coat and keep nice and warm.'

Sara managed to hide her emotions. Below the surface, she was distraught that her baby boy was going to the other side of the world.

* * *

The hooter blew and the ship slowly left the dock behind. Hovan waved goodbye until his family became tiny dots on the quay, and his thoughts turned to Marianne. Little did he know he would not be returning to Calcutta for a good ten years. There were to be many twists and turns for the young Hovan as he set out on his voyage called 'life'.

142

18

Emile Kaspar – WWII

During their medical studies in Switzerland, Emile and Chantal became increasingly aware of the rumblings in nearby Germany. At the start, and like everyone around them, they thought that the 'Authorities' would be able to sort out Mr Hitler and put him back in his box. Then it became clear that Mr Hitler wouldn't be going anywhere soon, and that war would be inevitable.

* * *

Emile's father Davit, died of pneumonia in August 1933. His mother Jacqueline died peacefully in her sleep on Christmas Eve 1938.

Davit had spoken extensively with his son Emile about the death of his own parents and his brother Vahan; how they had all died so tragically in a massive explosion in their house in Constantinople. Davit often spoke to Emile and his friend Konrad, of his own war experiences on the battlefield in Northern France. He told of the devastation caused by the nerve gas, the human suffering and complete waste of life. He expressed the need to stand up to brutality, and that it was the duty of every man to fight for what is right.

Davit had also communicated to Emile the lineage that had been passed down through the generations, referring to their distinctive birthmark behind their left ears. 'Be a good citizen and do what is right,' Davit would say repeating the exact words that had been spoken by his father Harat before him.

It was with a very heavy heart that Emile returned to the Kinderheim at Unterägeri. The lake was frozen over and the snow on the mountains made for especially good skiing. Emile was an excellent skier and took great solace gracefully descending the slopes. His dream was to ski in the winter Olympics but the recent debacle in Berlin had put an end to those dreams. The looming inevitability of another war was rapidly becoming a nightmare.

Then in May of 1939 came the takeover of the Sudetenland, followed by the taking of Poland. Europe was at war again.

* * *

Emile had hoped that he would see out the War in the peace of the mountain village of Unterägeri. 'Why can't this war just go away?' he would say to Chantal as they lay snuggled up together in their puffed-up duvet. 'There's more to life than fighting a war. Why can't the politicians just sort it out?'

Deep down reverberated the saying of his late father: 'Be a good citizen and do what is right.' He didn't want to hear the words and pushed them deeper into his subconscious. The inner struggle was tearing him apart. Working with the children up in the pristine Swiss mountains was all well and good for him, but what about the rest of the world. Each day the news from the front became more and more extreme. The bombing of cities and the desperation of the people was intolerable. Could he live with his own conscience?

* * *

Then one day came news from Lucerne of the death of his childhood friend Konrad. He had been fighting with the French army and had been killed on the battlefields of northern France. The telegram from Mrs Gottlieb finished with the words,

< KONRAD-DIED-KNOWING-WHAT- WAS-RIGHT >

Once again, these words resonated, throwing Emile totally off balance.

It was Konrad's death that pushed Emile into the decision to join the war effort. He joined the French medical corps and was sent to serve directly behind the front line. He was commissioned to tend to the wounded and dying. 'Your research into tropical diseases and immunisation will be more important than fighting wars,' he consoled Chantal as he left for the front.

* * *

Emile's war experience at the front was short lived. He was soon to be captured by the advancing German army that rampaged through the weak French lines of resistance. Paris was taken and occupied. It wasn't long before the Germans found out that Emile, not only spoke fluent German, but that he also had a 1st class medical degree from one of the best medical schools in Europe. Emile was forced to join the German army. He was quickly given a German army uniform and medical fatigues and soon found himself behind the German lines tending to their wounded and dying. The fact that they were Germans made the appalling conditions of the dying soldiers no less traumatic. Some of the German medical staff would confide with Emile, expressing their disgust for the war. His accent betrayed his foreign identity, and they often remarked that Dr Kaspar is doing a fine job in spite of not being a proper German. One rather sensitive doctor, a Dr Hans Gruberman once said to Emile that he appreciated the fact that Emile now worked for the Germans as a doctor even though he had chosen to fight for the French. Emile just replied rather bluntly, 'It was working for you guys or being shot. There wasn't much of a choice.'

As the allies pushed hard against a weakened German army, the wounded and dead were coming in by the truck load. Emile was working to save German lives knowing that some may eventually go back to fight and perhaps kill innocent French civilians. The wounded just didn't stop coming. It was one after another.

* * *

It was 2am on a cold November morning that he went outside for a breath of cold fresh air and to get away from the stench of the dead, the blood and stale urine that permeated the makeshift hospital. He strolled some eighty metres or so towards a nearby thicket. The moon

145

was full, and the cold night was silent. As he closed his eyes and took a deep breath, he suddenly heard what he thought was a stray bomb come spiralling down towards the camp and then bang it crashed on the roof of the hospital. A ball of fire rose twenty metres high as the whole camp was blown to smithereens. No one came out of the camp and for a moment or two all was silent. Then sirens went off and before he knew it, men dressed in mufti carrying machine guns appeared out of the bushes. Emile was told to stand still, or he would be shot. Emile realising that this was the work of the French resistance, replied in French. 'Don't shoot, don't shoot, I'm a Swiss national. I'm a Swiss doctor. I'm not a German.' He held his hands up high and a big burly French man who was obviously the leader said, 'Take him and make sure he isn't armed.' They captured Emile and tied his hands behind his back. Some of the men wore balaclavas and went into the camp shooting randomly as they entered. There was no response as everyone in the hospital had died.

Emile was marched off to a small truck that was hidden about a half a kilometre into the woods. There they blindfolded him and then drove him to a small holding deep in the forest. When they stopped the truck, they took off the blindfold but with his hands still bound, they directed him into a dishevelled timber shed. The blindfold was reapplied, and he was told to sit on a stool and wait. He waited for what seemed an eternity until some gruff French voices cursing and swearing came closer and closer. The three men were laughing and mocking each other. Then the leader of the gang removed Emile's blindfold saying 'Well what have we got here? Do you think he would be good to eat?' They all laughed except Emile of course. They spent at least an hour interrogating Emile, soon realising that he wasn't German but had in fact been captured by the Germans. They asked which unit he had been working for when fighting for the French army and after a quick call or two, it was confirmed that his story was indeed correct.

'I can release you on one condition,' said the burly bearded Resistance leader. 'I want you to help us in our fight. As a medical man who also speaks German and has a German medical uniform you will be very useful to us. Of course, if you decide you would prefer to work for the Germans, we can take you back to the camp in the forest, gag you, tie you up with a handwritten note to say that we have returned you as a traitor to both France and Germany. The note will explain that you alone were responsible for blowing up the camp and killing the entire medical staff and invalids. We know that the Germans will torture you and when they finally find that you have nothing to offer, they will blow your brains out.'

Emile once again found that he had no choice in the matter. However, this time it would be his wish to work with the French rather than last time not wanting to work for the Germans. He explained that he had a French father and a French wife from Lyon.

Emile spent the rest of the war fighting for the French Resistance. He soon became second in command to the bushy bearded Bertrand his captor. Bertrand would often consult with Emile and valued his opinions. His ability to speak fluent German helped in a variety of ways. Their daring sorties behind enemy lines became legendary amongst the Resistance and Emile became somewhat of a brigand with the nick name Count Kaspar due to his ability to vanish into what seemed thin air and turn up again in unexpected places. His command of English allowed him to also liaise with the British agents, but he remained his own man fighting for the freedom of France.

Once again, he started writing to Chantal. He was very cautious as to what he could put in his letters and signed them with 'Grosse bise, E.K.' They numbered the letters to make sure that they would know if any letters had been intercepted. They used the system of Poste Restante just in case. Chantal's father died of tuberculosis and her mother Christiane went to live with her daughter in Basel. Emile was pleased to know that they lived in the relative protection of neutral Switzerland and often contemplated upon the simplicity of life in the fresh mountain air of Unterägeri. He longed to be walking along the lakes edge with Chantal and to hold her in his arms once more.

* * *

One night Emile was busy intercepting a Morse code message from one German commander to another. Part of the message was about the bombing of the medical camp some five months previously. It was definitely the medical camp that he had been working at as a German doctor. The Germans had found the burnt-out camp and had eventually accounted for all the personnel except one. They had worked out that the missing person was a Swiss medical officer who had been captured and forced into the German army. The message confirmed that a certain Dr Kaspar was never accounted for and that he must have been the one who caused the explosion. It went on to say that they had no knowledge of his whereabouts or whether he had survived. Emile realised that he was a marked man and that if he got captured again, this time he wouldn't survive. The Germans kept copious records so his name would be marked for life. That night Emile got no sleep at all. He couldn't stop thinking of Chantal. He wasn't afraid for his own life, but didn't want Chantal to have to go through the loss. It seemed strange to think that way. He had seen how the ravages of war had destroyed his father and how this had affected his mother. He wanted to get back safely to the peace and security that he had known in Switzerland and let the rest of the world fight it out. This wasn't his land; this wasn't his war. The fighting was getting to him. He needed to get out.

The next day he felt awful. He was physically tired and mentally exhausted. Thinking was hard and he moved at a slow and deliberate pace. Bertrand confronted Emile saying in his crass manner, 'You look shit Emile, get your act together.' Emile explained that he hadn't slept all night and told Bertrand of the German message that he had intercepted. Bertrand immediately went into another gear, more sympathetic and understanding of the situation. 'Look if you need to take it easy for a few days, take a break at my sister Margot's cottage near the town of Viriat. I will give you her address. It's basic, but she will make sure that you get plenty of rest for a couple of days. Sometimes these things blow over but sometimes they hang around like a bad smell. If your demons don't fade away, then you're no bloody use to me. Let's see how you are after a couple of days.' With that he wrote a note and put it in an envelope. He wrote an address on the envelope and handed it to Emile saying, 'Here take this to Margot and I will contact her in a couple of days to see how you are going.'

* * *

Emile knew that Bertrand was right and thanked him for his understanding. He set off walking down the winding country laneway with a small pack on his back and the envelope in his pocket. He walked for at least a couple of hours before he was picked up by a farmer driving a truck that belched out black smoke as if it was on fire. It took the farmer a good five minutes to get his truck restarted but eventually they were on their way. The journey to Viriat took Emile a good eight and a half hours and by the time Emile found Margot's falling apart wooden cottage, it was already dark. He gently knocked on the door but there was no answer. He knocked a bit louder and then suddenly was aware of a gun pointing in his back. 'Who are you? What do you want?' said a woman with a strong colloquial accent. Emile spun around to find a fifty something woman with her front teeth missing standing in her nightdress and wellington boots.

'I'm looking for Margot Molineux,' said Emile frightened that the woman would shoot first rather than find out who he was. 'I have a note from her brother Bertrand,' he said handing her the note. The woman read the note and then laughed.

'Why didn't you say so,' said Margot with the same chuckle in her voice as her brother. 'You'd better come in and we will get you something to drink.'

* * *

Emile slept that night in the shed. The rats did their best to keep him awake but he slept right through, not even being woken by the rooster at 4:30am in the morning. At 10am, Margot opened the shed door with a creaking noise that finally woke Emile with a startle. 'Thought you might have died during the night,' she said with a smoker's chortle, 'You look a whole lot better than you did last night. I've got some breakfast and hot milk if you are feeling up to it.'

Emile spent two days with Margot helping her with various items around her small holding. He even had a look at the rash that she had around her waist and told her that she should not be wearing her tight woollen underwear as it was irritating the skin. 'Well, it's the woollen or nothing as I don't have a spare pair,' she told him. 'It'll be bloody cold in winter,' she laughed.

After the second day, he felt a whole lot better and thought he should get back to see Bertrand and the other brigands. He thanked Margot and gave her some money that she didn't want to take. 'Buy yourself some new cotton underwear and make sure you wash them on a regular basis,' he said with a voice of medical authority. She reluctantly accepted the money and said, 'Look after yourself Doc,' adding, 'You've done your duty here and you should now get yourself back home before it's too late.'

It took Emile just six and a half hours on his return trip.

It was daylight when he got back to the small house occupied by the Resistance, but no one was there. It appeared that they had packed up and left in a hurry. On the table was an envelope with the word 'Doc' written in Bertrand's oversized handwriting. The ink was still wet. He quickly opened the letter and thought he would find out where they had all gone. Instead, the note read.

'Go home Doc. It's too dangerous to stay here. Go home and have a good life. Vive La France,' it wasn't signed. Emile knew exactly what he needed to do and knew that he needed to do it fast. He left by the back door and ran into the woods. He heard the tanks heading up the driveway, but he just kept running.

* * *

Emile knew all the byways and found his way to Lyon. He considered stopping to see Chantal's friend Nadine but decided that it may implicate her if he was caught at her house. Instead, he continued towards Geneva, deciding to bypass the city and continue around the lake towards the small township of Nernier on the French side of Lac Leman. He had a medical friend called Claude Steiner who lived there. They had studied medicine together in Zurich. If anyone could help him get back to Switzerland it would be Claude. Emile gently knocked on Claude's front door and then hid in case Claude didn't live there anymore. Emile was fearful about being caught or even being seen by the Germans. He was still very disturbed by the intercepted message naming him as the perpetrator of the bomb blast at the German makeshift medical centre almost a year ago. Claude came to the front door and Emile softly called out his name. He felt safe with Claude and his wife Annette. They fed him a hearty bowl of onion soup and shared a bottle of red wine. At 1:15am Annette went to bed, leaving the two men to continue talking about the good old days and the horrors of war.

'I need to get back to Switzerland,' said Emile 'What will be the best way of getting there?'

'Not a big problem,' said Claude full of confidence. 'Leave it to me. I have a friend called Guillermo who has a small boat. He occasionally smuggles people over to Switzerland. He has a small hold in the cabin that you can hide in. He is a fisherman and is well known to the Germans. He'll take you hidden in the hold and if the Boche should be out on patrol, he will just tell them that the wind had blown him off course. Once he was taking someone and the German patrol caught up with him. Instead of getting into trouble the stupid Boche helped him to get back to France. They had to wait a week before they tried again. I will speak with Guillermo in the morning and perhaps we can get you over the border in a couple of days' time. In the meantime, you can lie low and help me drink my wine cellar dry.'

It was bitterly cold and raining hard the night that Emile and Guillermo set off across the lake to Switzerland. Luckily Emile only had a small sack with a change of clothes and managed to curl up in the hold. The cloud cover meant that there were no stars or moon to be guided by. Guillermo stood outside on the deck and didn't mind getting wet. A bottle of cognac and his pipe kept him warm but not dry. The trip over only took twenty minutes and they got to Nyon on the other side of the lake without an incident.

'We have arrived,' called out Guillermo in a rather slurred voice. Emile jumped into the waist deep water and scrambled ashore. He looked back to wave to Guillermo who had already disappeared into the night.

* * *

Emile, cold and wet, found shelter in a doorway, and slept curled up like a dishevelled hobo. The rising sun dried him off a little, as he made his way to the nearest police station. There he showed a policeman his Swiss passport and explained what had happened. He also told him that he didn't have any Swiss francs. The policeman made a call to Emile's wife Chantal in Zurich, who said that she would take the first train to Nyon.

The policeman then locked Emile into a cell saying because he hadn't been through customs or the proper immigration channels, Emile was considered an alien. Emile offered to walk to the nearest customs house, but the policeman wouldn't let him leave the station. It was somewhat of an impasse. He had to go through immigration procedures, but the police wouldn't let him out of the station in case he was a spy or wasn't who he said he was. Eventually the policeman organised for an immigration officer to come from Geneva, but it would take quite a while. Emile took the opportunity to have a few hours' sleep in his cell and was awoken by the immigration officer from Geneva, who examined Emile's Swiss passport and then took Emile's fingerprints for comparison with their previous copies. All was fine and Emile was a free man, back home in southern Switzerland. The immigration official told the senior policeman that he had done the right thing to detain Emile.

'Why don't I take you to the bar across the road and buy you a drink,' said the police officer to Emile. 'We don't want your wife to find you in a prison cell, do we?' he added grinning.

It was past 6:30pm before Chantal came to the bar. She saw Emile sitting at the bar with his back to the door. He was busy talking with the policeman, so she quietly crept up behind Emile and tapped him on the shoulder. Emile spun around and she flung her arms around him and burst into tears of joy.

That night they managed to get as far as Lucerne where they stayed for a couple of days before returning to Zurich. Chantal had completed her Ph.D. in Basel and had returned to Zurich to take up a position as a virologist with the Swiss Tropical Disease Institute. She had lived with her mother in the apartment and had cared for her until her mother passed away.

Lucerne felt like home for Emile as it was where he had grown up. It was like being a tourist in his own town. He went to see his old house and when he approached the house of his good friend Konrad Gottlieb, memories came flooding back.

'I wonder if Konrad's mother Mrs Gottlieb still lives there?' he said to Chantal. He knocked on the door but there was no answer.

* * *

It took some weeks for Emile to find his feet again. He had been away for more than two years, and fighting wasn't really in his blood. His sense of duty had been fulfilled and he wanted to put it all behind him. His dreams brought back many pent-up fears and anxieties. He would wake in the night screaming at someone. He tried sleeping in a separate room to Chantal, but the screaming was so loud that even the neighbours were woken up. Emile would struggle with the recurring nightmares for the rest of his life.

The war finally came to an end and the German army retreated. News of Adolf Hitler's suicide put an end to the war in Europe, but it still raged in the Far East. Two American atomic bombs closed the final chapter of what had been such a devastating time for so many people. Finally, the world returned to its senses and the mopping up phase started as sanity resumed. The war had torn so many people's lives apart. Chantal and Emile had come out of it alive but not without Emile's lingering traumas resurfacing. He wanted to get away from all the chaos. He wanted to get away from the voices. He was haunted by his interception of the communication between the two Gestapo officers. The message stating that Emile Kaspar's body had not been accounted for after the bombing of the medical camp and that he should be found and eliminated without trial. Emile felt his war never really ended.

19

Hana Kohl

ana Kohl was born in Jihlava, Czechoslovakia. The small town lies just slightly closer to Brno than to Prague, straddling the Bohemian and Moravian borders. Hana was an only child born to two academics who taught at different Universities. Her father, Robert Kohl, was a professor of mathematics at Prague University, while her mother Edith, taught art history at Brno University. Their compromise was to live equidistant from the two cities and travel by train to their respective academies.

* * *

Hana was born in the October of 1926. Her mother Edith, already in her late thirties, decided that she would give up teaching to become a full-time mother and part time artist. Edith's mother Gertrude, died two years after Hana was born, leaving her frail husband Josef alone in a large house on the outskirts of Pilsen, an industrial town, close to the German border. Pilsen, famous for its beer production and the headquarters of Bata, an international tanning and leather goods company meant that the town had a certain smell. Nevertheless, Edith and Robert decided to relocate to Pilzen to look after Edith's father, Josef. They took the downstairs of Josef's large house and made a separate self-contained apartment for him on the top level.

To begin with, Josef would babysit his granddaughter Hana but after a few years, the tide changed, and Hana was left to care for her ailing grandfather.

* * *

Robert found a position at the local Technical College. His research as a mathematician shifted from pure to applied mathematics. This allowed him to be at the forefront of the start of computer technology. Wages for a professor were sufficient to raise a single child family, enjoying a modest but fulfilling lifestyle. One compensation was that he no longer had to commute to Prague. Instead, he used the time to tend to his garden, where he produced an abundance of vegetables and an orchard of fruit trees. Edith was an experimental cook, who explored the benefits of a healthy diet. She delved deeply into exotic combinations of food styles, specializing in Middle Eastern cuisines with its variety of grains, pulses, fruit, and vegetables, all picked fresh from the garden. Hana wanted to eat the local foods that her friends enjoyed, but Edith would say, 'But dumplings have little nutritional value.'

Robert flourished in Pilsen and overcame his prejudices. He thoroughly enjoyed living the easy lifestyle. His younger brother Oscar, who held the chair of Botany at Vienna University, rather disdainfully asked, 'Robert, how can you stand living in that uncultured tin pot town? Vienna is so much more refined.' Robert would smile back at his younger brother and would answer sarcastically, 'Well Oscar, we can't all be as clever as you. Anyway, I prefer being a big fish in a small pond.' He didn't need to add the part about being a small fish in a big pond.

Robert was a talented musician playing the piano at a reasonable level. He badly wanted his daughter Hana to learn the violin, so they might play together. Edith was a visual person, with no inclination towards music. Robert soon realised that his daughter Hana wasn't at all musical either, but like her mother, loved drawing and painting water colours. Undeterred, Robert, every Friday evening, would take young Hana to the local Opera House or Concert Hall. Poor Hana suffered the likes of Wagner, Dvořák, Mahler, Janáček and Smetana to name a few. However, she did enjoy the Operettas of Mozart and Puccini.

Robert's thinking was; if Hana could only enjoy and experience music, she might one day, want to learn the violin. Alas, this was never to happen. The more Robert pushed the more Hana resisted. Finally, the impasse was resolved. Edith and Robert had taken the bus into town to go shopping and had left the ten-year-old Hana to practice her violin. Hana hated it so much that she threw her violin on the ground, leaving the broken pieces strewn all over the floor. When her parents returned, she held up the largest fragment saying that she had accidentally sat on her violin, and she never wanted to play the violin again. Sobbing she ran to her room. Robert was furious as it was obvious that the violin had suffered more than just being sat upon. Edith with her calming touch, spoke in no uncertain terms to Robert saying, 'She is only a child. You can't force this on to her. Let it come naturally. One day she will want to play the violin and she will be good at it.' Robert knew in his heart that he had lost. He knew, that not only would Hana never want to learn the violin, but if by chance she did, she would never be any good at it.

'Robert, go and console your daughter or she will turn against you,' said Edith. Robert politely knocked on Hana's bedroom door and waited for a response. Eventually he was allowed in to console her. He spread his arms around her and gently pulled her towards his oversized belly. 'No one will ever make you practice the violin again,' he said softly. 'One day if you want to play the violin again, we can always buy you a new one. Anyway, this one was getting too small for you.'

'Do you mean that I don't have to practice anymore?' said Hana, amazed at what she had just heard. She had won the battle.

'Never again,' confirmed Robert. 'Let's have some coffee with that spicy carrot cake that your mother has made.'

'Can we have cream with it,' asked Hana beaming from ear to ear.

Hana never took up a musical instrument but instead, was encouraged to concentrate on her water colours.

* * *

On another occasion, Hana took a large pair of scissors to her beautiful long hair; hair that she could sit on. It would take ages for her mother to plait her hair after it had been washed. Hana considered this to be a complete waste of time and on several occasion told her mother so. 'But your hair is so beautiful,' Edith would respond. Once again Hana took control, in her own somewhat contrary manner. Snip, snip and off came the plaits. When Edith came home Hana held up both 40-centimetre-long plaits, one in each hand, and with a grin said to her mother 'Look what happened to my plaits.' Edith was furious and once again sent Hana to her room saying 'Wait till your father comes home. He will have plenty to say to you, young lady.' Robert came home and Edith showed him the severed plaits. 'Don't worry my dear,' said Robert with a grin, 'I'm sure they will grow again.' Edith just laughed as she realised that Robert was simply returning the consoling position that she Edith had espoused during the violin episode.

Hana's wilfulness and determination would one day, stand her in good stead.

Life in the Kohl family was one of love and caring. Robert spent most of his time in academic and cultural pursuits, while Edith and her daughter Hana, followed more of the artistic and creative pastimes. Hana was surrounded by gardening, music, needlework, and water colours. Robert had bought a Blaupunkt radio that picked up radio stations from all over Europe. In the evenings they would enjoy listening to broadcasts of plays from the BBC in the hope that Hana would learn some English. Robert was a keen linguist and tried to speak English with both Edith and Hana whenever he could. He was aware that although his English was reasonable, it had its limitations.

* * *

It was soon after the incident of the plaits, that Robert and Edith decided to put an advertisement into a British newspaper for a live-in English au pair, with some minor domestic duties. The pay wouldn't be much but board and living expenses would be provided, with both skiing and summer sports encouraged. The response wasn't overwhelming but from the shortlist, they chose Susan Eastern, a nineteen-year-old fresh faced young woman from Stourbridge in the West Midlands. Susan was vivacious, fitting into the Kohl family as if she had always been there. Hana spoke English to her and helped Susan to learn German. Susan was childlike for her age and got on well with Hana, who, although twelve years younger, regarded Susan as an older sister. The introduction of Susan into the family proved to be a vital connection and one that would play a pivotal part in Hana's life.

After the Berlin games of 1936, tensions within Europe started to escalate dramatically as dark clouds gathered. Pilsen, situated in the west of Czechoslovakia, was close to the German border. Initially Sudetenland served as a buffer, but it soon became increasingly populated by Nazi sympathisers, becoming a threat, rather than a shield. Hana was relocated to a local technical school, where many of the children refused to speak Czech as their parents were Nazi supporters. The school didn't insist on the students wearing a school uniform, but some of the children chose to wear Nazi attire and sang Nazi songs in the playground. Hana was surrounded by aggression and witnessed adolescents brandishing knives and terrifying catapults. These children simply mimicked their parents who were strongly influenced by Nazi propaganda. The school was divided and the people of Pilsen became anxious as racism reared its ugly head.

The pressure from within became intolerable. Susan, the young English au pair returned home to the West Midlands having been accosted in a laneway. Thugs roamed the streets and rallies supporting the Nazi principles were held in parks and squares on a regular basis. Robert and Edith became increasingly aware that something was bound to happen and that they needed to prepare for a speedy exit. They realised that they themselves would be targeted, as the rallies spoke of death to five different groups of people. The Nazi's hounded Jews and intellectuals as they often didn't support the Nazi cause. They also threatened people belonging to Socialist parties, homosexuals, and gypsies. Although Robert was a practising Catholic and Edith had converted from Judaism to Catholicism, the Nazi's considered both Edith and her daughter Hana to be Jewish. Robert was in the firing line because not only was he an academic, but he had married a Jewess as well as being a long-time supporter of a Social Democratic party. Three out of the five categories spelt danger. Robert and Edith felt that they needed to act without delay.

In early December of 1938, Robert wrote a Christmas card to the au pair Susan Eastern from Stourbridge and addressed it to her and her family. He inserted a letter that described the ominous clouds that were rolling over the horizon. He asked if he could send Hana for a holiday and that he would come to pick her up once the dangers had passed.

He explained that Josef, Edith's father had become increasingly ill and wasn't able to travel. Understandably Edith wanted to stay with her father. Robert explained that an Englishman called Nicholas Winton, had visited Czechoslovakia and had become acutely aware of the plight of Jewish and other political dissidents. He had returned to England to persuade the British Government to harbour some of the children. Winton then demanded from the Czechoslovakian Government, who were at that time under Nazi control, to release children up to the age of fourteen. Remarkably the Czech Government agreed as they were happy to export as many children as Britain would take. One stipulation that both governments demanded, was that the children should have a written sponsor or guarantor that would take responsibility for the welfare of each child. Robert's note in the Christmas card asked for help to find a sponsor for young Hana. At the Christmas table, Susan showed the letter to her family and in particular to her older sister Olivia.

Miss Olivia Eastern was a geography teacher at a local all-girls high school in Stourbridge, and when school started again in early January, she showed the letter to the head mistress, Miss Day.

Miss Day was a true battle axe of a woman, whose formidable physique concealed her sympathetic heart. 'Leave it with me,' barked Miss Day to the slight and slender Olivia Eastern. The next day, Miss Day called Miss Eastern to her dark and foreboding office. 'Now I have spoken to the school board and have shown them the letter from Professor Kohl about his daughter Hana,' she explained to Miss Eastern, 'The board have decided that they would be prepared to assist with the schooling of Miss Kohl, with both of us as the signatories to the sponsorship forms and responsible for the housing and welfare of this Miss Kohl.' The young Miss Eastern couldn't believe what she was hearing from this dour, fierce headmistress. 'Now if you will sign here,' said Miss Day pointing to the form, 'I will sign here and will send off the forms to Professor Kohl this evening. I'm sure that he and his wife will be more than pleased.' The forms were signed in triplicate and then two signed copies were sent back to Robert and Edith Kohl.

It was in early February when Robert received the wonderful news that Miss Day and Miss Eastern had accepted to become the official guardians for Hana, with the school board agreeing to support her schooling.

Robert was ecstatic as he showed the signed forms to both his wife Edith, and their daughter Hana. Edith tried to console Hana saying that they would be coming to pick her up and bring her back home as soon as the dangers had passed. But Hana wasn't at all worried about leaving and thought of it as an adventure.

One set of the signed forms were sent to Mr Winton who was extremely busy putting things into action. In the March of 1939, Nazi tanks rolled out of the Sudetenland into Czech territory. The invasion had started. The children who were to be transported, were now termed refugees.

Hana was later to recall, 'When we woke up, I think it was 15th March, we put on the radio and there was no music playing. Just one announcement being repeated over and over. "Drive on the right, the Germans have invaded." We had previously driven on the left and the authorities were anxious that people should not cause or be involved in an accident.'

* * *

Mr Nicolas Winton had arranged for a series of trains that would transport the children across Germany to Holland, where they would be dispersed to various parts of the world. These trains were called "Kinder Transport". The first train left in late March and carried some 80 children. Then there was another train in mid-April, with Hana's train scheduled for early May. There were trains leaving in June and July, but the Germans decided to cancel the scheduled departures in August and September. In all, some six hundred and sixty children were rescued, avoiding their certain demise.

On the 6th May 1939, Robert and Edith took their only daughter Hana to Prague to board the train. Children, parents, and mountains of luggage were huddled everywhere on the platform. The children wore luggage labels around their necks, indicating their sponsors and desired destinations. Children as young as four years old were grasping the hands of their parents or sitting on their father's shoulders. The children saw it as an adventure not realising that most of them would never see their parents again. It was the parents that were beside themselves in anguish. A whistle blew to indicate imminent departure. With the children aboard, the windows had been fully lowered. The parents held their children's hand and were saying their last goodbyes. People were screaming with despair. Suddenly from the next compartment to Hana's, there was a commotion, as one anxious father, grabbed his six-year-old daughter through the open window of the train. Sobbing, he held her tight against his chest, not wanting his daughter to be taken away. Little did he realise that he was dragging his daughter to her early death, the only hope for her survival was to send her far away, into the distant unknown. Finally, the whistle for the train to depart blew and the guards ordered all the parents to stand well away. The guards had chained all the doors so the children couldn't escape but they were free to move around within their compartment. Hana would never forget her mother's eyes as the train slowly pulled out of Prague's central railway station.

* * *

There were only two adults sent to accompany the ninety children on the train. Hana being twelve years old, was one of the older children. She was given the responsibility to look after a five-year-old boy called Achim, who was being sent to a boy's home in central Wales. The young Achim sat next to Hana the whole way. He had a stunned look on his face and wouldn't say anything. He wouldn't let go of Hana's hand. They slowly made their way towards Dresden in Germany; there they would have to change trains. German guards with guns paraded on the platform and some got onto the new train to make inspections and account for all the children. There was a bit of a fuss because they couldn't account for the little girl that had been pulled out of the window by her father at Prague station. One of the adults explained repeatedly what had happened and eventually the German commander accepted her explanation. Then the chains and bolts were refastened, the train chuffed out of the station into the night, bound for the Dutch border. Achim slept peacefully with his head nestled into Hana's lap.

Hana had a couple of hours sleep before waking to glorious sunshine and meticulous German countryside. The patchwork fields that glistened in the early morning light, masked the darkness of their ominous journey. Hana thought of Beethoven's Pastoral Symphony and how her father had talked about the way in which Beethoven had contrasted and juxtaposed the goodness of peace with the evils of war. She thought of her parents as she looked out of the window.

Nearly all the other children were asleep except one little boy of around seven sat in the corner whimpering. Hana smiled at him, and he smiled back. Hana found it hard to keep awake and found herself drifting into a light sleep.

Suddenly the train came to an abrupt halt. Children started crying as they were awoken by the jolt. They had reached the Dutch border and once again German officials boarded the stationary train. They were going through endless checking and rechecking in a most officious manner. Achim came and snuggled in close to Hana and asked what was happening.

'I think we are going through the border patrol,' she whispered.

'Then can we go home?' whispered back Achim.

They waited for what must have seemed an eternity until the train made a lurch forward into Holland and freedom. The train snaked its way through the flat Dutch countryside, past windmills, and broken-down farmhouses until it came to its destination at Eindhoven in southern Holland. There the chains were removed, and the children were allowed onto the platform amidst cheers from the local people who had come to welcome the children to their freedom.

The Dutch people had put on a real party. The mayor of the town was there to make a speech, but none of the children understood a word that he was saying. The welcome speech was followed by music and food. Hana thought even though the food was awful it was the best meal that she had ever eaten. Then the children were grouped into the countries of their destination. All the luggage was put at one end of the platform and fifteen minutes prior to their train departing, the children were asked to pick out their own luggage and were given help to drag it to the other end of the platform. For some the wait was lengthy but Hana and her newfound friend Achim, were soon put on the train bound for Ostend, to catch a ferry to London. More officials at the Belgian border and again as they boarded the ferry from Ostend to Dover. At Dover, the officials once again welcomed the children. This time Hana was able to interpret for the other children, who had started to chatter amongst themselves. The officials smiled at the children and the children smiled back.

When their train finally arrived at St Pancras station around 3:30pm, Hana said goodbye to young Achim, as he joined the group of children bound for Cardiff. Hana was introduced to a Miss Enid Selway, a teacher at the school in Stourbridge. Miss Selway had been sent to receive Hana and immediately recognised her from the small photo that she had been given. Nicholas Winton was at the station organising the children into groups for the next leg of their journeys. On being introduced Miss Selway held out her gloved hand to Hana and in a most deliberate and stilted voice, formally welcomed Hana to Britain. It was something of a pleasant surprise when Hana replied in fluent English that she was very happy to be there.

Together they set off by train to Stourbridge near Birmingham. Once again, the journey involved a couple of changes, that seemed to take for ever. Hana was extremely tired and with the constant rocking movement, she couldn't keep her eyes open, nodding off from time to time. It was twilight by the time they finally reached Stourbridge, where they were met by a Mr Plunkett, the handyman and caretaker of the school. Mr Plunkett had an old car that belched out black smoke. After a couple of false starts, it managed to transport them through bleak roads, along dark laneways, to the house of the head mistress Miss Day and her companion Olivia Eastern. Hana was taken aback, by how much Olivia Eastern looked like her younger sister Susan, Hana's governess at home in Pilsen.

That night Hana was shown to what was called the "spare room". Hana lay on the soft bed with floral sheets and immediately fell asleep.

The next day Hana was woken up by Olivia and taken downstairs to the kitchen where Miss Day was preparing a cooked breakfast. 'You must have been very tired, as we found you fast asleep on the bed fully clothed,' she said with a chuckle. 'You will have some breakfast, won't you?' Hana wasn't used to a fully cooked breakfast, that swam in grease, and wondered, 'If this is breakfast, then what will the other meals be like.'

The three of them walked briskly to the school. Hana was asked to wait in Miss Day's dark, intense office. She could hear the other students arriving at the school and looked out of the window at the children arriving, all dressed in the same uniform. She wasn't used to seeing students in a uniform, nor having boys in the same classroom. Then Miss Day burst into the room, telling Hana to follow her. They went along endless corridors and eventually entered a classroom with about twenty-five students, all of similar age to herself. 'This is Hanna Kohl from Czechoslovakia,' announced Miss Day 'She will be a student with us, you will find that she already speaks very good English.' Then without any hesitation and quite directly, she explained that Hana would need somewhere to live and requested the students to ask their parents if they could accommodate a young girl from Czechoslovakia.

Hana spent the day with her class and felt different because she was the only one out of uniform. By the end of the day, she had made a number of friends and one young girl, called Alice Ward asked if she would like to come home with her. Hana was somewhat taken aback and replied, 'I would love to come and live with you, but you would have to ask your parents if they wouldn't mind.'

'My father is dead' said Alice bluntly 'But I'm sure my mother would love it.'

Early the next day, Alice and her mother Beatrice Ward, arrived before school started and asked to see the headmistress, Miss Day.

Alice went to her classroom where she found Hana sitting alone, pouring over a map of Europe. Together, they explored the route that Hana had just taken. Alice wanted to know all about Czechoslovakia and was somewhat amused by the spelling. They were both laughing at the pronunciation of certain cities. Pari or Paris. Rome like Home. Then quite abruptly, Miss Day, followed by Beatrice Ward, burst into the classroom, to formally announce that Mrs Ward had kindly offered to take in Hana, promising to treat her in the same way she treated her own daughter Alice, and that a small financial allowance to assist with living costs, had been agreed upon.

Soon the rest of the class arrived and noticed the smiles on both Hana and Alice's faces.

* * *

That evening, Hana moved into the loving home of Mrs Beatrice Ward and her daughter Alice. The two girls became closer than sisters. Both girls had gone from being an only child to suddenly having an instant sibling and in Hana's case an immediate stepmother. Hana had moved from one happy home in Pilsen to another happy home in Stourbridge.

* * *

Hana wrote letters to her parents in Pilsen but never got a reply. No one knew of their whereabouts. It was the not knowing and living in hope that delayed her grieving process.

Some 50 years later she found out that her parents had perished at Auschwitz concentration camp. Her pent- up sadness could finally be released.

20

Serendipity

Hovan Kaspar arrived at Southampton docks early on the 1st of August 1936, the day the Berlin Olympic Games began their dramatic opening ceremony. With just a small brown suitcase and the big heavy overcoat, he felt elated and ready to face the world.

The night before Hovan's departure, his mother Sara, had sown a hidden pocket into the lining of his overcoat. Into this concealed pocket, she had placed a written note with some Indian rupees. She knew that her youngest son Hovan was a heavy gambler, for which she blamed his father Vahan. She also knew that Hovan would only write home when he needed some funds, so to make it simple, she concealed some money in the lining of his coat. As she could neither read nor write, she had asked her eldest son, Zaven, to write a note, 'This is all the money that you are getting, so don't ask for anymore!' Sara had a simple but direct way about her. She couldn't understand why Hovan wanted to go halfway around the world to study Engineering. Once again, she blamed her husband Vahan for suggesting this stupidity. What was wrong with being a businessman and making lots of money close to home.

* * *

As Hovan walked down the gang plank, he questioned what he had done. This questioning lasted for less than a microsecond. Hovan never looked back at his mistakes, he was always looking forward, asking himself 'Where to next.' He was very quick at assessing situations and even quicker deciding which option to take. Life was a game, and he played it well.

His thoughts drifted to his friend Marianne, wondering if she would ever be able to walk again. The news from America had not been good. Her parents had taken her to the leading Polio specialist in a New York clinic, giving her the best chance for a full recovery that money could buy. The specialist had given her an outside chance of walking again. He thought if anyone would be able to make it, surely Marianne would be the one. He backed her spirit and although she came from an extremely wealthy family, she was down to earth. He used to say, 'She calls a spade a shovel.' She had told Hovan to forget her, and to get on with the rest of his life. She wrote to him saying 'Don't worry dear Hovan, if I do manage to walk again, I will learn to run so fast. So, watch out, because I will find you wherever you are.'

* * *

Thoughts about Calcutta, his family and Marianne were totally forgotten by the time he got to the bottom of the gang plank. He made a beeline to passport control and flashed his brand-new British passport. His father Vahan had applied to the Home Office for a full British passport as his father, Harat, spending more than five years as a student in England, had been entitled to become a British subject. Harat, having registered as a British subject, allowed Vahan and subsequently Hovan full entitlements.

Once through immigration and then customs, Hovan headed straight to the railway station, taking the next train to Waterloo. Everything seemed so ordered. Where were all the people? Where were all the beggars? Everyone looked refined, just like in the films that he had seen, except there wasn't any fog, and no Sherlock Holmes. At Waterloo Station he took the Northern line underground train to Kings Cross Station via Euston. He had never been underground, and as the train rattled through station after station, he wondered if he had taken a direct route to hades. Carefully he counted down each station to Euston, where he changed trains to get to King's Cross. Charing Cross, Leicester Square, Tottenham Court Road, they all sounded so familiar to the young man from the Empire's second largest city. Hovan had heard the names while playing Monopoly, but hadn't realised that they were actual places, not just names on a board game. One day, he would explore these places, and they would become his stomping ground. One day, he would become a true Londoner, but for now, he was just passing through.

At King's Cross station, he had a four hour wait for his train to Sheffield. He bought a copy of the *Daily Express* newspaper to read about what was going on in the world, in London and, of course, the local horse racing results. Much was being written about the Berlin Olympics and Herr Hitler. Nothing about India or more specifically his home city of Calcutta.

That night, he arrived in Sheffield, hungry and exhausted. It was too late to find anywhere to stay so he wrapped himself in his big overcoat that his mother had given him and slept on a station bench. He used his only tie to secure his suitcase handle to his wrist, wary that someone might want to rob him. The next morning around 4:30am a station guard nudged him gently and said in his broad Yorkshire accent, 'You still alive lad?' Hovan woke startled but soon realised that the guard was being helpful and was directing him to some toilets and a café. Hovan couldn't understand what the café owner was saying but somehow managed to buy a much-needed cup of tea and a currant bun.

By 9:30am that morning, dressed in his best attire, shaven and with clean shoes, he was knocking on the door of the engineering workshop where he had applied for the position of "Apprentice Engineer".

'But Mr Kaspar, we only got your application in the post yesterday,' said the deputy principal Jimmy Wilson, somewhat surprised at the apparition standing before him with a suitcase and heavy overcoat. 'We have had twelve applicants for the two positions on offer.' Hovan felt dejected but did his best to hide his disappointment. 'Where is this Calcutta you say you have come from?'

'Well Calcutta is in India, Sir. It is the second biggest city in the whole of the British Empire, Sir,' replied Hovan pleased that he could get a chance to mention the phrase "British Empire".

'You mean you have come all the way from India, on the off chance that we would offer you a position,' said Jimmy Wilson in disbelief.

'I thought you might like to see me in person, and besides, I will be the best person for the job, Sir,' replied Hovan with a beaming smile. 'I will try my hardest and you won't be disappointed.'

Luckily, Jimmy Wilson took a shining to the heavily Brylcreemed Hovan, eventually saying 'Well Mr Kaspar, seeing that you have come all this way and you look like a keen young lad, I am prepared to give you a go. When can you start?' He wasn't at all surprised that Hovan could start straight away and so called in Dave the supervisor and introduced Hovan as the new apprentice. Hovan asked where he could leave his coat and small suitcase and Jimmy Wilson said, 'If they don't fit in your locker, you can leave them under my desk for the day.' Hovan rolled up his shirt sleeves and never looked back.

That night, Dave the supervisor took Hovan to the local pub and introduced him to the British way of life. Hovan played darts for the first time, showing great promise. He told stories of his journey from Calcutta and soon had a small crowd around him all buying him pints of ale. He quickly became one of the lads, making Jimmy Wilson pleased with his decision to hire the young Hovan. He proved a great asset to the firm and Jimmy Wilson told his boss, 'Watch out that young lad will go places, he's got a lot of what it takes, even though he's not true Yorkshire.'

Dave and his wife had a spare room in their little cottage and offered it to Hovan for little rent, in return for help around the place at weekends, and cooking the odd Indian curry. Hovan found his way to the racecourse at Doncaster, limiting himself to the odd flutter. He simply didn't have the funds to put on any large bets and besides it would take time to study the form of the local horses.

Hovan soon took on a Yorkshire persona. One problem was that he couldn't drink as much beer as the other lads. They had been in training from a young age. It was simply one thing that he couldn't get used to. He would find excuses as to why he couldn't "Go down Pub" as they used to call it. Also, rugby league wasn't really his game. He preferred hockey but no one knew much about hockey up Yorkshire way. They told him that some of the girls down south played hockey but 'Not somet that we men folk play up 'ere lad.' He worked hard and played hard; he was popular, making several friends but none became particularly close.

* * *

The ominous black clouds from the Continent loomed heavily on the horizon. War it seemed, would be inevitable. All the lads around him were going off to war. Hovan wanted to join the Royal Navy and put in his application only to be refused because his grandfather hadn't been born British but had simply become British. Then one day, Hovan received some call up papers from the British Army. He was told to report to the Army barracks the next Thursday. He immediately wrote back saying that he wouldn't be enlisting for the British Army but would prefer to serve as an engineer aboard a British Merchant Navy vessel.

In his letter to the Army recruiting officer he argued, *'If I am considered a Turk by the Royal Navy, then I must be a Turk for the British Army.'* He reported to the docks in Liverpool on the Tuesday and was immediately placed on a merchant ship, heading for South Africa. They needed every engineer they could get.

Hovan's naval career got off to a rather shaky start. He had terrible tooth ache, so when the ship got to Cape Town, he went to see a dentist. The dentist fixed up the filling that was leaking and then said. 'But Mr Kaspar you still have some of your baby teeth at the back. We can easily remove them.' Then without permission, the young dentist proceeded to unsuccessfully hack away. With his knee on Hovan's chest for leverage, and a huge pair of pliers, the dentist started pulling as hard as he could. But those baby teeth were determined to stay. Hovan re-joined the ship in agony as his gums had been severely battered and bruised.

* * *

Hovan travelled as a ship's engineer throughout the entire war years. It was in 1941 that his ship stopped in Calcutta en route for the Far East. Hovan asked for some shore leave, and the captain granted it willingly saying, 'We will be going to Singapore, and then on to Hawaii. We can pick you up on our return.' Hovan enjoyed his time with family and friends, but missed Marianne who was still in America.

Hovan waited but his ship never came back. It was bombed by the Japanese in Pearl Harbour with no survivors.

Hovan was transferred to another merchant ship that also travelled the world picking up and delivering supplies. It was dangerous work, and the shifts were long. In the Far East he befriended a Chinese engineer who introduced him to many of the Chinese crew. A group of them played cards at every opportunity, and in a most expressive manner, slamming down their cards with all their force. Gambling was in their blood. There was one particular Chinaman who somehow by the end of each trip would end up with all the money. Hovan was intrigued on how he did it. He couldn't believe the risks that this Chinaman would take and get away with. Hovan spoke often about this Chinaman as the mythical gambler that always came out on top.

On one occasion, his ship was torpedoed off the western coast of Ireland. The crew were lucky to be rescued, after spending thirty-six hours in a little life raft, adrift in the Atlantic Ocean. Hovan would tell of his many adventures around the world and always spoke of how beautiful the beaches were in Rio de Janeiro or how he loved the harbour and the little coves of Sydney in Australia. Hovan spoke of the splendours of the Mediterranean, and how in Beirut one could be water skiing in the sea, and then forty-five minutes later, be snow skiing in the mountains.

Eventually, the war came to an end and Hovan went back to England. He managed to find a job in London, working as a mechanic in a large car yard. He missed the ocean waves and the excitement of exploring new ports around the globe. London having been heavily bombed, after the initial euphoria of winning the war, descended into a rather dark and dismal place. There was so much repair work to be done. The winter of 1946 was bitterly cold, and Hovan seemed to be getting nowhere. He decided to wait till after the monsoon had broken in Calcutta to return to see his family and friends. He hadn't been home to Calcutta for ten years, except for that disastrous stopover in 1941. His brother Zaven had written to him saying there would always be a job for him if he returned to Calcutta.

* * *

It was a cold, dark Saturday morning in February 1946, when Hovan got in his car to travel up to Birmingham to visit a friend, whom he hadn't seen for quite some time. Hovan had crossed paths with Stanley Davidson, also an Engineer on Merchant Navy vessels, on numerous occasions. Stanley had invited Hovan for the weekend to go and see his favourite soccer team, Aston Villa.

After the game in which Aston Villa lost to Wolverhampton Wanderers, Hovan and Stanley went to a nearby pub to drown their sorrows. Hovan wasn't a big drinker but enjoyed the rowdy pub atmosphere and especially a game of darts.

The two lads were walking home when they passed a dance hall with a crowd of young people queuing up to get in. They joined the queue to pay their money. The place was packed and really bopping to a lively swing band.

'Just what I need a good dance,' said Hovan. 'You never know, you might meet the girl of your dreams.'

'Fat chance here,' replied Stanley, still smarting at Villa's loss.

Once they got into the hall the music took over. Hovan saw a young woman across the dance floor and said to Stanley 'She looks like the one for me,' as he made a bee line straight for her.

* * *

It would be a weekend that Hovan would always remember, even if his beloved Aston Villa had lost to their neighbours and rivals Wolverhampton Wanderers. It had been a chance meeting that would change his life.

21

The Proposal

It was 7:45pm on that cold Saturday evening, when Hana Kohl and a couple of her nursing colleagues, arrived at the dance hall. The sound of the band playing swing music seeped out of the hall as they queued up to pay their two shillings entrance fee. Under her mid-length toggled duffle coat, Hana was wearing a simple dark blue dress with small white polka dots, a heavy red cardigan and her latest acquisition, a pair of stockings with seams at the back. She wore a red beret tilted slightly in a French mode and around her neck lay a fine gold chain with a small diamond pendant that her school friend Alice had recently given her. As she walked into the dance hall, the little pendant caught the light that bounced off the revolving mirror ball and a spark of excitement emanated from her radiance. Out of the shadows a young man in a rather baggy 1930's suit and colourful tie came directly up to her and asked with confidence, 'Excuse me, my name is Hovan. May I have the pleasure of the next dance?'

Without hesitation and as if she had known him all her life, she followed him to the dance floor. They danced and danced, oblivious to anyone around them. They were already in their own cocoon from the moment they met. It was as if they were made for each other, and secret forces were bringing them together. They danced, laughed, and then danced some more. After the final waltz, Hovan accompanied Hana back to the nurse's quarters. They walked hand in hand in complete silence;

wanting to take in as much of the moment as they could. Time stood still for both of them until Hovan asked, 'Do you have a middle name?'

'Yes,' replied Hana. 'It's Maria.'

'Well, my middle name is Michael,' said Hovan with a big grin on his face. 'We both have the same initials H.M.K. don't we?'

'So, if we were to get married, I wouldn't have to change my initials,' said Hana suddenly realising that she had been far too forward. 'No, I didn't mean it like that,' she started to say trying to back track as fast as she could.

'I suppose we will just have to discuss it over lunch tomorrow,' said Hovan putting her at her ease, 'I have the day free but must drive back to London around 4:30pm. What if I come and pick you up around midday and we find one of those country pubs that do such scrumptious roasts.'

'That sounds terrific,' said Hana 'I will be here at noon on the dot.' She laughed as she pointed to her polka dotted skirt. She couldn't believe what was happening. She bent forward and gave him a little kiss on the cheek and then turned around skipping towards the hostel gates repeating, 'noon on the dot.'

She heard her polka dotted skirt make a squishing sound as she ran up the stairs into the hostel. She felt as if the skirt wanted some sort of appreciation for making the evening so successful.

Hana was out on the pavement a good fifteen minutes before the agreed time. She didn't want to be late. Her anxiety grew as time marched on. What if he doesn't come? What if it was all just a dream? The nearby church bell struck 12 o'clock and as if by magic a green Morris Minor pulled up with Hovan in the driver's seat. He immediately jumped out from the driver's door and started tugging the passenger door handle. Initially Hana thought that Hovan was being a gentleman and opening the door for her but soon found out otherwise. He pulled harder on the handle, but the door wouldn't budge. Eventually Hovan pulled really hard. He pulled so hard that the door handle came off in his hand. Reeling backwards, he finally arrived at a stationary position, seated on the pavement. Hana couldn't help laughing and Hovan just sat there seeing the funny side to his predicament.

'Good job I'm a nurse,' said Hana as she gave Hovan a helping hand.

'Hope no bones need mending,' she added as Hovan dusted down his trousers and regained his dignity.

'Come on,' said Hovan as he opened the driver's door so Hana could sit in the back seat. Hana couldn't stop laughing as she said, 'I feel like a princess being driven around by a chauffeur.'

'Well, that's good,' said Hovan 'because we are off to The Whittington Inn for lunch where, it's said that King Charles II took refuge following the Battle of Worcester.'

Hana felt so special as she rode serenely in the back seat of that little green Morris Minor. They had a wonderful meal together and they talked and talked about their families and their aspirations.

'Now as you said last night, you wouldn't have to change your initials if we got married,' said Hovan with a smile on his face. 'Do you think that this would be a good enough excuse to get married?'

'I would need a proper proposal and perhaps a ring if that is what you have in mind,' said Hana cheekily.

'Well as a matter of fact I was thinking that way, but perhaps it is all a bit too hasty for you,' said Hovan. 'Hana I would love to marry you and I think I would not only cherish you always but also make a good father to our children. I am a hard worker, reliable and you would always have food on the table.'

'You don't need to sell yourself,' interrupted Hana 'But I do need you to put that as a question.'

'Hana, will you marry me?' asked Hovan.

'Yes of course I will, you old goat,' said Hana. 'But I will need a ring to seal it, won't I?'

With that Hovan tore a strip off his white paper serviette and rolled it into a length about three inches long. He then took Hana's hand and wound the thin roll of paper around her finger and tied a knot to form a ring. He fluffed up the ends to make it look like petals saying, 'There, will that do until I see you next with a proper engagement ring?'

* * *

Hovan took Hana back to the nurse's hostel and then drove on back to London, where he worked as a garage mechanic in Brentford. As promised, a couple of weeks later, he returned to pick up Hana and take her to see her official guardians, Miss Eastern and Miss Day, who had moved to a small cottage in a Cotswold hamlet called Guiting Power. There, Hovan formally sought their approval for Hana's hand in marriage, which was duly given with their blessings. Then, all celebrated the happy occasion, with homemade cake and a pot of tea. Hana was beside herself with excitement, but sad that her parents weren't there to witness the event. She knew that they would have wholeheartedly approved.

'We have decided to get married in Calcutta,' said Hana to her two elderly guardians. 'It is going to be a big wedding with more than two hundred guests, and we would love both of you to be there.' Hana realised, as she completed her invitation on a descending note, the incongruity of discussing weddings in faraway places such as Calcutta, whilst in the cramped but polite, little country cottage. Especially with the two elderly spinsters, sitting in winged armchairs before her.

'We will have to see,' replied Miss Eastern. 'Calcutta, how exotic,' she said turning to Miss Day.

* * *

The following weekend Hana had two consecutive days off and asked the matron if she could have an extra day so she could go down to London. Hovan shared a small house in Fulham with his sister Agnes, who was studying the piano at the Royal College of Music. Most of the day Agnes was practising for her final examination. Knowing that she would pass her exams, she was driven to be the best student in her year. Agnes had music in her veins. She would go round singing popular tunes, then play them on the piano and as if she was sight reading. Even her examiners were impressed by her musicality, her ability to sight read, her perfect pitch and her ability to immediately play back music after hearing it just the once. Hovan was very proud of his elder sister and Hana enjoyed her company. In turn, Agnes was impressed by Hovan's choice and welcomed Hana into the family. 'We are a mixed bunch,' said Agnes 'but we all come with a generous heart.'

Hovan was practical and extremely good at planning. His organisational skills were to stand him in good stead, especially in his business. It was a quality that Hana would come to admire in Hovan. He had a direct approach to life and a man of few, but effective words.

Hovan and his sister Agnes had a lease to rent the house in Fulham until the end of April. Agnes intended to return to Calcutta, with hopefully 1st class exam results, around the middle of March. Hovan had previously decided that he would also vacate the house and return to Calcutta to catch up with his family for a month or two. He had been in constant correspondence with both his father and eldest brother, but he hadn't been home for a number of years, and it was time to take a few months holiday. Hana initially thought how exciting it would be to go with Hovan on a cruise ship all the way to India. She had never been on a ship except the ferry crossing of the English Channel, but that didn't count. She wanted to experience the notion of the word 'Passage' rather than simply 'Crossing'. She wanted to experience the booking clerk asking 'Madam, will you be going POSH?' Port side out and starboard side home. 'Oh yes,' she would reply, 'And can we have a suite rather than just a cabin,' she dreamed, until Hovan brought her down to earth with his sense for the practical.

'Now, I intend to be marrying a State registered nurse,' said Hovan with a smile on his face, 'not just one of those "also ran".'

Hana looked quizzical as she hadn't heard that expression before.

'"Also ran" is a horse racing term,' he explained for horses that didn't make the grade. 'It is most important that you finish your nurses training. You only have a couple of months to go before your finals and besides I will be waiting for you in Calcutta and getting everything ready for our wedding.'

Hana could see the sense in his words, but they didn't really cushion the thump back to reality. 'Yes, you are right but how can I possibly exist without you and for a full two months,' she replied with a sarcastic smile of acceptance. They laughed with happiness as their world overflowed with joy.

The following weekend, Hovan came to pick up Hana and together they went to Wollaston near Stourbridge, to see Alice and her mother Mrs Ward. Both approved of Hovan but were disappointed that the wedding would be held in Calcutta. It seemed so far away and rather exotic to people that had only been as far as Coventry. They discussed the problems of Hana not having a passport but only papers proving her refugee status. There would be a lot to get sorted, especially getting temporary visas without a passport.

Agnes took her music exams and passed top of her year. Two weeks later Hovan and Hana took Agnes to Heathrow airport to catch her flight back to Calcutta. The three of them, with Agnes's entire luggage squashed into Hovan's little Morris Minor. It was the first time that Hana had been to an airport, and she couldn't believe the size of the planes and how they could take off, carrying all those people and their luggage. Once Agnes had departed, Hovan and Hana made enquiries about flights for Hana. The wedding had been set for the third Saturday in June, which Hovan considered would give Hana enough, but not too much, time to settle into the way of life in Calcutta. Before the wedding Hovan would be staying upstairs with his father while Hana would have her own room in the larger downstairs flat with Hovan's mother Sara, and his sister Agnes. Arman, Agnes's twin brother, would have to move upstairs into the spare bedroom of the oldest brother Zaven and his wife Victoria. It all sounded too complicated for Hana but luckily, Hovan had given her a family photo that showed all the members of the family, so Hana had a feeling she knew them before she met them.

* * *

She wondered how she would be accepted but if Agnes was anything to go by, all would be fine. She did find it strange that Hovan's parents were separated but lived amicably in the same block of flats. Although they avoided each other as much as possible, they behaved in a civilised manner in each other's company. This was more than could be said for many separated couples.

22

Chicago

Emile and Chantal had been working in a Zurich hospital for almost two years after the war had ended, when Emile saw in one of the American medical journals, an advertisement for a physician to work in a hospital in Chicago, Illinois. That evening, he discussed it with Chantal, who agreed that he should apply for the position. The pay would be excellent, and they agreed that they should see it as a two-year working holiday rather than a commitment for life. Chantal wouldn't have to work and could spend her time at the galleries and looking at Frank Lloyd Wright's Architecture, which she so much admired. She thought she might even enrol at his school in Taliesin West for a subject, but then found out that the school was now in Arizona many miles away from Chicago.

Emile applied for the job and before they knew it, they were packing their bags and taking a flight to Chicago. They had committed themselves for a couple of years after which they could decide whether they would stay or not.

* * *

They both loved it in Chicago and after the two years were up, they both wanted to stay. Chantal had found a well-paid research job at the hospital, researching a cure for Malaria. The small research unit had connections with the Swiss Tropical Institute in Basel. Malaria was killing thousands each day in India, Africa, South America, and throughout the tropics.

She published papers, and attended conferences all over America, but soon gave lectures around the world. She quickly became a highly regarded research leader in her field. On occasions she went to conferences in Europe and made a special effort to spend a day or so in Basel with professor Egon Hilgenberg; he had been so influential at the start of her career. She had well and truly surpassed his abilities, but she always respected that it was he, who had taught her the basis of good research, and that without his help, she wouldn't have achieved very much at all. Egon Hilgenberg was now in his 80s but would keep abreast of what was happening in the field of Tropical Medicine. His wife had died some years ago, but he kept himself busy and his mind active.

On one such trip to Basel, Chantal made her way to see Egon in his tiny little flat. He had asked her for dinner and his carer had prepared a special fondue that Chantal loved so much. Egon had put out a lot of candles and put on a gramophone record of one of Mahler's symphonies. He had rather over done things; she thought perhaps he was trying to seduce her. He was now in a wheelchair and his thoughts ran far from any form of seduction.

'Chantal, I have a proposition that I want to present to you,' he started and then continued, 'As you know, I used to be the head of the Swiss Tropical Medicine Institute and have now been made a Lifetime Honorary Member. The other day, I was asked to suggest a suitable candidate to head up our new branch in Caracas, Venezuela. It will require a lot of field work as well as liaising with Head Office here in Basel. They are looking for a leader for a research unit, exploring a cure for Malaria. I have taken the liberty of speaking with Professor David Sonderling and asked him if he would be amenable to releasing you for a two-year stint in Caracas. The work would be hard but very rewarding. A lot of the work would be carried out deep in the Amazon close to the Brazilian, Venezuelan borders. Most of the field work would be co-ordinated in a small place called Tama Tama on the Orinoco River. He has indicated that he would be prepared to release you should you want the position. Of course, the final decision would be totally up to you.'

'Of course, it would be up to me,' she replied rather tersely. She had been rather taken aback but somewhat honoured by the invitation.

'I am a married woman you know, and I would have to discuss it with my husband. How long before you need an answer?'

'They want someone there within a month. Six weeks at the most,' he replied.

'And how long would the research be expected to take?' she asked, immediately aware of the stupidity of her question.

'Research can't be subjected to a timeframe,' he replied. 'Research takes as long as it takes to find an answer to your field of enquiry. It could be two weeks or forty years. Who knows? At this stage I think they just want someone to start up the program and then it will be taken from there.'

'Emile and I will have to think about it,' she replied. 'Anyway, I will need a full job specification before I can consider anything.'

'I had hoped that you would say that,' he said handing her a large envelope. 'You should find everything you need to know in this package.'

* * *

On the flight back to New York, Chantal looked through all the documents and the more she read the more exciting the project became. By the time she got to meet Emile at New York's La Guardia Airport, she was brimming with excitement. That weekend in New York was filled with Art Galleries, a Concert, and some fine dining. Chantal was so pleased that Emile was also excited about this new venture in South America. He said that when they got back to Chicago, he would cable his friend Wolfgang Bernstein, who worked in a major public hospital in Caracas and see if Wolfgang couldn't help with getting him a job interview. Wolfgang Bernstein was a diminutive Austrian Jew from Vienna; he had trained in Zurich to be a gynaecologist. After the war Wolfgang had spent some time with Albert Schweitzer in Gabon, this had prepared him for work in equatorial climates. After a couple of years of service with Schweitzer, Wolfgang had decided that he needed to explore his own pathway and found himself in Caracas, Venezuela.

Chantal and Emile flew back to Chicago, where Chantal formally gave in her notice to her boss, Professor Sonderling. It wasn't as if she was leaving her employer but rather relocating to a new location and overseeing the setting up of a new research field unit. David Sonderling was only too pleased that Chantal had accepted the challenge, although he was sorry to see her leave his department, she would always be welcome back in Chicago. He refrained from telling her that he hoped she would come back to take over his position when he retired.

Chantal and Emile packed up and left for Caracas within the month. They managed to squeeze in a ten-day trip around the Yucatan Peninsula, Mexico, exploring some of the Mayan ruins. Chichen Itza, Uxmal, Tulum, Palenque. It was a whirlwind trip that became a bit of blur. They learnt some Spanish along the way and Emile, who had a gift for picking up languages was able to string some sentences together by the time they got to Caracas.

* * *

Caracas quickly became their home, where they would reside for almost thirty years. It was where they would flourish and raise their three beautiful children. That is until they met face to face with what was to be a fatal tragedy.

23

Deep in the Jungle

Emile and Chantal thrived in Caracas. Emile had a dark complexion that could take the scorching sun, while Chantal applied copious amounts of cream to her delicate skin and wore an extensive selection of broad brim hats with colourful flowing ribbons. They soon fell in love with Venezuela and wanted to play a part in the development of the emerging republic. Venezuela was a country of contrasts. Everything appeared exaggerated. Extreme wealth adjacent to abject poverty.

But it was the energy of the people, that they found appealing. It seemed that even the beggars, begged with a smile on their face. People sauntered with a syncopated rhythm in their step. In the squares, they sang beautiful love songs, played music from the heart, and danced as if there was no tomorrow.

* * *

At the beginning, Emile worked in a central hospital in Caracas, while Chantal was busy setting up the programme researching a cure for Malaria, that had become particularly virulent in the jungle near the Brazilian border. She would be flown down to the makeshift airstrip at Tama Tama and would come back to Caracas every other weekend. Emile would often fly down to Tama Tama on a Friday evening to spend the weekend with Chantal. They loved exploring the Orinoco basin and would make trips on a dug-out tree, called a "bongo", to explore all the little side tributaries of the Cassiquiare river. These "bongos" were working vessels, used to transport goods up and down the river. Weekends were just not long enough for them to go any real distance, so from time to time, Emile would take a few days off work, allowing them to explore further upriver and into some of the little tributaries. Together they ventured deep into the Amazonas territories but were aware that they shouldn't go too far away from the river. The river was the lifeline of the jungle. It was the internet, the superhighway through which people communicated. Distances were measured in days travelled by "bongo" rather than miles or kilometres.

Emile soon realised that his services as a medical physician were much sought after in the jungle, and the deeper he went, the greater was the demand. He was confronted with another world of health care that challenged the very foundations of western medicine. Religion and mysticism held a greater influence than an understanding of how the body functions. Rituals and rites of passage with their ceremonial and theatrical performances abounded and completely threw Emile's knowledge of medicine out of the window. Belief systems, hallucinogenic remedies using potent concoctions of jungle fruits, and animal sacrifices, all played a role in the wellness of individuals.

As they travelled further up the rivers and deeper into the jungle, they encountered indigenous tribes of Indians, each with their own language, rituals, and customs. The tribes knew little of each other as the distances were great and unlike other tribal peoples around the world, they were not particularly nomadic. The jungle provided adequately for each tribe. As Emile and Chantal entered the jungle areas, they would initially come across the Makiritare tribe, as they penetrated deeper, they would come across Piaroa Indians, and then close to the Brazilian border, the Yanomami Indians. It would be more accurate to say that the Yanomami would come across them. The Yanomami are hunters and are acutely aware of any animal that ventures into their space, long before the intruder would be aware of them. The Yanomami fiercely control their section of the jungle, swooping from their hiding place to kill any unwanted interlopers, usually with poisoned spears or arrows.

The Yanomami Indians live in what is called a Shabono, a communal open hut that is built with leaves, vines, and tree trunks, found in the surrounding rainforest. The hut would usually house about one hundred or so tribal people, and was basically a clearing in the jungle, with an elliptical, fifteen feet wide, thatched roof, creating a large central communal open space. Under the thatched roof, the Yanomami would swing precariously in hammocks. The only wall to the Shabono, was an external perimeter barrier used primarily for protection from animals or other intruders. Being made of logs and tree trunks, this wall was also used as a supply of wood for the constant smouldering fire beneath the hammocks. The nights can be cold in the jungle, so the smoke keeps the tribe warm at night and repels the mosquitoes by day. The hammocks are made of reeds from the jungle, with strands that only go lengthways. Heaven knows how the people don't fall through the strands of reeds onto the smoking fires below. Some of the hammocks are big enough for a whole family to sleep in.

Each morning the men replenish and rebuild the external walls of the Shabono with wood from the jungle, before going off for the day to hunt for whatever moves. A couple of the older men stay to guard the Shabono, and the women who look after the children. The men wear only a cord around their stomach. This cord is used to hold their penis up against their body. No one wants a penis dangling around the place and getting in the way when trying to hunt.

Many of the Yanomami speak a language called Waika (pronounced Gwaika). In Waika, there is a word for 'one' and a word for 'two'. After that there is a word which sounds like *'bruta'* meaning 'many'. Their culture has had no need for numeracy, thus the words for one and two are quite sufficient. They don't have personal possessions as everything is shared. If a Yanomami man comes back with lots of fish from the river, the tribe will eat well. If no fish are caught, then perhaps someone else has been successful with snaring some wild animals or birds. The river is full of Piranha fish which aren't edible but will devour you completely within a matter of minutes.

When a Yanomami person dies, there is much wailing mixed with sounds of joy. Crying and laughter are both cross cultural reactions shared by all of humanity. The dead body is laid to rest on a pyre, with a tribal elder removing the bones just before they get too charred. He will hand them to some of the younger men who will pulverise the bones to a fine powder. This powder will then be mixed with a liquid concoction of fruits, berries and leaves that the women have prepared. Then with great excitement, the tribe will sit randomly in the open space of the Shabono to drink the concoction. It is considered that the spirit of the person is within their bones, and the drinking of their bones allows that spirit to re-enter the tribe; thus, the spirit lives on and is passed on from generation to generation.

* * *

Chantal was completely captured by the things she saw during her time near the Brazilian border, but never lost sight of the bigger picture of finding a cure for Malaria. Hers was a worldwide search, with global significance. Through her scientific research, she became a highly decorated and renowned virologist. Each year, for a short period of time, she would emerge from the depths of the jungle, giving lectures at eminent Universities on her findings, and share her progress in the field. She became highly sought after and was awarded numerous honorary doctorates from universities around the world. She was careful not to speak about the culture and tribal peoples of the Territorias Amazonas as she desperately wanted to keep the Yanomami people safe from the savages of so-called Western Civilisation.

She wanted to maintain the trust of the Yanomami, keeping them safe from both the Anthropologists and the Evangelical missionaries such as the 'New Tribes Mission'. The sole purpose of the missionaries was to seek out any 'New Tribes', to teach them the 'Word of God'. These evangelical missionaries believed that if the 'Word of God' and 'Christian Thought', were the first encounters that an unknown tribe experienced with western culture, then somehow the whole tribe would miraculously be converted forever. There appeared to be a race between the missionaries and anthropologists to see who could get to the hidden tribes first.

Chantal never spoke to anyone, except her husband Emile, about the Yanomami people. She gained the tribes trust through a basic sign language that she developed with them; she was accepted as an adjunct to the tribe. Through these secret hand gestures, a senior elder of the tribe told Chantal that when she died, they would drink her bones. Whilst she was very honoured by her acceptance by the tribe, she did feel a little disturbed by the thought of them all sitting around drinking her bones.

* * *

Chantal spent more than five years deep in the jungle, coming up for air in Caracas for short but regular intervals. She enjoyed being in Caracas with her husband Emile for a week at a time but couldn't wait to get back home to the jungle. The research went well but the work was hard and the conditions difficult. After five years Chantal was ready to return to so called civilisation, exhaustion was catching up with her and becoming pregnant with her first child changed everything. Luckily the research was at a point that she felt comfortable with handing over to her senior assistant. Chantal returned to Caracas to be with Emile and start their family.

24

Dum Dum Airport

Hana's ticket to Calcutta proved much more complicated than was originally envisaged. As she only had refugee status, she couldn't get a passport until she got married to a British subject. Finally the Indian immigration authorities agreed to grant a two-month visa; just long enough to arrange the wedding.

Getting visas to transit through certain countries was straight out impossible, while other countries said it would be fine if Hana got clearance from the next country on her itinerary. It was a bureaucratic nightmare with countries giving transit approval, but with impossible conditions. In those days the passenger planes didn't fly at night. Eventually Hana managed to arrange her ticket to Calcutta, using three different airlines.

* * *

Hovan had already purchased his flights some months before meeting Hana and had arranged his departure to coincide with the termination of the lease of the house in Fulham. He liked to coordinate every detail to the minute and decided to go in advance so he could organise their wedding arrangements.

On the morning of his departure, his friend Ronnie, who worked in the same garage, would pick up Hovan and take him to the estate agency to return the house keys and to also collect the bond. Then Ronnie would drive him to Heathrow airport to catch the 10:35am flight to Cairo. Hana wanted to see him off, but she was on duty that day, so they said their farewells the previous weekend. 'Of course, I will be there to meet you at the airport,' said Hovan. She hadn't known whether to believe him, when he told her that the name of the airport in Calcutta was called 'Dum Dum'. She thought he was joking but then he showed her his ticket and itinerary and there in black and white was written 'Arrival at Dum Dum airport, Calcutta'.

Hovan's flight had only two stops. First at Cairo, then early the next morning on to Karachi where he would be able to transit for one hour before taking a flight to Calcutta. Hana's itinerary would be much more involved. First, she would have to fly to Paris, and then the next day, take a flight to Cairo. The Egyptians would accept her coming from France but not from England. Similarly, the Pakistani authorities insisted that Hana make a stop in Kabul before going on to Karachi. From Karachi, Hana could fly to Delhi, and then the next day a flight to this Dum Dum airport. It would take her a full five days with a 06:05 hours departure time from Karachi arriving at Dum Dum at 10:35am.

* * *

Hana took her final nursing exams, then stayed with her friend Alice and her mother for the last couple of days before taking the train to London. Alice and her mother came to the station to see Hana off. 'You will be back shortly,' said Alice, 'and write as soon as you get there, won't you.' Mrs Ward was silent. She couldn't understand why Hana was running off to the Far East. She felt a sense of betrayal and a great sense of loss. She had treated Hana as her other daughter but felt that Hana hadn't fully accepted her as a mother. As the time came for Hana's train to leave, Alice gave Hana a warm embrace, but Mrs Ward coldly put out a hand for Hana to shake. Hana took her hand and then bursting into tears embraced Mrs Ward saying spontaneously. 'Don't worry mum, I will be back soon.' It was the first and only time that she had called Mrs Ward, 'mum'. Mrs Ward remained stiff and awkward with the same distraught eyes that Hana had witnessed from her actual mother, when she had left Prague. The departure whistle blew, and Hana jumped on the train. As the train slowly pulled out of the platform, she leant out of the window to wave goodbye. In the distance she could see the two woman waving and then a minute or so later she saw Mrs Ward slump onto the platform. The train continued wending its way through the grimy back streets of Birmingham. Hana, feeling completely helpless, could do nothing but find her allocated seat. Closing her tearful eyes, she wondered what this second journey into the unknown would have in store for her. At not quite twenty years old, she had experienced more than most people do in a whole lifetime. Now, she was on her way to the man she loved.

* * *

The next day she presented herself, and her little brown suitcase with her initials H.M.K. painted on the outside, at Heathrow Airport. Even though she had never flown before, she boarded the small plane to Paris with the confidence of a seasoned aviator. She had a window seat at the back of the plane and the only time she felt an ounce of fear was when taxing up the runway for take-off. She spent the night in a small hotel near the airport as her departure to Cairo would be early the next morning. She had to wait two days in Cairo before getting a flight to Karachi via Kabul. She found Egypt fascinating. She had never experienced the hustle and bustle of the local bazaars. She felt the unwelcome stares from the men, but continued walking at pace, as if she knew where she was going. She kept well away from the tourists' spots and tried in vain to meld into the background. She heard French being spoken and found it to be the best language for her to communicate with the locals.

Then on to Kabul on an even bigger Pan Am flight. Once again, she was sitting towards the back of the plane where she befriended an attractive Danish woman who was travelling with her four-year-old son. To be completely correct it was the young boy Victor that befriended Hana, wanting her to read a children's book to him. He couldn't understand that Hana couldn't speak Danish but just carried on as if she could. Somehow, they managed to converse in what appeared a meaningful dialogue, both speaking their own language.

'I'm so sorry,' said the mother as she grabbed the young boy and his books. 'He is at an age when he wants to explore.'

Hana and Isabella Jensen struck up a friendship on the flight as they exchanged snippets of information about themselves, as well as enquiring about the other. Hana explained that she had just qualified as a nurse but was on her way to Calcutta to get married to the most marvellous man. Isabella said that she was a medical doctor but now a full-time mother. She and Victor were on their way to Delhi. Her husband was the undersecretary to the Danish ambassador in Delhi. They showed each other small black and white photos of their respective partners. The two young women got on famously, never running out of conversation. They ascertained that they would both be on the same flight to Delhi and the time passed quickly as their conversation flowed from topic to topic. Hana was taken by the demure Dane, her poise and beauty. Isabella found the youth and exuberance of Hana refreshing.

After a two hour stop in Kabul, they were guided across the tarmac to a waiting plane that would take them to Karachi. After a turbulent flight, and a bumpy landing, the small aircraft taxied down the Karachi airport runway, finally coming to a halt at the terminal. The transit passengers were ushered into a small room, where there was an official sitting behind a large and imposing desk. The noisy ceiling fan did little to alleviate the heat and stifling humidity. The room smelt of sweat and stale curries, and a single cord suspended from the ceiling, held a naked dim light bulb that did nothing to brighten up the oppressive atmosphere. The official looked down at some papers and didn't look up as he said, 'Next.' Hana presented her papers and the moustached official read them slowly. Without looking up at her he beckoned his assistant saying something to him in Urdu.

The young assistant guided Hana to an even smaller room which didn't have any windows but just a high-level grill on one side, and wooden chairs along the opposite wall. 'You wait here,' said the assistant and then left the room. About five minutes later, an elderly dapper Italian gentleman was brought in and told to wait. After another ten minutes or so, Isabella holding the hand of the crying Victor, and a teddy bear in her other hand, were also ushered into the room. 'What's happening?' Hana asked Isabella. 'I'm not sure but I fear we are going to miss our connection to Delhi,' whispered Isabella in case the walls had ears. Eventually the moustached official from behind the desk in the first room, burst in telling them in no uncertain terms that they were going to be sent back to Cairo, because they didn't have landing permission to arrive in India.

The Italian gentleman exploded and was taken off gesticulating as Italians often do. His loud voice diminished as he was carted further down the corridor, he was not to be seen again. The official started shouting at the top of his voice at the two young women and as far as they could make out, he wanted a considerable amount of money from them. Isabella started to shout back at the official and then she too was taken off down the corridor with Victor yelling and screaming at the top of his voice. Hana froze as she wondered what would be happening next. Time stood still for her. Her thoughts went this way and that. If only Hovan was here, he could sort it out.

The humidity dropped as evening fell. She could hear the propellers of aircraft, starting at a low pitch and then rumble past on their take off to foreign lands. Would she ever get to leave? What was happening to Isabella and little Victor?

Suddenly the door of the cell flew open, and a female assistant entered the room, followed by Isabella with Victor asleep in her arms.

When the assistant left, Hana asked, 'What's happening?'

'No need to panic. It's all got sorted out thanks to this little one,' she said as she looked down at the small sleeping child.

'What do you mean?' asked Hana in a hurried tone of voice.

'Well, first I explained that we are all travelling together. I told the official that you were coming with us as a nanny for Victor. I told him that my husband worked for the Danish Embassy in Delhi and gave him a number to call. I wrote the number down on a piece of paper and as I was handing it to the official, Victor who was standing next to me, suddenly vomited all over his shoes. The official went ballistic, but about ten minutes later, his assistant came back with a broad grin on her face and told me to follow her back here. Apparently, we are going to be deported but somehow on to Delhi instead of back home. I hope you weren't planning on coming back here any time soon.'

Hana was greatly relieved. The two young women and little Victor stayed in the room under guard for what seemed for ever. Their connecting flight to Delhi had departed some hours before but apparently there was a flight at 10:15am the next morning. Eventually they were taken by car to a hostel and shared a very shabby room with a toilet in the corner. The night was silent but at least it was cool. Hana slept for a few hours but was woken early by a rooster and other exotic sounds. The room didn't have windows, just high-level openings with only a mesh for protection from the outside world. Victor also woke early and wanted to play. Isabella slept well but was woken by Victor pretending to read his book yet again. He knew the words by heart and recited them out loud, with the same intonation as the adults before him.

It was only 6:45am when a young woman came with some inedible breakfast and told them to be ready to be taken to the airport in thirty minutes time. The ride to the airport in what was a clapped-out army jeep took around twenty minutes along potholed roads. Finally, they arrived at the airport with two hours to wait. Hana tried to find a public phone to ring Hovan, but no such thing existed. Hana presented her papers that were this time accepted. She asked about connecting flights from Delhi to Calcutta and was told that the only flight would be at 15:45 hours which would give her just under an hour to make the connection. Isabella assured Hana that she would phone through to Hovan in Calcutta from the Danish embassy in Delhi. 'It should give him enough time to pick you up from the airport in Calcutta,' she said reassuringly.

Hana managed to sleep on the plane for an hour or so, but still concerned that she hadn't been able to inform Hovan directly of what had happened. She felt greatly relieved that she was on her way, leaving Karachi well behind her. High above the clouds she dreamed of her parents waiting for her at this Dum Dum airport. Her father looked worried, and her mother had lost a lot of weight. Both appeared vague as if dementia had set in, neither of them recognised her, looking puzzled as she spoke to them. She was pleased to be woken by Victor, wanting her to read his book to him yet again.

* * *

The plane arrived ten minutes late at Delhi, giving Hana just enough time to make the connection to Calcutta. Luckily, she had been able to send her large suitcase directly from Heathrow straight through to Calcutta and was travelling with simple hand luggage. Would it still be waiting for her she wondered, as she would be arriving in Calcutta more than twenty-four hours behind schedule. Delhi airport was madness. So many people buzzing around as if they had a purpose. Hana, being in transit, was separated from Isabella and Victor at an early stage. Isabella had warned Hana that this might happen, so they had already said their goodbyes. The two young women had exchanged contact details and vowed to keep in touch. 'Please send us photos of your wedding,' said Isabella, 'and remember to expect everything to go wrong. After all, this is India, and one has to "go with the flow".' These words 'go with the flow' proved to be wise advice, Hana would remember them well for the next five years.

Finally, her little plane touched down at Dum Dum airport and the second of her long and arduous journeys had come to an end. The first had been by train across Europe, and this one by plane, to a new and complex land, that would prove to be different from what she was used to or what she could have possibly imagined. It was July 1946 and India was in turmoil. Hana showed the Indian immigration officer the letter she had received from the Indian High Commission in London granting her a sixty day stay in India unless she was to get married. This suited her well and although tired, she felt a sense of excitement. 'Welcome to India madam,' said the slight immigration official with a shake of his head from side to side. 'I hope you have a jolly good stay. Oh yes, please collect your luggage and proceed to the customs lounge.' She couldn't get over the head movement from side to side and put it down to the poor man having a peculiar tick. She was to become accustomed to this movement of the neck and soon learnt that is a form of garnering approval.

It was with great relief that Hana found her little suitcase waiting for her in the customs lounge. The customs officer rummaged through her meagre belongings, then waved her through, once again with that shake of his head.

'Thank you' she said hurriedly. She couldn't wait to go through the swing doors and rush into the arms of her fiancée.

* * *

On the other side of the doors, she was met by the smell of sweaty beggars, sprawled bedraggled on the hard floor. Some of the beggars came hobbling up to her on crutches, with their crooked hands held out in front of them. Hovan wasn't there. He was nowhere to be seen.

* * *

Hana circled round and around looking for Hovan. Finally, she decided to stand in the middle of the arrivals lounge and let him find her. She didn't want to believe that he wasn't there.

Then, out of the babbling crowd, appeared a wizened old Indian woman, wearing a ragged, dishevelled sari, no shoes, and a red dot on her forehead. She approached Hana saying something in Bengali but soon realised that Hana didn't understand. The old woman, with a gnarled index finger, pointed at Hana's suitcase and then into the distance. Hana looked and saw a man slumped asleep on a chair. Next to the man was a white placard with the letters 'HMK' written in red. Hana looked again. It was Hovan. He had fallen asleep while waiting for her.

She rushed to where Hovan was asleep with the bare-footed woman in pursuit. Hana gently tapped Hovan on the shoulder, saying 'Fancy meeting you here Mr Kaspar.'

They embraced but were soon interrupted by the old woman prodding Hovan in the ribs. 'Money,' she said in Bengali, holding out her hand. Hovan dug deep into his pocket and handed her all his loose change. The old woman beamed, as she disappeared back into the crowd.

* * *

'She must have noticed your placard and the initials on my suitcase,' said Hana and then asked, 'How long have you been waiting here?'

'Well, I thought you were coming yesterday, so about thirty hours or so. I was starting to think you might have changed your mind.'

PART 3

Never say never

West   East

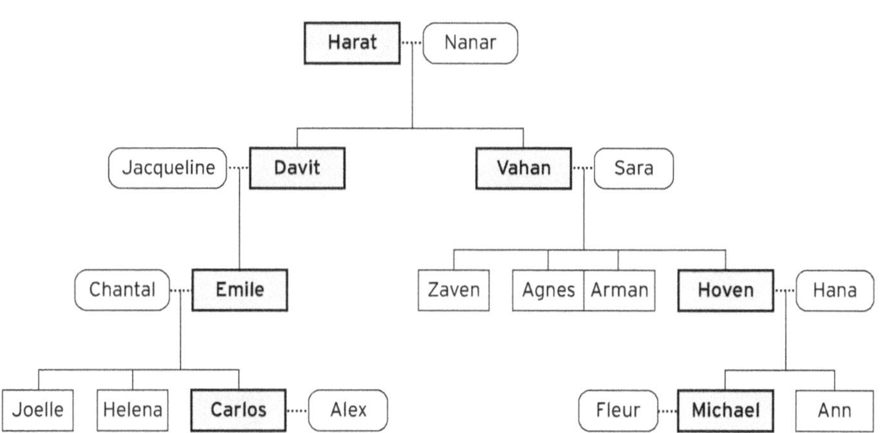

25

On Top of the World

My mother always told me that I was a most considerate child. Well, that is compared with my younger sister Ann, who apparently came into this world like an explosion. When I asked my mother what she meant by 'considerate', she replied that I was born at 11:10am, just in time for both of us to have lunch. Food it seems has always played an important part in both of our lives.

I was born in Calcutta, India on 23rd September 1947 in time for both lunch and the partition of the sub-continent, happening all around us. India was certainly a turbulent place but having just been born, I did not really know too much about the partition of a nation and the separation of religious groups. I was, I suppose, much more concerned about lunch, rather than the political or religious issues. Being born on the autumn equinox meant that the world was also in the balance from an astronomical perspective, but that didn't seem to register with me either.

Some couple of years later I was baptised at the Armenian Holy Church of Nazareth in Calcutta and given the name Michael Kaspar. My father Hovhannes Kaspar was proud to be of Armenian descent as was my mother Hana Kaspar (née Kohl) proud of her Czech origins. The result has been that I am a product of a mixture of cultures and that mixture has become even more layered as time has gone by.

My first memory of life was filled with drama, and I can still see it quite clearly today. Sometimes people think that they can recall things from a very early age, but often, it is just a memory jolted by a photograph or a home movie, not the actual event. There are no photos nor movies of my first memory, as it was an incident that happened on a truly personal level when I was three and half years old. My cousin Peter, who always reminded me that he was seven months and one day older than me, had come with his ayah – Indian nanny – asking if I wanted to go with them to the park opposite our house. I hadn't finished my breakfast, but my mother said I could go with them. Toast in hand, I waddled off with them across the road and into the small park. All I remember is standing alone, some paces behind them, looking up into the clear blue sky and seeing a bird circling around and around. Suddenly, the hawk swooped coming directly towards me. I can still sense that bird coming closer and closer, and then taking the piece of toast out of my hand. It must have been a full twenty seconds before I realised what had happened and then burst into tears. Peter's ayah took me home and still crying, I whimpered to my mother 'That birdie took my toast.'

'Never mind,' she said, 'we will get you another one.' I learnt that day, that not only was my mother extremely practical but that she also knew, that as far as I was concerned, food would console all.

My sister Ann was born soon after my encounter with the hawk, and the attention that had previously been bestowed solely upon me, suddenly found another focus. Pushing my baby sister in her pram and feeding her bananas, was my way of welcoming her to the world.

* * *

It had never been the intention of my parents that they would stay in India for too long. When I was two years old, my mother and I made a six-week trip back to Stourbridge. She had felt very isolated in Calcutta, and wanted to get back to what she called home. She wanted to show me off to her friend Alice and Alice's mother, Beatrice. She felt that they were now her true family, with Stourbridge her adopted home. I was too young to remember anything of the trip, but photos show that my father managed to join us for a few weeks' holiday in Devon.

My father Hovan, finally managed to sell his motor repair business in Calcutta, enabling us to move back to England for the foreseeable future. It was in early June of 1953, when my mother, Hana, boarded that BOAC plane with her two young children, back to "England's green and pleasant land". My father, Hovan, set off by boat the next day, with all the heavy furniture and other bulky items. My mother, Hana, would initially take my sister and me to Switzerland, where she would drop us off at a Kinderheim in the mountains, before re-joining my father in London. There, they would buy a house in Acton, a suburb in West London, and my father would start up his car business in Putney, south of the river. It was easier for them to organise everything without having to cater for two small children in tow.

* * *

We set off, saying farewell to Calcutta and the sub-continent, and my mother was relieved to finally be travelling down the runway at Dum Dum airport. They had stayed in Calcutta for longer than they had originally envisaged, although growing accustomed to the way of life in India, my mother wanted to get back to the country that had so generously adopted her in her time of need. Hana felt English, even though she had retained a slight European accent, her mannerisms and aspirations were those of a true British national. Marrying my father meant that she was entitled to a British passport. Her origins and upbringing in Czechoslovakia were now in the distant past. Mixing with my father's family wasn't easy. With their Armenian culture and Indian ways, they seemed doubly foreign. During her time in Calcutta, she had learnt conversational Armenian and Hindi.

The BOAC plane heaved its way into the sky as India would soon become just memories. Finally, Hana could sit back and relax, wondering what life would have in store for them. They were no more than half an hour into the flight when a very British voice came over the plane's speakers.

'Ladies and Gentlemen, this is your captain speaking. I would like to inform you that we have just been asked to make a detour to New Delhi to pick up some VIP passengers, on route to London. We shouldn't be too long at the airport, most probably a matter of forty-five minutes or so. We apologise for any inconvenience.'

A buzz went round the cabin as we wondered who these special people might be. They must be extremely special that required a mid-flight detour to pick them up. Perhaps a film star or an Indian Maharajah suggested my mother. We arrived in New Delhi and were asked to stay on the plane. Then out of the window we could see a group of about twenty burly fresh-faced men with just a handful of women, making their way across the tarmac. The men all had large packs on their backs with ropes and pickaxes. The women, presumably their partners, carried small suitcases as hand luggage. They turned out to be the mountaineers of the British expedition that had just climbed Mount Everest for the very first time. They were travelling as a group to London to be congratulated by the young queen. There had been quite a commotion back in London about the first ascent of Everest. Would they be able to reach the summit before the queen's coronation on 2nd June? The ascent was finally achieved on 29th May 1953, and it wasn't until the morning of the Coronation, that news arrived in London, of Colonel Hunt's successful expedition. The British had raised their flag on top of the world. What a way to start the reign of a new monarch.

Among the mountaineers that climbed the rickety steps to board our small aircraft, were Edmund Hillary and Tenzing Norgay, the two climbers that had reached the summit of Everest. Also coming on board were the rest of the expedition led by John Hunt. The eleven mountaineers were accompanied by the *Times of London* correspondent, James Morris (later to be known as Jan Morris). It had been his job to get the news of the ascent back to London, in time for a newspaper print run, on the morning of the queen's coronation.

Hillary and Tenzing were the stars of the show, soon to become household names, but there had been a large cast of people to make it possible. We remember the names Armstrong and Aldrin as the first men on the moon in 1969 but ignore the hundreds of people who assisted in the background.

Tenzing's wife sat next to my mother on the flight, while her two teenage daughters played games with both Ann and me. My mother spoke Hindi to Mrs Norgay, and they seemed to enjoy each other's company. Of course, the attention was all about the mountaineers, but I do remember Edmund Hillary talking with me.

My mother, my sister and I got off the plane at Rome, we were on our way to Zurich where my mother had arranged to take us to a Kinderheim, to be looked after. The night had caught us up, so it was dark by the time we got off the plane. I recall being very frightened as the plane backfired a jet of flames, letting out a dragon like roar. It was just too much excitement for a tired young boy.

The following day we took a plane to Zurich. Only a short hop for such well-seasoned travellers. A train ride to Zug and then a local train to the town of Unterägeri, where we were to stay for a while in a Kinderheim.

* * *

The Kinderheim at Unterägeri was run by a middle-aged Swiss doctor and his wife. Dr Lukas Schriver had taken over from his parents, both of whom had died in their mid-70s. Lukas had married Helga his childhood sweetheart, and together with the help from three full-time carers, an office manager, and a variety of part-time helpers, had continued the work that his parents had started. The Kinderheim had accommodation for thirty children. The children stayed around six weeks at a time. Many diplomats, military personnel or sometimes aid workers, would deposit their little darlings in the safety of the Kinderheim, while they themselves, worked in remote or dangerous parts of the world.

Lukas and Helga had two sons. Simon aged nine and Noah seven, both went to the local school, but also participated in the activities with the children in the Kinderheim. I'm not sure why, but Ann and I were treated as part of the family rather than going into a dormitory with the other children. By day, we participated in all the activities but in the evening after a high tea, we were ushered into the private quarters of the Schriver family home. There we played cards and other such games. During the six weeks that we were there, I learnt to speak Swiss German and a bit of French. Swiss German came naturally to me, so much so that I completely forgot how to speak English. Children at that age, learn languages effortlessly, but also forget them with the same ease with which they were learnt.

Time at the Kinderheim went fast as there was never a dull moment. I remember the first night that my mother left for London, having a nightmare. I must have woken Mrs Schriver, as I remember the warmth of her nightdress as she enveloped me with kindness. I also recall playing on the swings and pushing my little three-year-old sister Ann much too hard. She would scream with fear or was it exhilaration? When I stopped pushing, she wanted more. One of the child minders caught me and reprimanded me, saying that it was dangerous and threatened that if I did it again, I wouldn't be allowed any after-lunch chocolate. Large chunks from huge bars of Suchard milk chocolate, with a mug of fresh hot milk were given to us for dessert each day. I never pushed my sister again in fear that I wouldn't get my chocolate. It was my first taste of crime and punishment; in this case, it was the love of food that would prevail.

* * *

There was an elderly gentleman in his eighties who came to play with the children. I say it was play, but it was more like instruction. Dr Albers had been an engineer and had lost his wife soon after the war. To occupy his time, he set up a little workshop at the Kinderheim and instructed children in making items. One of the amazing things that he made for us were little aeroplanes made from balsa wood for the body and stiff paper for the wings. We would throw the planes with all our force to a point about ten feet in front of us, and the little planes would miraculously take off high into the sky, looping sometimes a hundred feet or more before returning like a vertical boomerang. Dr Albers was fascinated with flight and built a hot air balloon that rose high into the sky, before dramatically catching alight.

Dr Albers was my hero. He could do anything. He recalled that some years previously, there had been a boy called Emile Kaspar at the Kinderheim, and asked if I was any relation. I didn't know of any Emile in my family but thought it to be a rather strange name. When my mother came to pick us up, Dr Albers apparently asked her the same question, but she confirmed that there hadn't been an Emile in our family, as far as she knew. They concluded that it must have been a different Kaspar family.

Pleased to see my mother again, I wanted to show her everything that had been happening. She must have been surprised that her little darling had totally forgotten English and could only speak Swiss German. Luckily, we could communicate as she spoke high German and although they are two separate languages, we could make ourselves understood. My excitement and enthusiasm to show her around must have been a bit daunting for her. It meant that we had been having a good time, but it must have also set a standard for our entertainment.

Then another plane ride to London, where we were picked up by our father, Hovan. He must have been quite shocked to find that I couldn't speak English and that he couldn't converse with me.

I recall it being late at night, when the headlights of our car shone up our driveway and my mother saying, in German of course, 'This is where we live.' Our parents had filled a cupboard in the breakfast room, full of toys. We were home at last. The toys took precedence over everything else.

* * *

Within two weeks I was speaking fluent English again, but in the process, lost all the Swiss German that I had picked up so quickly. It must be locked away in the back of my brain, because when I hear Swiss German being spoken, it certainly sounds familiar.

I started school at Birchdale primary, soon after we arrived in Acton, just before my sixth birthday. The school was within easy walking distance, so my mother could take me there and bring me back. School was as much a social event for the mothers as it was for the children. Lifelong friendships were formed between parents as well as the children. There were two young French sisters that also learnt English in a hurry. Isabelle was in my class, and I immediately fell head over heels in love with her. It annoyed me immensely that she always wanted to sit next to Adrien Colbert. What could she possibly see in that lump, who always had snot coming out of his nostrils? Anyway, I was a much better dancer than him and tried my best to impress her.

Adrien was a single child of a single mother. Adrien's mother was a very pleasant woman and was the cook at the school. Toad in the Hole, Bangers and Mash and something called Bubble and Squeak. With a mother like that, I suppose Adrien couldn't be so bad after all.

School was always a great struggle for me. It was soon apparent that I suffered from dyslexia, having great difficulty with both reading and writing. My mother would spend hours with me after school helping me to overcome my slow start and I felt that both writing and especially reading was a punishment rather than a pleasure. I made up for it in mental arithmetic except for when I got some of the numbers back to front.

* * *

At the age of seven and a half, it was decided that I should go to a new school, as Birchdale only took children up to the age of nine. I had learnt a lot during my time at Birchdale, but my father wanted me to go to a boarding school. He mistakenly thought that it would make me a proper gentleman. Besides, he wanted to be accepted by the English establishment and where better to start than by getting a proper education for his son. Money was not an issue. He always said that education was paramount, and somewhat of an investment, paying like an annuity, dividends for life. He would have chosen Eton College, but it was already too late to put my name down, so it was decided to send me to a rather pukka, military school near Cheltenham Spa in the Cotswolds. The English call them Public Schools, but in fact they are very exclusive.

Told that their junior school didn't have any places at that time, an alternative Preparatory school was found that would prepare me for the Common Entrance examination. My parents and I visited several Prep schools around the country, but we finally decided on one near Kidderminster.

Hartley Hall was set on a two-hundred-and-fifty-acre mixed farm. The elegant Georgian manor house had been built in 1723, but now housed the classrooms and dormitories for sixty boys, with an average class size of just twelve boys per year. The mile long drive wound its way up past the private chapel and walled gardens. The school year had just begun, so it was agreed that I could start the following term, in early January. My mother took me to Harrods, a department store in Knightsbridge, to be kitted out for 'The Oaks' preparatory school.

I was feeling excited but with a twinge of anxiety as my parents drove me the hundred and fifty miles to drop me off for the first day of boarding school. I was just eight years old but felt very grown up as we drove up the single lane driveway, crossing a series of cattle grids. Four feet of snow had banked up either side of driveway, but luckily, we had a clear run and didn't meet any on coming vehicles. It was 4:30pm and already getting dark. On the steps up to the Big Hall as it was known, my father shook my hand passing me a pound note and my mother gave me a big hug trying to hold back her tears. She told me not to worry and reminded me that I should write long letters telling them how I was getting on. I waved goodbye and then followed the matron into the Big Hall to meet my 'Substance'.

* * *

I had crossed the threshold into a new world as I started the next chapter of my life.

26

La Sirène #2

Emile and Chantal named their first daughter Joelle, who was followed two years later by a second daughter, Helena. Both daughters had Chantal's fair features with blond hair and blue eyes. Then in 1954, their son, Carlos was born. He was just like his father Emile, with dark Middle Eastern features and thick eyebrows. When Emile noticed that his son Carlos carried the Kaspar birthmark behind his left ear, he quipped, 'At least I know he is my son.' Emile had been told of the family birthmark and how it had been handed down from father to son.

With his colleague, Dr Wolfgang Bernstein, Emile started a private medical clinic in a suburb called La Charneca, one of the poorest areas of Caracas. Wolfgang was a Jewish gynaecologist from New York, who before the war, had worked with Albert Schweitzer in French Equatorial Africa. The La Charneca clinic expanded rapidly, and they soon had to move to larger premises. Emile serviced a wide variety of patients, becoming the doctor for the rich and famous as well as the poor and infamous. He charged like a wounded bull to those who could pay but offered a free service to the poor and needy.

* * *

Success came to both Emile and Chantal, but they worked long and hard for it. Emile's medical practice went from strength to strength. Soon, Emile and Wolfgang invested in a purpose-built medical centre that had plenty of room for expansion and consulting rooms for allied medical practitioners. They based the rent on the turnover of each consultant, with only a minimum, set monthly fee. The clinic had a very good manager who set high standards, always demanding quality medical care. The money kept rolling in. As soon as her three children became of school age, Chantal became the head of Scientific Research at the University of Venezuela in Caracas. Her role was to oversee and co-ordinate all the PhD research students and her links with both North American and European universities became invaluable. It involved some travel to both continents, but she was fortunate to have a most capable live-in nanny called Amelia, who became part of the family, managing the household for the busy parents.

Amelia was a young woman in her mid-twenties when she was hired for the job. She had come from one of the Barrios that surrounded Caracas. The Barrios were the shanty towns perched on the hillsides. During torrential rain, the houses of the Barrios, known as ranchos, would get washed down to the bottom of the hill. Violent crime and abuse were prevalent in these haphazard shanty towns, and life had been particularly difficult for poor Amelia. Her father had been a petty criminal drug dealer, who had witnessed a violent shootout between two rival gangs. He had become a target for both gangs to silence, with a race to see which gang would put him out of his misery first.

Amelia was in her late teens when one morning, she went out to work in a local shop. On her return home at lunch time, she found that the police had cordoned off her house as a crime scene. Her mother, father and little sister had been brutally attacked and murdered. Amelia had approached the house and asked a policeman what had happened. The young police officer was in tears as he explained the brutality of the attack. 'They are all dead, they are all dead,' he told Amelia, not knowing that she also lived there. Amelia had the presence of mind to say nothing but slowly walked around the corner and then ran for her life. She managed to escape and lived with her uncle in Barquisimeto a town some four-hour drive west of Caracas. This uncle came home drunk one night and tried to rape Amelia. She returned to Caracas and had lived on the streets. Then one day, she heard about the job at the Kaspar household. She went for the interview with Chantal, who asked for references. Somehow Amelia realised that she had no hope of lying her way through, so she told Chantal what had happened. Chantal looked at Amelia then got up and hugged her. Both women were in tears.

Once the tears had stopped flowing Chantal asked 'Well what are you doing now? Would you like to come with me to the kindergarten to pick up the children?' Amelia went with her, and she never looked back. She fitted in perfectly. Somewhere between the children's older sister and Chantal's much younger sister. Amelia had found a new home and knew she belonged. She had her own quarters and even had it cleaned each day by one of the maids. Her job was to organise the help around the house. Coming from the Barrios, she had seen first-hand the stealing that had gone on and well aware of the effects of the poverty. She knew how the cook would buy extra food so he could steal it for his children. She was the go between and understood the situation perfectly. Often, she would explain to Chantal that a particular servant was a good worker, though not totally honest. The pilfering was minor, and Amelia could keep it under control. Both Emile and Chantal were understanding of the situation and happy to turn a blind eye. They saw their job as bringing in the money to pay the poor people for the work they performed. It was no use telling the servants not to steal, as it was something they just did.

The three children, Joelle, Helena, and Carlos, grew up in a happy household despite both parents, Emile and Chantal, being extremely busy and dynamic. Much of their success could be attributed to their super nanny Amelia, who was always there for them. Both Emile and Chantal spent quality time with the children, but the day-to-day care was provided by Amelia. It was very seldom that both parents were present at the same time.

*　*　*

Emile had branched out and had bought a little Cessna plane to make trips around the small Caribbean islands and deep into the interiors of the Venezuelan jungle. His business model changed to incorporate work for various Government agencies, providing medical support for people in remote areas. Although this work didn't pay as well as his private work, it was a good deal more challenging and satisfying. He set up a small clinic at Puerto Ayacucho on the Orinoco River, flying there at least once a week. Sometimes he had to go further afield, depending on the severity of the situation. Often it was just a case of preparing the patient for their long journey to Caracas. On critical cases he would have to accompany the patient to the nearest district hospital. There were numerous occasions when the patient wouldn't complete the journey and the day would end with a delivery to the morgue.

His reputation as a flying doctor became legendary, flying through severe electrical storms, with a critical patient and nurse on board. This happened more often than he would have wanted. On these occasions, his nurse had to be more than just a medical person, they would also act as a navigator, guiding him through tropical storms when all ground communication had been lost. They didn't have time to worry about the danger they were in as they bounced around in hazardous tempests.

Often, it wasn't possible to land in the small central airport of Caracas, so they were forced to fly on to a safer landing strip some eighty kilometres away. Emile would contact ground control ahead, asking them to arrange for an ambulance to take them the rest of the journey by road. Emile knew the dangers to himself and his nurses, so he made a conscious decision to spread the risk between his team of three assistants, ensuring that that they were chosen in strict rotation. It was somewhat cold and calculating when he sent out a message to each of the nurses that should anything tragic happen on one of these rescue missions, 'The show must go on. I would like one of the other two nurses to take charge and make sure that this important work continues.' The message went on to say, 'You can decide which of you becomes the boss by the tossing of a coin.' Such was his direct approach to life and in this case, to death.

Emile's astute business sense, coupled with hard work and a great deal of expertise, meant that his success knew no bounds. They certainly weren't short of a bob or perhaps it should be Bolivar or two.

* * *

As their three children grew, Emile and Chantal realised that they would need to move to new and bigger accommodation. Their flat above Emile's clinic had served its purpose. The clinic had been purpose designed by a famous Venezuelan architect called Graziano Gasparini who had a comprehensive understanding of the climatic and cultural nuances of living in Caracas.

Chantal had other ideas. It wasn't that they had fallen out with Graziano, but Chantal had always admired the organic approach to architecture of the celebrated American architect, Frank Lloyd Wright. She thought that his prairie houses wouldn't sit well on the piece of hillside that they had purchased but she wanted to use Wright's *'Fallingwater'* house at Fayette County, Pennsylvania, as a starting point.

'But we don't have any water' protested Emile. 'That building relies on the water.'

The arguments went on for weeks and Emile realised that it was an argument that he was never going to win. Chantal didn't seem to mind that Wright had died in 1959 but said she would make a trip to Taliesin West in Arizona, where Wright had set up his school of architecture.

Emile had other concerns to worry about, so after putting together a financial framework around the design and construction process, he left the details for Chantal to organise. He couldn't understand how a scientist of Chantal's calibre could get so caught up with the emotions of the design process.

'I want a building that incorporates Wright's philosophies,' she told the head of the school of Architecture at Taliesin. 'Could you recommend a past student that we could interview?'

The head of the school took some details and said that he would send Chantal a shortlist of six Architects that he would recommend. He had read Chantal perfectly as one of the names incorporated fourth on his list of ex-students was a Swiss architect called Franz Steiger. Steiger was originally from Zurich but as a boy of nine, his family had moved to the United States. After graduating from Taliesin, he had moved back to live and work in Bern. In Chantal's eyes, he was the man for the project.

* * *

Franz Steiger duly came to Caracas for the month of August and sat for many hours on the hilltop site that Emile and Chantal had purchased. He did his overall scheme and showed it to the family for comments.

Chantal was concerned that Amelia had her quarters attached to the main house and suggested that she might like her own little abode near the main entrance gates. Chantal had seen in England, how the impressive country properties had a small gate keepers lodge adjacent to the main gates, separate from the main manor house. Their son Carlos wanted a swimming pool and Emile asked if the music chamber room could be expanded to seat sixty people for a concert.

Emile's partner Wolfgang Bernstein saw the preliminary plans and asked if Steiger could also design a house for him and his family. Steiger did preliminary designs for both families and got their tick of approval to take them back to Switzerland for design development and detailed construction drawings. The two houses were quite different. Emile had his chamber room for music soirées, while Wolfgang asked for a hermetically sealed, wide corridor to house his exclusive art collection.

Construction of both houses were duly completed within two years and both families were extremely happy with their own house design. Friends and relatives from both families attended the opening ceremony, in the music chamber of Emile and Chantal's house.

Franz Steiger gave a speech saying, 'I am so pleased that each family likes their own house best. Wouldn't it be terrible if you both liked the other house better?'

Emile interjected, 'Oh no it wouldn't be a problem, we could just swap houses. The problem would be if we both liked the same house. Then we would have to fight it out to see who got to live in it.' All laughed at Emile's suggestion.

The champagne flowed and it was suggested that they should do it all again the following week at Wolfgang Bernstein's house, but this never happened as Franz Steiger and his assistant were booked on a flight back to Switzerland the next morning.

All went well for Emile and Wolfgang as their clinic grew from strength to strength, offering an ever-wider range of medical services. Emile got tied up with more and more administrative work and less as a physician. He came to terms with it and as long as he could make time to fly down to the Orinoco once a month, he was more than happy.

* * *

From time to time, Emile would take a whole week off, and with Chantal and their children, they would fly in his Cessna plane to an island in the Caribbean. From there, they would hire a local man with a motorboat, to take them with a week's supply of food, to a small, deserted coral reef, giving him strict instructions to pick them up a week later. There, they could swim and snorkel, sleep in the afternoons in their hammocks and live completely in the open air. At night they would sit around a campfire and tell stories or play charades. Carlos loved playing charades and always said he wanted to be an actor. Emile would say looking up at the sky, 'Instead of a five-star hotel we are staying in a five-billion-star hotel.' They would return home to Caracas wind swept and tanned by the sun.

On one such evening around the campfire, Emile suggested that they should name their new house in Caracas.

'Yes, what shall we call it,' said Joelle. 'How about Kaspar's hideaway' suggested Carlos. In the end they all agreed to call it 'La Sirène'. This had been the name of the house that Emile's grandfather had built so many years ago. It gave Emile a chance to tell the stories that his father Davit had told him as a child. The stories of a distant land, how Davit had survived but his parents and his identical twin brother Vahan had fallen to the fatal bombing and subsequent fire at their house in Constantinople. Emile had also received the gift of storytelling that had been passed down from generation to generation. The children listened opened mouthed to the stories being told to them around the fire. One by one they dropped off to sleep.

'La Sirène # 2' became the name of the house and Joelle made a clay plaque of a mermaid with a painted handwritten 'La Sirène' written below. The plaque was positioned at the front gate but not everyone who visited the house knew of the significance of the name. It didn't really matter because the people who lived in the house knew about it.

* * *

Emile and Chantal worked hard and played hard.

27

From Shadow to Substance

New boys at The Oakes Prep School were referred to as 'Shadows'. They were each designated an older boy called a 'Substance', whose job it was to look after their Shadow for his first term at the school. The 'Substance' not only showed his 'Shadow' around the place, but also made sure he wasn't being picked upon by anyone. Consequently, bullying wasn't a problem. With only sixty boarders, of which a couple had special needs, the system ensured harmony.

* * *

The school was run by two brothers and their wives. Mr Philip Enders was the elder brother and was referred to as Mr Philip. He was mainly involved with the running of the farm, teaching Latin and Greek to the older boys, and playing music at a professional level. He played keyboards, both harpsichord and pianoforte, as part of a celebrated quartet and the double bass for the Birmingham Symphony orchestra.

The younger of the two brothers, known as Mr Graham, organised the running of the school. He set the curriculum and coordinated the entire teaching programme. He taught French and geography, while Major Williamson taught history and English. Science was taught by Mr Philip's wife Barbara, known as Mrs Philip, while art and country dancing were taught by Mr Graham's wife Esther, Mrs Graham. The two wives also shared the looking after of the five Enders infants.

There was a young, rather attractive riding mistress called Miss

Conway. She never failed to get boys to help her mucking out of the stables or dubbin the saddles and bridles. Mrs Warner was the matron but was usually referred to as 'Matron'. She saw to our minor medical needs in the sick room, and had an old jalopy of a car, which she drove in a somewhat crazy manner. No one wanted to be too ill and need taking to the village doctor, or worse, the nearby hospital. Mrs Warner spoke with a heavy South African accent. She had been married, but there was no sign of a husband. This led the boys to all manner of speculation.

The impressive manor house had a central three storey section with two storey wings either side. The northern wing housed five classrooms, a small gym, and a shower block. The southern wing housed living quarters for both of the headmasters and their families, some administration spaces, a kitchen, and dining room. The two wings wrapped around substantial inner courtyards, while the main central building, housed on the ground floor numerous formal reception rooms, with two levels of the boy's dormitories above. On the ground floor the large Chamber Music Room, referred to as The Big Room, seated comfortably ninety people, and with a stage at one end, it was an ideal location for Mr Philip's quartet to practice and perform on. Often, I would sit quietly and enjoy the quartet practicing for an evening performance. I began to learn the language of music and enjoyed the intensity of discussion between the performers such as 'Less vibrato or exaggerate the crescendo.'

A formal library was also used as a green room for the performers. The shelves were filled with many leather-bound historical books and the doors to the library, were clad with the spine covers of books, making the doors blend with the shelves. The two front reception rooms either side of the Big Hall had become Mr Philip's study and a smaller performance space. Mr Philip had a harpsichord and a baby grand piano in his office, as well as a sophisticated Grundig reel to reel recording system. On Friday evenings, we had what was called 'Music Appreciation' club and were invited into his office. Often, he would have twenty or so young boys sitting cross-legged on the floor, being totally mesmerised by the imparting of his considerable musical knowledge and talents. Playing a piece of a Beethoven symphony or some other grand opus on his reel-to-reel Grundig, he would suddenly stop at a particular junction, saying, 'Listen to how Beethoven changes key.' Then winding back the recording a few bars, he would play the relevant section again before sitting at his piano to illuminate the transitional chords and interplay with the melody line.

We had musical quiz nights with prizes. He would ask questions on all sorts of music and composers. What does Andante mean? What is Diatonic Harmony? Who was born first or sometimes who died first? Who was born first, Bach or Händel? Apparently, Handel was born just thirty-six days before Bach. It was claimed that Georg Friedrich Händel had visited Hartley Hall a couple of times to enjoy concerts in the big Chamber Room. I soon became immersed in music and although by the age of eleven, I had taken my grade six Theory exams, I lacked concentration as far as practicing for the piano playing exams. During the school holidays I was sent to a music teacher down the road, who successfully managed to completely put me off. I had a good ear and could pick out popular tunes, and with my knowledge of harmony, was able to put chords around it. As a ten-year-old boy, I would proudly show her what I had taught myself during the week. To my disappointment she wasn't at all impressed and would dismiss my efforts with, 'Well let's see how Mr Liszt is going.' Luckily, I did take up music some forty or so years later but found myself playing Jazz and improvising purely for my own enjoyment.

As to be expected, the boys at the school came in all shapes and sizes. One friend of mine a certain Billy Mollett was extremely tall for his age. He became a lifelong friend of mine as we somehow followed each other from one institution to another. He was later to be called Bill by his first wife and then becoming William when he remarried. To me he will always be just Mollett.

* * *

The Enders had a very strong philosophy about life, which permeated throughout. They didn't push their environmentalist attitudes but lived them to the full. They looked at our planet in a holistic way, and this had a strong influence on their style of education. They believed that each student should be allowed time to find their own pathway and that self-discipline was the only form of discipline worth aspiring to.

During my first summer school holidays, my parents invited the two Swiss boys, the sons of Dr Lukas and Helga Schriver, from the Kinderheim at Unterägeri, to come and stay with us in London for three weeks. The arrangement was that the two boys, Simon and Noah, would stay with us in London for three weeks, then all four of us would fly back to Switzerland together, where my sister Ann and I would be their guests for three weeks. At the end of the holiday, Ann and I would fly back to London by ourselves, having taken in the fresh mountain air, and eaten a bit too much Swiss milk chocolate. This was a rather ingenious plan set up by my father. Not only were Ann and I fully occupied, but it also gave my parents three weeks in which they could go away on a holiday together.

Ann and I loved going to Switzerland. We loved the hiking through the woods, the fishing by the lake and the general camaraderie of the other children from around the world. For me it wasn't much different from going to boarding school, but I was surprised how Ann seemed to enjoy herself, having her own group of friends, separate from her older brother.

* * *

I was almost eight years old, and Ann would have been just four as we set off for our first holiday in Switzerland. At Heathrow airport, my mother bent down to give me a kiss and said, 'Try and make some nice Swiss friends who don't speak any English so you can relearn your Swiss German.'

I was too excited to take it in and felt very important as I walked across the tarmac and up the stairs to find my seat on the plane. An air hostess had been assigned to accompany the four of us onto the plane before any of the other passengers came aboard. She seemed quite surprised to find out that I was already a seasoned traveller. I precociously told her that I had met Hillary and Tenzing on a flight from India and asked if there would be any famous people travelling with us. As the plane took off for Zurich, I waved out of the window at my parents on the viewing deck.

My parents went to the Greek Islands that year, while Ann and I had a wonderful time with our friends. To my surprise not only was Dr Albers still there, but so were a few of my other friends. I became good friends with a young Jewish boy called David Freiberg, from the Bronx in New York. This totally put paid to the idea of me returning home bi-lingual but instead, much to my parent's chagrin, I had traded my countrified English accent for a broad New York twang.

My father had sent me with a £50 note in an envelope to give to Dr Schriver. The envelope also contained a request to help me to buy my first Swiss watch. When the time came for us to return home, the Schrivers took us back to Zurich airport. We were there in plenty of time for us to look at duty-free watches. I was so proud of the new Tissot watch on my left wrist. Ann had chosen a Swiss doll which started an extensive dolls' collection from around the world. There was still a bit of money left over, so it was decided to buy my mother a present. After much deliberation, I decided that my mother would like a small Swiss chalet that had a hinged roof as a lid. When one opened the lid, it played a little Swiss ditty. The musical box doubled as a cigarette box. I thought it would be something my mother would greatly admire even though she didn't smoke. Well, I liked it and that seemed to be important.

I placed the little chalet into my BOAC shoulder bag. This was the same bag that I had previously travelled with from India. When we presented ourselves at the baggage counter, we were assigned another young air hostess to look after us. Once again in my excitement I told her all about my flight with Hillary and Tenzing. Once again, she seemed suitably impressed. We were shown to our seats towards the front of the plane, and I let Ann have the window seat. The BEA Viscount Discovery taxied up the runway and soared into the skies. My feeling of importance grew as the plane ascended.

A different air hostess brought us some juice and some colouring in books with a packet of coloured crayons. Then came sandwiches and more juice. I was in heaven.

These were days prior to the use of photocopiers. Gestetner machines were around at the time but clumsy to use. The British Customs and Excise office wanted to inform incoming passengers arriving by plane, exactly what could be taken in duty free, and those items needing to be declared. Rather than printing off numerous lists for each passenger, they devised a simple system in which one typed list was glued onto a backing sheet of cardboard. This typed list was handed to the passengers at front of the plane who, after reading it, passed it to the passengers, behind.

I was handed the list and read through it. As the list was in alphabetical order, the very first item was 'Antique Musical Instruments valued over £100,' needed to be declared. My eyes just saw 'Musical Instruments' and I totally panicked. I didn't bother to read any further down the list but passed the list back to the people behind. I leant over to my four-year-old sister and whispered in her ear, 'it says we can't take in any musical instruments, so we are going to have to smuggle in Mum's present as it plays music. Leave all the talking to me and don't say a word.' With that, I climbed up to the shelf above and carefully brought down my trusty BOAC shoulder bag. When no one was looking, I stuffed the little Swiss chalet down to the bottom of the bag and then returned the contraband back to its original location on the shelf above. The rest of the flight was petrifying. I couldn't smile and didn't want to speak.

We arrived back at Heathrow, and with the help of an air hostess, we located our two little suitcases. We dragged them to the customs hall, and I heaved both cases up onto the stainless-steel counter. I held Ann's hand very tightly and made sure the BOAC shoulder bag was behind my back and hidden from the customs official's view.

'Hello' said the official with a broad grin on his face.

'Good morning,' I replied tersely with a solemn face, not knowing if it was morning or afternoon.

'Are you travelling alone Sir?' enquired the official.

'No, I'm here,' pipped up Ann. Why did she have to say anything I thought to myself. She's sure to blow our cover.

The customs officer leaned over to find an even smaller child hidden behind the cases on the counter.

'I meant where are your mummy and daddy?' asked the official thinking that surely our parents would be following behind.

'No, we are all alone,' I said with my best poker face and showed him our passports and boarding passes.

'Where have you come from today?' asked the official.

'Switzerland,' I replied.

'Did you have a nice time?'

'Yes.' I answered rather too sharply.

More questions and then came the thunderbolt.

'And did you buy any nice presents for mummy and daddy?'

I was totally stunned and squeezed Ann's hand tightly. I'm not sure if she thought my silence or the squeezing of her hand were her cue, but she blurted out, 'We bought them a house.'

Her comment and my bursting into tears caused a wry mirth on the official's face.

We had been sprung. My ruse had been foiled. My tears flowed freely, as I thought we would be sent to prison. I emptied the contents of my shoulder bag and finally managed to find the offending item. The official suddenly burst into laughter as he realised that the little chalet, was in fact the house that Ann had referred to and not a property in Zurich.

I opened the roof of the little Chalet and showed the official that it was indeed a musical instrument. He laughed even more, and I realised that we weren't going to be sent to prison. His laughter was infectious and proved to be the best medicine. A lesson that would one day save my life. But that is a story for a bit later.

Out of the corner of my eye, I saw my father behind a sheet of glass, waving at us profusely. He had watched the proceedings and hadn't known the ordeal that I had put myself through.

Finally, Ann and I got the all clear from the amicable customs official and ran with our little cases and my shoulder bag towards my father.

'Look at the new watch I got at the airport,' I said to him innocently showing him the new watch on my wrist.

* * *

A week or so later, it was back to school for me and the ritual of going to the Carvery at the Cumberland Hotel, before taking the train from Paddington railway station.

On the platform, I proudly showed some of the boys my wrist sporting my new Tissot watch. No one seemed that impressed and most seemed more captivated by the latest Swift or Eagle comics, bought at Paddington station.

At quarter term, our parents could come and take us out for the day. This was an opportunity for my mother to get away from London and to visit her friend Alice in Stourbridge for a few days. My mother and sister would go by train on the Friday afternoon to Birmingham and then make their way to Stourbridge. Typical of my industrious father, he would take the opportunity of travelling into the countryside on the Sunday to buy a car or sometimes two on the way. Cars in the country were that much cheaper than cars in London. He would set off from London very early in the morning with Lofty, his five-foot-tall driver, and sometimes with Ronnie, his chief mechanic. They would meet up with some car dealers from the Midlands where my father might buy a car or two, depending what was on offer. He would send Lofty the driver back with the car that they had set out in, and Ronnie might drive the other bought car back to London. This meant that my father would continue his journey to pick me in a car that he had just bought an hour before he arrived at the school. He liked to test it out and sort out if it needed any mechanical work on it. This meant that my father would arrive at the school not being able to tell me which car he might arrive in.

After Sunday morning Chapel, it was customary that we sat down at our desks and wrote letters to our parents. Mr Graham would come round to each desk and read the letters before they were sent off to our parents. It was his way of keeping control of the information that went out. At quarter and three-quarter term breaks, letter writing wasn't necessary as we were being collected by our parents to be taken out for the day. Instead, the boys, who were being taken out, went to the Big Hall and waited for their parents to pick them up. There was always great excitement amongst the boys as they could see their parents' car way off in the distance coming up the mile long driveway. 'Look out for a blue Rover,' one boy would say. 'Papa has got a green Jaguar,' or such like would come from another boy. I would only find out my dad's car when he stepped out of it. It could be a van or a Humber, a Mini, or a Ford Escort. Eventually I worked out that it was bound to be my dad if no one else claimed the car. Once he arrived in a big left hand-drive Chevy. White and pink with lots of chrome it looked like something out of an American glamour movie. The E type Jag caused a bit of a stir too, but the car I will always recall was a 1928 Rolls Royce that my father had bought from some old friends of theirs from India.

* * *

The two brothers, Mr Philip and Mr Graham didn't believe in pushing the academic side of teaching in their school but were more interested in imparting a well-rounded education with honest values. Farming, music, horse riding, and sailing were encouraged. The classroom was a necessity but not the main objective. Instead of homework we could attend various activities such as music club, sailing club, debating and poetry reading. Instead of competitive sport we could choose farming, horse riding or tending of the 'Walled Garden' for exercise. Not that competition was shunned, it was just that, boys who weren't competitive could chose other physical outlets to pursue. We harvested most of the food that we ate, and life was simple. We were totally oblivious to the world around us, and it came as somewhat of a shock to have to leave that little patch of paradise and pass on to a school with quite a different agenda.

28

The Brigadier

It was early one morning, when Emile's assistant took a call from a senior official of the British Embassy in Caracas. After lunch, Emile called the number and found to his surprise that it was the British Ambassador's direct line.

The phone was answered abruptly with a single word, 'Chapman.'

'Ah, Sir Peter,' replied Emile rather taken aback. 'It's Emile Kaspar here, I was given this number to call.'

'Emile, thanks for ringing back,' replied the ambassador in a more friendly tone of voice. 'I'm just wondering if you can help us out with a tricky situation. You see, we have here at the embassy a retired British Brigadier, a George Collins who is attached to one of our Trade delegations. He's been rather ill for a couple of years now and is costing us an arm and a leg, what with your hospital fees. We were wondering if you might find the time to accompany him back to London so he can be put on the NHS. He has no dependants but wants dearly to die back in the old country rather than on foreign soil.'

'Well, I would need to check on his condition first and then discuss the logistics with you,' said Emile.

'Yes, of course,' replied the ambassador. 'We are completely in your hands and would appreciate any help you can give us.'

'I will go round and assess him later this afternoon and should be able to pop in to see you around 6:30pm this evening if that is ok with you,' said Emile.

'Fine I'll wait here for you. I've got a nice drop of Glenfiddich 18 single malt that needs opening,' replied the ambassador knowing full well that Scotch whisky lasts forever.

Emile went to see the Brigadier in the hospital but found him to be in a much worse condition than expected. Later at the appointed time, he went to see Sir Peter and explained that transporting him all the way back to London wouldn't be an easy task.

'I'm not looking for any guarantees, but I need him out of our hair so to speak,' said the ambassador.

The next day, the undersecretary Sir Eric Noble, phoned Emile and told him of the arrangements that he had made for the transportation.

'We have arranged a flight with a Peruvian Airline for this coming Friday. The plane is coming from Lima and will arrive in Caracas early in the morning. We have booked eight seats in the central aisle, at the back of the plane. These seats will be removed with a privacy curtain to be installed, so the patient can be laid out horizontally. The first stop will be Madrid where they will stop for forty-five minutes to take on extra passengers and refuelling. Take off for London at 14:35 hours with an estimated arrival of 16:45 GMT. An ambulance will be ready to take you through to Guy's hospital. By the way, the ambassador asks if you would like to stay at his house in Belgravia for the weekend. His son, Sir Toby and daughter in law, Susan will be there and look forward to catching up with you. I booked you back on the Concorde, Monday evening. How does that suit you?

'All fine with me,' replied Emile.

'Good all sorted then. I'll send round a CD car to pick you up at 05:45 hours on Friday.'

'I'll be packed and ready,' replied Emile.

* * *

A car arrived at 5:43am to take Emile to the airport. He boarded the plane, going straight to the back to check on his patient. Take off all went smoothly. Emile sat in a seat near to the Brigadier and every twenty minutes or so, went behind the privacy curtain to check on his patient. They were most of the way to Madrid, with another thirty minutes to go, when Emile went to see his patient for the last time before landing. Poor George Collins hadn't made it. Emile went casually back to his seat as if nothing had happened. They arrived in Madrid with a corpse in the back, and only Emile being aware of the situation.

The refuelling and pick up of new passengers progressed as normal. Take off to London wasn't going to be a problem as the man had already died. About fifteen minutes into the flight to London, Emile got out of his seat and strode casually up the passageway and politely asked the chief steward if he might have a word with the pilot.

'Anything wrong,' enquired the chief steward.

'No nothing wrong just that my patient, the Brigadier has passed away peacefully in his sleep,' replied Emile in a very matter of fact tone.

'Oh, I see' replied the steward. 'Come with me and I can code you in to speak with the pilot on the emergency phone.'

Emile explained the situation to the pilot and told him that there was no need to alert the other passengers or crew of the situation as the patient had already died.

The pilot wired ahead and alerted Heathrow to prepare the ambulance to take the corpse to the airport hospital. The hospital at Heathrow has a morgue and after sorting out the official paperwork the body was handed over and Emile was free for the weekend to explore what London had to offer. The ambulance had been set up to take both Emile and his patient to Guys hospital but luckily the driver didn't mind taking a detour via Belgravia. Emile hadn't sat in the front seat of a London ambulance with the alarm siren blaring away. They made the journey in record time and in time for dinner with Sir Toby and his wife Susan.

'Well, I had been paid to bring him back to London,' explained Emile to his hosts over dinner. 'So, I brought him all the way. Friday afternoon in Madrid, all those coroners would be in the bars having a drink. We would have missed our flight to London, and I wouldn't have accomplished my mission. Besides I have booked some tickets to see Oscar Peterson at Ronnie Scott's later this evening. I hope you are free.'

They all thoroughly enjoyed the show at Ronnie Scott's, and on the Saturday, they went out to a West End theatre to see a performance of the musical *Hair*.

Early on the Monday morning, before leaving for Heathrow airport, Emile bought some gifts for his three children from Carnaby Street, then made his way to Harrods to see if he could find something special for his wife, Chantal. Having lost sight of the time, he decided to take a taxi to Heathrow, urging his taxi driver to go faster. 'Sorry Guv,' said the driver, 'I would lose my license if I got caught for speeding. What time is your flight Guv? I'll see what I can do.' Emile recalled how fast it had been by ambulance and vowed that next time, he would take an ambulance rather than a taxi.

* * *

The three children, Joelle, Helena and Carlos soon became teenagers and all three were excellent students. Joelle excelled at mathematics and became absorbed with logic and statistics. She decided that she wanted to become a Human Rights lawyer. Helena loved animals and to begin with thought she would either like to be a farmer or a vet. The grades that she was achieving at school were outstanding, she could have done anything that she wanted. With a little persuasion from both Emile and Chantal, she decided to take a medical degree first, and then see where it would lead her.

Carlos was the artist, the creative person. He decided he wanted to study drama, saying the best place to study was at RADA in London. Swinging London seemed very enticing. He was more interested in hanging out and being part of the scene than studying. Besides, he had met some young actors who had come from London as part of a troupe performing a Shakespeare trilogy. Carlos had become smitten by Sally, who played Hermia in *A Midsummer's night dream*. She had invited him to come and stay with her in her flat in West Kensington and Carlos was more than keen to take up her offer.

Emile made some calls to RADA and for a small incentive, managed to secure a place for his son to study drama. The academic year would start towards the middle of September, which was less than three months away.

In early September, the day arrived for Carlos to be driven to the airport to catch the plane to London. To his mother Chantal, he looked so young. He kissed his two sisters and mother goodbye, having previously said his farewells to his father Emile, earlier that morning. Emile had a full day of surgery.

* * *

As Carlos strode off with his little shoulder bag over his left shoulder, clutching his boarding pass and passport firmly in his right hand, he turned around to wave to the three women of his life. Little did he know of the tragedy that was about to unfold, and that he would never return to the happy home he was leaving behind.

29

Angus Gorton

I started at Millswood College, an English Public School in the heart of the Cotswolds, in the January and I certainly wasn't anticipating its military regime. My prep school, The Oakes, had been so relaxed and somewhat idyllic. It certainly hadn't prepared me for what was to come.

Millswood College was based on a military structure of always knowing one's position in the hierarchy. Senior boys punished the junior boys, and it was expected that when a junior boy did rise through the ranks, he would get his revenge, delighting in punishing anyone below him.

This vindictive process was all somewhat of an anathema to me, and they soon found out that I didn't play their game.

The school was very proud that its Cadet Force was entitled to parade the Queen's colours. Marching up and down in the rain to some senior boy screaming out orders seemed futile to me. Learning how to fire 303 rifles that had been left over from the First World War gave me the shivers as well as a damaged shoulder.

Luckily, I found my niche within these military exercises. I became a bugler in the Corps of Drums. This suited me as I managed to exercise my musical talents and practice my pacifist leanings. I had thought about becoming a drummer but who wants to lug around a drum when a bugle fits easily in the gloved hand.

* * *

Angus Gorton was also a new boy who had started at Millswood College that January. I was in Burnside House, whilst Gorton was in Mowbray, a bit further down College Avenue. About one week after the start of the school term, we happened to be sitting next to each other in the big Dining Hall. After introducing ourselves as Gorton and Kaspar, there was an awkward silence before we struck up what was to become a memorable conversation.

'I come from London, where are you from?' I asked trying to break the ice.

'I come from London too,' replied Gorton and then asked, 'Which part of London are you from?'

'I come from West London; whereabouts are you from?' I enquired just making small talk.

'From West London, a place called Acton,' replied Gorton.

'So do I,' I replied adding, 'I live not far from Ealing Common tube station.'

'So do I,' he replied.

'Do you know Burford Avenue?' I asked but wasn't expecting the reply that I was to get.

'Yes, I live at number 91, Burford Avenue, at my grandmother's house,' he replied.

'Well, we live at number 34, so it's not that far away,' I said nonchalantly, trying not to appear too startled.

Just then, the gong was struck by the duty senior prefect. This signalled that the evening meal was over and that we all had to make our way back to our respective houses, for an hour and a half of prep. We had just eight minutes before prep started.

That evening I wrote a letter to my parents telling them that I had met another new boy who says he comes from Burford Avenue. I added that I didn't know whether to believe him or not, but he does seem to know the area.

My mother replied by return post, 'That's nice. Now you will have someone to visit during the school holidays. Make sure you get his telephone number.'

The rest of the term went by and although we acknowledged each other when passing in the quadrangle, neither of us seemed to want to make anything of furthering our friendship. The holidays came and were almost over, when my mother asked me if I was going to phone Gorton to ask him if he wanted to come to tea. I phoned and two minutes later he appeared at our doorstep. It was the first time we met out of school uniform, but it certainly wasn't the last.

* * *

At school we addressed each other by our surnames but out of school we were Angus and Michael.

Angus lived up the road with his Irish grandmother and grandfather. Aunt Molly as his grandmother was affectionately known, nursed her aged husband who lived in a room upstairs. He was in the last throes of Parkinson's disease and was to succumb a few months after I had met him.

Angus had been born just four months after his mother, Sandy, had been informed of her husband's fatal plane crash. Dirk Gorton had been a pilot in the Fleet Air Arm and had miraculously survived many dangerous sorties during the war. The planes were slowly being decommissioned and Dirk would have joined the civilian ranks some three weeks after that crash. Drastic times required drastic measures. With just four months left of her pregnancy, Sandy, totally devastated, went to live with her mother and father in Acton.

* * *

It was not long after we met that Angus and I had a rather unplanned adventure. After the war had finished, my mother contacted her younger cousin called Helga, who lived in Gmunden, Austria. A glorious scenic tourist town, Gmunden is situated at the head of the Traunsee, one of the many lakes of the Salzkammergut district. The Sound of Music is everywhere. With the Traunstein and Grunberg mountains towering above the crystal-clear lake and their reflections shimmering in the transparent blue waters; Gmunden is one of the most picturesque places on the planet. It's no wonder that for centuries, the kings and queens of Europe chose to have their summer residences nearby.

My parents had decided to take a couple of week's summer holiday in Gmunden, staying in the big Hotel on the esplanade of the lake. After the

231

war, Helga had got married and had studied to become a master leather trouser maker. She had taught her husband Hans, to also make leather goods and together made personalised leather items for people who could afford them. They were crafters of the highest calibre, with clients coming from far and wide to have bespoke items created for them. They exhibited in Paris, Milan and Vienna and were considering that they should open an outlet in London and then perhaps New York. Helga spoke very limited English but seemed to manage with facial expressions and her infectious laughter.

My parents had arranged for my sister and me to go on holidays with them. This meant I would be wandering around by myself, and without my best chum Angus. It was decided that I should ask Angus if he would like to come with us. Angus had never been out of the country and quickly busied himself with getting a passport. My mother wrote to her cousin Helga and asked if it would be okay to bring Angus. Helga and Hans had a little apartment above their shop which had been where Helga's mother had lived until her death a few years previously. 'The boys are most welcome to use the flat if they want to,' she replied. It was decided that Angus and I were to travel by train to and from Salzburg rather than fly, it would save some money and make it all financially possible.

Angus's mother Sandy saw us off from Victoria train station, assuring us that the train, boat and then train to Salzburg would be relatively easy. Meanwhile my parents, with my sister Ann flew to Salzburg and would pick up Angus and me from the railway station. The five of us would then drive in a hired car to our destination of Gmunden.

I would soon turn fifteen years old whilst Angus a couple of months older had already become fifteen. The journey to Gmunden had been a breeze. My parents were at the end of the platform at Salzburg station ready to meet us and after a lunch, a visit to the Salzburg castle and Mozart's house; we drove to Gmunden in a hired Ford Taunus estate car. Once again, there was much laughter to one of my father's infamous stories, that somehow always seemed to miraculously last exactly the length of the journey.

We had a wonderful two weeks. We spent time at a place called Strandbad, a lakeside luxury swimming pool complex. We went on the teleferico, up the Grunberg Mountain. We spent afternoons mucking about on the pedaloes on the lake and eating long lunches with plenty of merriment. Wiener schnitzel washed down with Apfelsaft, followed by Salzburger nockerl, Viennese cakes and pastries and the odd tasting of homemade Schnapps filled our days and stomachs. Helga and Hans were the perfect hosts and the town of Gmunden was the perfect backdrop for what was a memorable holiday for all.

Then came the journey back to London. My parents drove Angus and me to Salzburg and waved us goodbye as the train drew out of the station. We had reserved seats in a self-contained, eight-seater compartment, where we found a rather sullen looking man with his young peroxide blonde female companion, occupying the seats opposite us. The woman would have been around twenty years of age and the man would have been old enough to be her father.

The train slowly wound its way through the Austrian Alps on its way to the Swiss border. The young woman and the older man spoke Swiss German to each other, and I didn't let on that I could sort of understand what they were talking about.

It was about 3:30pm in the afternoon and we were getting close to the Swiss border when Angus decided to get something from the overhead rack. Just as he was stretching up, there was a sudden screech of the brakes and an almighty thud and bumping as our compartment and three others came off the rails. Angus fell backwards and found himself sitting fairly and squarely on the young woman's lap. Stunned he seemed to sit there for what seemed an eternity. Eventually Angus managed to get up from the young woman's lap with his apology being accepted by a coy smile. Shaken, we all managed to make our way out of the carriage which was leaning towards a steep ravine.

Our carriage and two of the others had come completely off the rails. Everyone was walking up and down by the side of the train. It was all a bit chaotic as there seemed lots of people taking charge, but no one really knew what to do. The cook was remonstrating by the side of the tracks, his apron covered in soup. Eventually, it was decided that the front part of the train, which was still on the tracks, should be decoupled and take all the passengers to next station. There it would wait till the derailed carriages had been put back on the tracks. Luckily no one was badly injured but one elderly woman sobbed uncontrollably. Angus and I thought it all rather exciting.

We must have waited at least two hours on the platform of the small rural station. A woman brought around refreshments but there weren't many seats on the platform. Finally, to the cheers of all the passengers, the carriages that had now been re-railed came pushed by another engine. The recoupling to the train seemed to take for ever but eventually we were on our way again. People went back to their original carriages to their allotted seats. It was already getting dark when we got to Zurich where many people disembarked much to the joy of the people who had come to meet them.

When Angus and I moved back to our original carriage, we found that a rather overweight sour looking elderly couple had taken the seats, left by the young woman and her companion. We decided to explore further up the train to see if we could find an empty compartment to spread out for a proper night's sleep. Towards the front of the train, we found just what we were looking for, a vacant compartment all to ourselves. Angus decided he would do things in style and got out his Lilo. He blew it up and put it out on the floor between the seats. I tried to sleep spread out on four seats. The train had slowed to a snail's pace as it slowly wound its way into Basle station. Lots of shunting and commotion had no effect on Angus as he slept like a baby. We seemed to be waiting at the station for an eternity. Then to my surprise appeared the original carriages of our train, on the other side of the platform. I recognised the sour looking couple sitting upright and noticed on the side of the carriage was the number D34. This had been the carriage in which Angus and I had originally started our journey. It struck me that perhaps we should be on the other part of the train. I decided to check it out and walked up the tight corridor to find an official. I showed him my ticket to London and in my broken childlike Swiss German, asked him if I was on the right part of the train.

'No, no,' he replied. 'You should be on that part of the train,' he said, pointing to the other side of the platform. 'This part of the train is going to Paris.'

As he said it, the train on the other side of the platform heaved itself out of the station. I rushed back to see Angus who was still fast asleep and shouted at him in somewhat of a panic, that we were on the wrong part of the train and would soon be on our way to Paris.

Angus and I decided we needed to leave 'Tout de suite'. Paris certainly wasn't on our itinerary! Hurriedly we opened the window, and I rushed out onto the platform to receive our luggage that Angus was throwing out as fast as he could. No time to deflate the Lilo, so out it came, still fully inflated. Angus managed to jump out, just as that section of the train left for Paris.

Our train disappeared into the distance as a deafening silence ensued. The large railway clock at the end of the platform showed it to be just past 11:30pm and the night was very cold and still. Angus put on his shoes and there we stood in a completely empty station with our luggage strewn around us.

Undeterred, we picked up our belongings and went to see if we could find any signs of life. We came across a train timetable and discovered that there was another London bound train coming from Milan at 4:15am the next morning. Filled with positive hope, we could at least sit it out and wait for that train. Knowing that both of our mothers would be expecting us at Victoria station around 1:10pm the next day we wanted to let them know that we would be about five hours late.

'Let's try and phone them,' I said to Angus. We walked further up the platform leaving our luggage near the timetable and started to look for a phone. As luck would have it, we found a phone box and because we didn't have any Swiss Francs, I tried to make a reverse charge call. No luck as I couldn't get an operator. Then out of the blue came a portly middle-aged gentleman who asked us if we needed any assistance. He spoke broken English, so we told him that we were trying to make a phone call to London. He told us that we couldn't make international calls from that telephone, but if we wanted, we could use his home phone which was just around the corner. We wanted to take our luggage with us, but Angus's Lilo wasn't fully deflated. The man told us that we wouldn't be long and best to leave the luggage on the platform. As gullible kids, who should have known better, we followed him, as he got into his car.

He assured us that it was just around the corner. We drove for what seemed an eternity before we came to a block of flats with a private garage at the bottom. The roller door opened automatically, as he drove into the garage. Then the roller door closed behind us. We were trapped.

'Come don't be afraid,' he said to us as he got into his personal lift that took the three of us directly into his apartment on the fourth level. There was no way out.

At this stage, the man was quite civil and asked if we needed the bathroom. Neither of us accepted his invitation.

'Are you related to Emile Kaspar' he asked to my surprise. He must have seen my name on the label on my shoulder bag. 'He is a marked man you know. The neo-Nazis are still looking for him. There's quite a bounty on his head.'

'I've never heard of him,' I replied rather confused.

'Has your mother ever told you not to get into a car with a strange man?' whispered Angus to me as we followed the man into what would have been his study.

'Bit late now,' I replied, as I secretly showed him the little knife I had in my pocket. Angus and I had only a couple of days previously been to a street market in Gmunden and had bought six identical pocket-knives. We thought that they might have a good resale value at school. They had a blade that folded back into a groove in the painted wooden handle. My knife was green, Angus smiled as he showed me his red knife. We both smiled at each other.

The overweight man sat behind his desk and told us that it was too late to make a call so we would have to stay the night and then we could perhaps call in the morning.

He said that we should take off all our clothes as he pulled out a trundle bed from beneath the sofa in the sitting room. 'You can sleep here, and I will look after you,' he said and then started breathing heavily.

'We are not staying here,' said Angus to him in a direct tone. 'No, we are going back to the station so you can take us back now.'

'There aren't any trains till tomorrow, so you might as well stay here,' he replied with a grin on his face.

'You will take us back now,' I said in my most assertive voice. At that we both took out our knives from our pockets. The grin on his face melted.

'Let me see when the next train to London will be,' he said as he thumbed through a train timetable.

'4:15am this morning so you will take us now,' shouted Angus at which the man visibly cowered as he knew that the two of us could overpower him, especially with the knives in our hands.

The man realised that we meant business and slowly we retraced our steps back down into the garage. Angus and I got into the back seat, as he drove us at a snail's pace, back to the station. Once again, it seemed to take for ever.

Finally, we saw the station coming towards us, and then we were alongside it. He stopped at a traffic light and that was our cue to get the hell out of there. Angus and I looked at each other and we both knew it was time to go. Before the man could do anything we both jumped out of the car and made a run for it.

We were at the other side of the station from where we had departed. The man called out after us and tried to give chase, but we just kept running. He soon realised that he was no match for us and gave up. I recall that there was a peasant woman sitting on the ground and he decided he would speak with her before slinking off.

There on the other side of the station was our train some six platforms away. It had to be the 4:15am from Milan. It was still dark, and the station was poorly light. We just kept running. The platforms weren't that high so we could hurdle them like Olympic steeplechasers. When we got to our original platform, we could see our luggage was still on the seat that we had left it. It wasn't much of a problem that someone had placed a railed barrier across the platform between us and our luggage. One stride and we were over the barrier only to be confronted by military Swiss guards with rifles. They came out of the train and ordered us behind the barrier.

'But that's our luggage and we've got tickets to London,' we told them with some urgency.

'You have to wait the other side of the barrier,' said the guard pointing his rifle at us. Pocket-knives certainly wouldn't have been a match.

Finally, the guard explained that the train was going through customs and that we wouldn't be allowed on the train until the customs procedures had been completed. He looked at our passports and said to me, 'Are you related to Emile Kaspar?'

'I don't think so,' I replied. 'Who is he?'

'I went to University with an Emile Kaspar,' said the guard. 'He disappeared into thin air after the war. I heard he went to America to avoid the neo-Nazis.'

His comments fell on deaf ears. I understood his Swiss German, but he might as well have been speaking Japanese for all the sense he was making.

Eventually, they took away the barrier so we could get our luggage and find a seat on the train.

The train pulled out of the station into the new day. We both gazed out of the window saying nothing but staring into space. The blood seemed to thump through my veins as I thought how lucky we had been. What if we hadn't bought those knives at the market?

We arrived at Victoria station just five hours behind schedule. My mother Hana was at the head of the platform seated on a bench. She had been waiting all five hours and when we finally arrived, she calmly said 'Oh hello, we thought you were never going to come.' She must have been so worried but didn't show a morsel of panic. Angus's mother had initially been at the station but when we didn't arrive had gone back to her office to call the police, who had in turn alerted Interpol. We called Angus's mother Sandy, and it was decided that we should make our way back home. We caught the District line tube back to Ealing Common. It was the London rush hour and I recall us telling my mother what had happened. She appeared outwardly calm, but I know internally she would have been horrified. At one point I looked around to see the other passengers on the train flabbergasted at the tale.

* * *

Angus and I were to experience several other European adventures together, but those are another story.

30

The Chauffeur

My father Hovan was a man of few words. Sometimes I could hear his mind ticking over as he considered all the possibilities, then suddenly announcing his decision with alarming clarity. Like the other members of his family, he was a gambler. He gambled on everything. If we were in the lobby of a large building waiting for a lift, he would want to gamble which lift would come first. To him life was a gamble. The only difference between my father and the other members of his family was, he could afford to gamble.

* * *

I remember my father once telling me: 'You know Mikey, I would be a very rich man if I didn't gamble.'

'Then why do you gamble? Why don't you just give it up?' I replied in a self-righteous tone.

'Well, if I didn't gamble, I wouldn't have any money,' was his response. 'If gambling is in your blood, it's not something you can turn off and on.'

What he meant was, the whole of his life had been a gamble. His business was his biggest gamble, but there, he was the ring master with complete control. The profits from his business more than adequately paid his bills and left a substantial surplus to spend at will.

He was also an extremely good poker player, playing twice a week at a respected poker school in the city. 'You can't win all the time,' he would tell me, 'But a better player, will overtime win more often than the others.'

He had a series of greyhounds which ran at the White City stadium. One of the greyhounds won the greyhound Derby for which my father received a large trophy with a large cheque in it. Our house was littered with trophies. Sometimes he would take us to the 'Dogs', to watch our greyhound in a big race. As an owner, he and his visitors were treated to a red-carpet treatment with a silver service dinner all laid on.

The thing that I most admired about my father was his ability to get on with everyone that came anywhere near him. He was self-assured, mixing with rogues or royalty, with a spontaneous joke that would always break the ice.

He was a member of 'The London Motor Trade', a group of twelve car dealers that met monthly to discuss business. Out of the twelve members, he was the only non-Jewish member but as he had the biggest showrooms south of the river he was fully accepted into the fraternity. Together with some of his colleagues, they set up the London Automobile Auctions near Frimley in Surrey. Wednesday was auction day when a group of car dealers, would turnover their part exchange vehicles to the unsuspecting public.

* * *

My father, through his work, seemed to know lots of people. Many of them owed him favours and often paid in kind.

A struggling artist wanted to buy a car to transport some of his paintings to various galleries. He was a young man just out of art school and seemed delighted that my father wanted to do a deal with him. I recall going to see the artist's studio with my mother and father. On the way, my father said, 'Don't look at the prices, just choose what you want.' Frankly the paintings were not that good, and my mother struggled to choose any of them. My father only looked at the back of the paintings to check the prices. As the artist went out to make us a cup of tea, my father told my mother 'Look he's a struggling artist and may one day become famous. Just choose any three paintings and I'll get my friend Harry to auction them off. He'll put an exorbitant price on them, and the punters will think the paintings are worth something. Harry's a great manipulator of the market. You wait and see, the paintings that you have chosen will soon triple in price.' It's true to say that my father didn't really appreciate art, but he liked that, in some cases, art would appreciate. It appealed to his gambling spirit.

Through the late 60s to the mid 70s, some of the Australian tennis players playing at Wimbledon used to hire cars from my father at bargain prices. It started with Neil Fraser, but soon spread to other competitors. Each would in their own way want to thank him. Rod Laver gave my father a box of signed Wimbledon tennis balls, which was unfortunately kept on top of the piano. Angus and I hadn't realised the significance of the gift and used the balls to have a hit of tennis at the local courts up the road. We lost one of the balls and the others soon lost their pristine white to become a dirty grey colour.

* * *

Even though my father knew lots of people, he somehow could make each person feel special. He had a kindness about him and brought out the best in everyone. He referred to himself as just a 'tradesman'. He mixed with everyone in the same congenial manner.

One day a tall man in a pinstriped suit came to the showroom and asked to see the boss.

The young salesman said, 'Wait here sir, I'll go and see if he's available.'

'Gov, there's some geyser out the front, says he wants a word with you,' said Bert to my father.

'What's he want?' replied my father with his head buried in paperwork.

'I dunno,' Bert replied. 'He wouldn't say. Says he wants a private word.'

My father looked through the half glass door and said, 'Well Bert, you better show him in.'

'Take a seat sir, what can I do for you on this beautiful sunny day?' said my father to the man.

'I need to know the price of that blue estate car you have out the front,' said the man with a strong Liverpudlian accent. In those days the price and other details didn't have to be shown on the car.

'Yes, that's a low mileage and the asking price is £699. What were you thinking of using it for?'

'Well, I'm only the chauffeur,' said the man. 'But if you look at that green Jag parked over the road, you might see someone special sitting in the passenger's seat. Yes, it's Ringo Starr and it's him that wants it to carry around his drums. I can go and tell him that its £799 and he won't know the difference. Extra fifty quid for each of us.'

'I don't care who you've got in that car,' replied my father. 'You can go and tell him the price I've just told you and if he wants it, he can come and see me directly.'

Five minutes later Ringo came to inspect the car and then asked to see my father. The deal was done, and Ringo went into the office to sign all the paperwork. He must have felt comfortable with my father as he off loaded a lot of his concerns. Ringo had been ill and had decided not to go on the Beatles tour of Australia. He had needed some time off to put things in perspective.

'What the tax man doesn't take, the sharks seem to be helping themselves,' said Ringo 'We're being ripped off everywhere we go. I sent my driver in to talk with you about the price of the car because otherwise you would have recognised me and put up the price. Recently I invested £100,000 into a construction company that lasted three months before it went bankrupt. I was left a beaten-up old Land Rover. I get worried about things.'

Ringo left a good deal happier and drove off to pick up his drums in his new acquisition. My father felt sorry for the young kid, as he referred to him. He didn't have the heart to tell him that his own driver was ripping him off.

As it happened some thirty-five years later, I was working as an Architect and had to check lots of drawings that the drafters had done for me. Purely as a cost saving exercise, they would reduce the A1 size drawings down to A3 which meant that I needed a magnifying glass to see them properly. It was time to get my eyes checked so I went to see my optician. He told me to bring along some reduced drawings so we could make sure I could see them properly. As it happened, I had some reduced drawings of a project that I was doing called 'The Cavern Club' where the Beatles used to play. The Liverpool Cavern club had given out the naming rights to four locations as a test to see how franchising the club might go. I think there was to be one in Los Angeles, another in Berlin, one in Tokyo and one in Adelaide, Australia. We had found a suitable venue and were well into the construction in Adelaide when I took the drawings with me to the opticians.

'Oh, the Cavern Club,' said the optician when he saw the drawings. 'Of course, I know about the Cavern Club. In fact we were in Liverpool last year and my cousin who lives there took me to the new Cavern Club. My cousin used to be Ringo Starr's driver many years ago and knows everything there is to know about the Beatles.'

'I'm sure he would,' I said to the optician but didn't add anything more to the story. It later transpired that the optician's cousin had indeed been Ringo's driver but at some years after the pinstriped gentleman who had tried to rip him off. I always wondered if Ringo eventually found out about the crooked chauffeur and had to replace him with the optician's cousin.

* * *

In the summer of 1966, England was hosting the soccer world cup. A car dealer friend of my father's had a brother who was at that time, the current Chairman of the Football Association. He had given my father tickets for the matches to be played at Wembley stadium. My father and I went to see the controversial quarter final game that England played against Argentina. The Argentinian player Antonio Rattín was sent off and it was later reported that Alf Ramsay had called them 'Animals'. Then came a close semi-final win against Portugal who were captained by Eusebio. England were through to the final. My father went back to his friend and managed to get only one ticket for the final match against West Germany. As he handed me the ticket he said, 'Consider this as your birthday present. It will be a once in a lifetime experience.'

It certainly was an experience. I was sitting some ten rows or so behind the Queen and her royal party. The atmosphere was electric. I think West Germany was the favourite, but England had the home team advantage. There was a strong rivalry, and it was only some twenty-one years after the end of the war. For both sides, it was more than just winning a soccer match. The game was played in good spirit and England were winning by one goal with just ten minutes to go. The crowd was starting to thin out as many of the spectators, anticipating an English victory, wanted to avoid the end of match crush. I wanted to stay to the end. I wanted to soak it all up.

Then, in the last minute of injury time, West Germany scored a controversial equaliser that put the match at 2-2, with an extra 15 minutes each way to be played. England through Martin Peters scored twice, and Bobby Moore was presented the Cup. What a day for English sport, what a day for the nation.

I took my time going home so I could savour the moment. When I did get home, I found my mother watching the 2nd half and extra time replay on our black and white television. See if you can see me behind the Queen,' I said with pride.

* * *

My father had a very stable workforce and treated them all with the utmost civility. He always told me that the secret to the Motor Trade is in the buying of cars. 'Any fool should be able to sell cars as they usually sell themselves. But buying cars, that is a different matter.'

Big John, the sales manager, was allowed to take cars in part exchange but my father was the only person that could buy cars.

Irish Paddy was one of the senior salesmen who had been with my father for many years. Paddy had the gift of the gab and frequently received a bonus for the highest number of cars sold in a month.

Unfortunately, Paddy had a couple of vices that stopped him going places. One vice was that he was a constant follower of the nags. That is, he always had to put a bet on the horses. This in no way bothered my father as he would ask Paddy to go and put a bet on for him at the same time or pick up his winnings. The second vice was more difficult to control. Paddy would occasionally go on a massive drinking binge.

These would usually happen when he had had a bad run on the nags. He would go and get himself totally paralytic and not turn up for work for a week or so.

It was after one of these occasions that Big John, the sales manager, came in to see my father and told him the news about Paddy.

'Gov,' he said 'Paddy has been on one of his benders again but this time he's really spoilt his copybook good and proper. There's £200 missing from the safe and I'm afraid he's totally blown it this time. He's up to no good and not worth bothering about. My advice is you've got to give him the sack once and for all.'

'Thanks for your advice' replied my father. 'Let's wait a day or two and see what he does.'

Three days went by and no sign of Paddy. My father called Big John into his office and asked if he knew where Paddy lived.

'Yes Gov, I know where he lives but there is no point in trying to get your money back cause he ain't got none. He needs his job back but is too ashamed to come and speak with you.'

'I'm not worried about the money, but I am worried about Paddy's welfare and besides I don't want to lose a good salesman. I've thought about it and have come up with a plan.'

'What's the plan Gov?' said Big John with a bit of a smirk.

My father went to his safe and took out £200, giving it to Big John.

'Here, you take this money and give it to Paddy this evening. Pretend it's a loan coming from you. Tell him that he must come tomorrow to see me with the £200 and give me back my money. I will take back the money and ask him to come back to work, saying that this will definitely be his last chance. Paddy can then repay you directly from his pay each week, the £200 loan that he thinks he owes you, in £10 instalments. As he pays you each instalment, you will then give it back to me. That way you gain a friend in Paddy, Paddy gets his job back and I get my £200 back as well as a good salesman.'

* * *

The plan worked perfectly. Paddy never knew that my father had been instrumental in the setup and thought the world of Big John. Big John in turn had great admiration for my father.

31

To pass with E's

I was failing rather badly at school and the more I tried to fit in with their military controls, the worse it became. It wasn't the school's fault; it was just that I didn't uphold any of their values. I couldn't come to terms with the notion of inherited wealth, knowing that half the people in the world were struggling for an existence. Try as I might, I seemed to be spiralling downwards and couldn't find enough stimulation to satisfy my creative needs.

* * *

At the age of fifteen, I already had a reasonable tenor voice and enjoyed being part of what was called the 'upstairs choir'. Each morning, dressed in a white surplice, the upstairs choirboys had to shuffle up an enclosed stone spiral staircase to the organ and choir balcony. One morning, I noticed that a door that continued the spiral stairs, had been left slightly open. I could see more steps that I assumed would lead up to the roof of the chapel.

My curiosity got the better of me. I went to see my friend Tony Hogarth, the son of a Major General. Hogarth had a most devious if not criminal mind, that could manipulate things to his advantage. His large bunch of keys would get us into almost anywhere we wanted to go. Hogarth didn't even ask why I wanted to open the door. For him it was the challenge. That night at about 2am, we climbed the first set of spiral stairs up to the organ balcony and he tried some of his keys to open the small, locked door. None seemed to work. 'Don't worry,' said Hogarth. 'There's always a way.' He then picked the lock without a problem, so he could open the door. Removing the lock mechanism, he inspected it carefully by torch light. 'Do you want me to alter the mechanism and make a new key, or do you want to use the same mechanism?' he asked with that mischievous grin. 'No don't alter the lock.' I said in a whisper. 'I only want to go up there the once.' With that we started the climb up the second set of steep narrow stone stairs, spiralling up towards the roof.

The chapel was a small version of Kings College chapel at Cambridge. We could look along the gothic rib-vaulted ceiling towards the alter with its stained-glass window beyond. The intricate pattern of the slender rib-vaults disappeared into the distance and glistened in the moon light that seeped through parts of the stained-glass window.

As we climbed slowly up the second set of stone stairs, the space became narrower. It spiralled like a corkscrew for what seemed an eternity. Finally, we arrived at a small circular space about six foot in diameter and eight foot in height. I shone my torch around the space and above my head was a wooden trap door with yet another padlock. 'Damn,' I thought, 'we have come so far and foiled at the last hurdle. And then I saw something that just blew me away …'

High up on the stone wall, near the wooden trap door, was scrawled a piece of graffiti which said, 'Harat Kaspar' with the numbers 3663 below. It was as clear as daylight in the torch beam. I was totally stunned. What was my great-grandfather's name doing up there and what did the number 3663 mean? I couldn't take my eyes off it. Finally, I turned to Hogarth and said 'Come on mate, we have to get out of here. We can't go any further. Abort the mission!' We turned around and made our way back down the spiral stairs. I couldn't get out of there fast enough.

I climbed back up the external fire escape of my boarding house to crawl in through the window that I had left unlocked. I found my pyjamas where I had left them, changed back, and walked back down the long dormitory as if I had just been to the toilet to have a pee. No one stirred and I was back under the blankets around 3am but just couldn't get back to sleep. My head was spinning. What was my great-grandfather's name doing there and what did the numbers mean. I knew that my great-grandfather, Harat, had been sent to boarding school in England, but I didn't know which school or exactly when. At around 6am, I was about to doze off when it hit me as clear as a bell. I thought 'What do they normally put with the name scrawled in graffiti?' Of course, it must be a date. It must mean the 3rd of June 63. But that is today! How come he had put today's date? Then I realised that it didn't actually say 1963, it just said 63. It must have meant 1863. To think my great-grandfather had explored this secret staircase exactly one hundred years ago to the day.

Later that day, I went to the college library and found the College Book of 1863. Towards the front it listed all the boys alphabetically in blocks of five years, and indicated which house they belonged to. I looked under K for Kaspar. There in black and white, it said 'KASPAR – Haratyan – Burnside House – 1860–1865. Not only had Harat been at the same school, but he had also been at Burnside House.

* * *

A year or so later, I was about to take my Ordinary Level GCE exams when the careers master called me into his office to ask what I had decided to study at university.

'Surely I need to decide a career and then consider if I need to go to university or even sit for my A Levels.' I was hoping to somehow get out of school all together.

'Well, Kaspar, whatever it is, we need a decision by next Tuesday,' replied the careers master condescendingly. 'I suggest you have a chat with your father this weekend and come back to me with your decision.'

That weekend, my parents were taking me out for Sunday lunch. I told my father, 'the school has given me an ultimatum about my career choice. I don't have a clue what I want to do.'

After lunch, my father sat me down, starting the conversation with, 'We had better make a decision, hadn't we? Have you had any thoughts as to what you might like to do in life? You know you can come and work with me, but I suggest you get yourself a profession first. Being a lawyer would be useful, but being an accountant would be even better. Yes, accountancy would open up lots of possibilities even if you didn't want to come and work with me. Everyone needs a good accountant. What do you think?'

I could sense his frustration growing, as none of his suggestions met with a positive reaction from me.

'Well, what do you think you want to do? He asked again in his conciliatory tone.

'I want to be a photographer or perhaps an artist.' I suggested.

'Those won't get you anywhere, besides they aren't proper jobs that you can be proud of. I'm not supporting you for the rest of your life.' He paused and then asked, 'What do you like doing in your spare time?'

'I spend a lot of time in the carpentry workshop designing furniture for the other boys to make.' I said, thinking he might quite like my entrepreneurial qualities. 'Perhaps I could be a furniture designer.'

'Why don't you design big things like roads or bridges, tunnels or ships or large buildings? There's a lot more money and prestige in big things rather than small items of furniture.'

'What if I became an Architect?' I said thinking of some of the one-off houses and other boutique modern designs that had appealed to me. They seemed to me like an extension to furniture design. Some architects even designed the furniture for their clients. I had always admired the chairs designed by Mies van der Rohe, Frank Lloyd Wright, Le Corbusier and especially those of Marcel Breuer.

'Now you're talking sonny boy,' he exclaimed smiling from ear to ear. 'Go and tell them that you are going to be an architect. My son is going to be an architoke!' He laughed at his own joke, no doubt thinking that I would be designing massive skyscrapers or significant monumental edifices around the world. Perhaps planning new cities like Brasilia.

And so, it was decided that I should be an architect. To ease the pain, I just went along with it. The next holidays, I worked in an architect's office in Victoria. They were designing a sizeable development for my father, so he asked the senior partner if I might get some work experience with them. My father was building a new double storied car showroom with a car lift in Putney. Above were to be three floors of flats, that could be sold off the drawings. Perhaps secretly, he thought that I might become a developer, but having an architectural qualification would be a good start. I must have been such a disappointment to him in those days.

At the architect's office in Victoria, I soon found myself in the basement making photocopies of specifications and dyeline copies of the drawings. The machines were very temperamental and the paper kept getting jammed. It wasn't exactly my fault that photocopier started belching out smoke and then stopped all together. I was really pleased when the three weeks were up, and I could enjoy the rest of the holidays building box carts or some such thing.

The career's master knew nothing about being an architect. Like most people, he thought one had to be good at mathematics. It was decided that I should take maths, physics, and chemistry 'A' Levels. I went to various 'red brick' universities for interviews and showed them my portfolio of sketches. Eventually it was decided that I should go to an art and design college to study architecture. This was far more down my alley. They couldn't care less about 'A' Level results, but the Royal Institute of British Architects (RIBA) required a minimum of two 'A' Levels at any grade. I sat the exams and scraped through obtaining the required two 'A' Levels both with the minimum grade of 'E'. I could therefore legitimately say that I had passed my A' Levels with 'Ease'. The problem was I couldn't keep the smile off my face, so most people got the joke.

* * *

At the interview at Kingston School of Art and Design, just south of the river, I was asked if I had ever worked in an architect's office. I replied with a simple 'Yes I have.'

'So how did you get on?' was their follow up question.

'I thought it was pretty boring and I didn't learn anything new,' I responded, being perhaps a little too honest.

'Then why are you here?' asked the bald headed, bearded man, wearing round rimmed spectacles and a floral shirt.

'Well, I don't think it was a good representation of an architect's office,' I replied, bringing a smile to their faces.

Later, I would learn that most architects' offices are mundane and boring establishments; the office in Victoria had been typical, rather than an exception.

* * *

I was very pleased to see the end of my school days. Angus and I decided to take a final trip around Europe before he went to Bristol University to study civil engineering and I, to what at that time was called Kinston School of Art and Design, to study architecture.

Neither of us knew that the trip around Europe, would be our last adventure together.

32

The Emperor's New Clothes

While queuing up to enrol for my first year of architecture at Kingston School of Art and Design, I became aware that for the first time since the age of eight years old, I would be studying with females in my class. Having been deprived of such company, I felt rather awkward, but soon got the hang of it.

Out of the fifty-five students enrolled for the first year, there were only five female students. These five young women were rather studious, compared to the fifteen young women and one rather effeminate young man of the fashion department. The fashion students were all rather 'way out'. This was a 60's expression meaning outlandish. The fashion girls were all over the one young man, teasing him as they felt comfortable in his company. How I wish I had been studying fashion rather than architecture!

* * *

It was just two weeks into the first semester, as I was striding along a corridor, on my way to some lecture, when I saw walking towards me a familiar face. It was Mollett, Billy Mollett. A blast from the past.

'So, what are you doing here Mollett?' I asked. 'You seem to be following me everywhere like a bad smell,' I laughed as we had become good friends having endured both The Oakes Prep School and Millswood College together.

'I have just started the Foundation Year and hope to get into graphic design. What the hell are you doing here Kaspar?' he replied with a grin.

We arranged to meet for a coffee at 1pm in the college canteen to catch up with what had been happening.

* * *

Over time, the ice between the various departments showed signs of cracking, but our heavy workload kept us apart. At the end of their final year, the fashion students used to put on a Fashion Show. With Mary Quant, Carnaby Street and a host of young fashion houses, London had become the centre of the New Wave of fashion. Many art schools were a buzz with young up and coming talent, experimenting with the trends of tomorrow.

Much work was put into this final fashion extravaganza. A big hall had been hired and an elaborate set had been created with a stage and a long catwalk for the models to parade in front of an invited glitterati and representatives from the 'Rag Trade'. Tall, elegant models paraded up and down the catwalk to pumping music and psychedelic lighting. The students had chosen a wide range of themes. One theme was 'Food' another was 'Films'. Then there was a section entitled 'The Moon Walk', inspired by the recent missions to send astronauts to the moon.

Alice Juniper, a senior lecturer in the fashion department was an elegant woman wearing completely black, with red rimmed glasses and severely cropped silver hair. With a microphone in hand, she described what each of the models was wearing.

'Here we have Chantal, wearing a gorgeous orange with random green splashes jump suit designed by Rebecca Cohen. I love those little white plimsolls and it's all beautifully contrasted with that crepe turquoise turban with an offset gold star brooch. Well done, Rebecca.'

'And now we have Mimi and Katya wearing ankle length evening gowns adorned with strands of multi coloured ribbons. These designs by Gabriella Evangelista are simply sumptuous and I love the way the simple bandanna has a perpendicular tail. Soooo expressive. Well done, Gabriella, exquisite, simply divine.'

'Oh, what do we have here?' queried Alice Juniper, as two of my friends Peter Davies and Nigel Smithers from the third year of architecture appeared arm in arm, completely naked, except for black masquerade face masks hiding their blushes. They walked slowly down the catwalk to the gasps of a totally stunned audience.

'Yes, now here we have Vincent and Shamus in their Emperor's new outfits,' adlibbed Alice Juniper in her perky Oxfordshire accent, as if it was all part of the show. 'It doesn't exactly say here what material they are wearing, but whatever it is, it is very transparent and gorgeously revealing. And those masks are simply divine. I think these outfits could be considered as one of the many highlights of this show. And now we have …' as the parade continued.

Most streakers in those days would run as fast as they could but these two fine young specimens of manhood, strolled with deliberation to the end of the catwalk, turned as ballet dancers, and walked gracefully back along the catwalk as if nothing unusual had happened.

* * *

Art school suited me. For the first time in my life, I really enjoyed studying.

33

The Troubadour Club

Carlos flew from Caracas to New York, where he stayed for three days in a crummy hotel on 54th Street and Broadway, before continuing to London. His father Emile had offered to take him in his small Cessna plane as far as San Juan, Puerto Rico but the twenty-year-old Carlos wanted to be independent. He was ready for adventure.

* * *

Overwhelmed by the height and scale of Manhattan, he walked non-stop, experiencing all the famous sights as well as some of the not so famous. He went to see a college basketball game at Maddison Square Gardens, he walked through Central Park, he took a ferry to the Statue of Liberty, and a lift to the top of the Empire States building. At night, he walked till 2am in the morning or until he couldn't walk any more. The plumbing at the hotel would have woken the dead, but Carlos slept through till 8am each morning, had breakfast at a nearby café and then the walking started again. He walked as if he had a purpose but spoke to no one, and no one spoke to him. Although there were millions of people buzzing about, he felt totally isolated.

Tired and having experienced three concentrated days of the Big Apple, he just about managed to climb up the steps onto a TWA flight bound for Heathrow. The Big Apple had already become a memory. The flight was through the night, and he managed to sleep the whole way. It was early on a grey London morning, that the plane landed at Heathrow airport; once again he was ready for more adventure.

Unaware of the morning rush hour commuter traffic, Carlos took a bus from the airport to Hounslow West tube station, from there he could take a packed Piccadilly line train straight through to Earls Court. His mother Chantal had booked Carlos into the Earls Court YMCA Hostel for three nights, so he could find his feet and perhaps make some friends. Getting a part-time job would be his primary aim. It would be a good two months before he could start his full-time studies at RADA; getting a part-time job would help him to become immersed in the swinging London scene.

The hostel was basic, but Carlos knew that it wouldn't be for long. At least he could have a shower and have a place to sleep.

By midday he had already started his walking routine again. Luckily, he was a fit young man and had good footwear. His tanned skin, long shiny black shoulder length hair, colourful bandanna, calf length leather boots and collection of leather bangles around both wrists gave him that striking South American appearance. Later, these would be replaced by a pair of sneakers, torn flared jeans, and a simple black Tee shirt to give him a degree of anonymity.

Once again, he found himself walking through the busy streets with a false sense of purpose. He walked through Soho then around the Serpentine on his way to Notting Hill Gate. On the second day he found new and exciting places where many young people hung out. The Round House at Chalk Farm, The Kings Road Chelsea, and Piccadilly Circus all made Carlos feel that London would be his kind of town. He felt he had arrived.

* * *

That night as he returned to his hostel, he passed by a folk club that looked enticing. The club was called the Troubadour Club, on the Brompton Road, Earls Court. The club had started in 1954 and had been the home of the London folk scene. It had hosted a wide selection of influential folk musicians, many of whom had gone on to become huge celebrities. Paul Simon and Bob Dylan had both played there and so had Bert Jansch, John Renbourn, Martin Carthy and Davey Graham to name a few. In fact, anyone who was anyone in the Folk or Blues world had at some time performed there.

Tired and hungry, Carlos had a bite to eat at a roadside café, before making his way downstairs to a small intimate performance space of the Troubadour club. The audience of about twenty-five people were listening to a striking young woman singing original ballads. The young woman introduced herself as Roberta Anderson from Canada, who would later record under the name of Joni Mitchell. On weeknights, the venue was open house, which meant that after the main performers had finished, spectators from the audience could play if they wanted to. Performances were limited to ten minutes, unless by mutual consensus the audience wanted to hear more. This was a way for up-and-coming performers to show their potential to a bevy of recording scouts that frequented such places. People were drinking and smoking and later in the evening serious musicians that had been performing in other clubs came to catch up with fellow artists. Carlos feeling completely at home, borrowed a guitar and asked if he could sing a few South American songs. Declan the owner and organiser said 'Sure, help yourself.' And so began his lifelong connection with the Troubadour Club.

Carlos was a true performer. He would introduce his songs with stories about the characters he knew in Caracas, especially those in the Barrios, where crime and kindness lived side by side. His large hands with long fingers glided over the frets of the borrowed guitar and with chords that would have made John Renbourn or Bert Jansch envious, he accompanied his melodious voice with simple ballads that enchanted the small audience. At the end of his gig on stage he thanked the audience and then with a big grin on his face, he stepped off the little performance stage into the small appreciative gathering.

'That was really great man,' said Declan in his heavy northern Irish accent. 'Can I buy you a drink?' Declan was in his forties and introduced Carlos to the young woman behind the bar. 'What will you be having?' she asked with her Irish smile of kindness.

Declan and Carlos chatted for hours. Carlos explained that he had come to London to study at RADA, arriving a few months early to enjoy the London scene before starting his studies.

'Acting is hard in London,' said Declan. 'You better have a back-up to earn a bob or two.'

By the end of the evening, around 2am the club was closing. 'That hostel won't let you in at this hour,' said Declan. 'You had better come upstairs to me flat, to have a bit of a kip on the sofa. Just be sure you don't snore too loud, cos I don't want you waking me missus.'

The next morning, Carlos was woken by Rachel, Declan's partner. 'How d'you ave your coffee?' she asked.

'Just black,' replied Carlos.

'That's good, cos we don't have no milk or sugar,' replied Rachel in her cockney accent. 'I heard you woz pretty good on guitar, playing them foreign type songs.' Declan came out of the bedroom in his underpants, made himself a coffee and sat down in an armchair opposite them.

'Rachel and I have been thinking we need some help with running this club, and thought you might like to assist,' said Declan out of the blue. 'See Rach is in the family way and wants to bow out of helping too much. We need a strong young lad like you. The money won't be great, and the jobs will vary from cutting sandwiches, cleaning the toilets, and running the show a couple of nights a week. What d'you think? We could clean out our junk room so you could kip there as part of the payment. You don't need to give us your answer straight away; you might like to think about it.' Carlos thought about it for all of two seconds and then said 'Yes.'

'Does that mean you want to think about it a bit more, or you want to take up the offer?' said Declan.

'It means that I have thought about it and my answer is yes, I would love to be part of the club.'

'Well, the first job is to help me clear out the junk room so you can move in there. It only has a roof light window, so you must make sure it is closed properly, or the rain will come in.'

* * *

By 4:30pm that afternoon, the small box room had been cleared, and Carlos had collected his backpack from the hostel. Declan then took Carlos down to the café below and showed him how the coffee machine worked, together they set up for the evening's performance. A Scottish folk singer called Eric Bogle would be playing, Declan seemed confident that he would attract quite a crowd. Eric was a rising star and would one day become an international celebrity.

Carlos soon learnt the ropes of running the Troubadour Club and was left to do most of the work from Tuesday through to Friday. At the weekend he was free to do as he pleased, but often, he chose to hang around the club to see some of the big-name stars.

'Don't book anything for next Saturday cos you better come and see two of the greats performing here,' said Declan to an enthusiastic audience. 'We'll be honoured to have Sony Terry and Brownie McGhee playing. You won't want to miss em.'

Carlos was in his element. So much so that he forgot the purpose of going to London in the first place. September rolled around before he could blink and the thought of going to RADA to study acting became somewhat of an imposition. 'Who wants to be an actor anyway?' He wrote to his parents back in Caracas, intending to defer RADA for six months, until their spring intake. To his surprise his father Emile replied, 'We aren't surprised at your decision to give up being an actor. You are now twenty years old and must live with the decisions that you make.' Carlos had expected a different reaction, especially from his father and felt a little uneasy. He knew that Folk music was not for him in the long run, but also knew that he had plenty of time to find out what he really wanted to do. In the meantime, helping at the Troubadour was what he wanted, and he was experiencing a world of different characters, all with differing opinions. He would have plenty of time to sort out his life, or so he thought.

* * *

It was during this time at the Troubadour that Declan hired a young 19-year-old local girl from Barnes to help in the Kitchen, and to serve food and drinks. Alex Peters was a fresh-faced girl straight out of school.

Her father David had died of cancer just two weeks before she was born. David had been an amateur folk singer and had left her some reel-to-reel tapes that he had made for her to remember him. He had known that he didn't have long to live but had hoped to have lived long enough to see his only child. Just in case he did die before the child was born David and his wife Jane had decided on naming their child Alex. This could be either a shortened form of Alexander or Alexandria. Alex was the name he used on the tapes and to be on the safe side he made the tapes some three months before he died. As he sang the songs to his unborn Alex, he did so in a very matter of fact way. No hint of sadness in his voice, just a sense of love and a hope that all would go well. 'Alex, I hope you will enjoy these little songs that I have written for you. I hope you will know that I will always be with you.' He said at the beginning of the tapes. Alex hung on to every word, every chord and played the tapes repeatedly. David had made a book of handwritten poetry and little pen and ink sketches to go with each of the songs. He also wrote out the notes and words of each song and hoped that Alex would take up the guitar and sing them to the world. Her mother Jane had brought up her child in the little house not far from the river that she and David had lived in together before Alex was born. Alex felt a presence and grew up feeling that her father would one day reappear as if he had only gone away on holidays. She had a wall of photos of her father in her bedroom and would say 'Goodnight dad' before she went to sleep.

Alex had learnt all the words and music to the songs that had been left to her by her father and it was on one of those audience participation evenings that she asked Carlos if she could perform her songs. Declan was in the audience and was completely blown away by the tenderness of the songs and the way she performed them. It was the first time that Alex had performed in public, feeling nervous before she started. She introduced herself and songs by saying 'I am Alex Peters, and I would like to play a couple of songs that my father left for me. I never met my father as he died two weeks before I was born, and I know he won't mind that I am sharing these songs with you.' She played a few minor 7th chords and then sang with a clarity that was completely overwhelming. No one in the audience moved until she bowed her head and said quietly to herself 'Thanks Dad.' The audience was stunned, and she heard no applause. Those couple of seconds of complete silence were deafening. Then to her amazement the audience called out 'more, more, more'. She played a total of five songs introducing each of them with her father's words and phrasing that she had heard a million times before on the tapes.

After her performance Carlos went to Alex and told her how moving her performance had been. They talked together till past midnight, so Alex had to be taken home as the buses had stopped around 11:30pm that night. Declan offered to drive her home, but Carlos said he could do it and assured Declan that he would be back in time to close up the club.

That night was a full moon and the light danced on the river as they crossed Hammersmith Bridge on their way to Barnes. As Carlos pulled up outside Alex's house on St Ann's Road, both knew that something magical was in the air. 'What are you doing tomorrow?' asked Carlos 'Nothing much, just washing some clothes and cleaning the house while Mum is out at work,' she replied.

'What if I come around 12:15pm to grab a pint and a bite to eat at the Bulls Head not far from here?' asked Carlos.

* * *

They met the next day at the front bar of the Bulls Head, and they never looked back. Together they became a major part of the London Folk scene until tragedy struck its cruel blow.

34

Palanca

My third year studying architecture at Kingston soon flashed by. It was full on studying. Projects to get out on time, Crits to face and those twenty-four-hour nonstop stints at the drawing board were both exhausting and yet exhilarating. Tertiary education is more about discipline than the digestion of information.

Fifty years ago, no one had a computer let alone a mobile phone. The idea that one day we would be presenting our designs with the use of Virtual Reality would have been met with a chuckle and responses such as 'And I suppose you believe in Telepathy as well.'

The practice of architecture has changed more in the last fifty years than it had in the previous thousand years. No wonder it has become the mantra of the universities that they are more involved with 'Learning how to Learn', rather than the cramming of facts that will soon be out of date.

* * *

During my studies, there were a couple of books that made big impressions on me. One was a book entitled *The Future Shock* by Alvin Toffler. It explored the trajectory and acceleration of change that the world would soon be experiencing and the psychological effects that would result from this unfettered acceleration into the unknown.

Another book that I read, was in stark contrast and altered my perceptions of what architecture was about. The book entitled *Housing in the Modern World* and subtitled – *Man's struggle for shelter in an urbanizing world* by Charles Abrams, made a deep impression on me. It introduced me to the social responsibility that an architect might pursue rather than the notion of building monuments that would somehow make the world a better place to live in.

At that time, the course in architecture took seven years to complete. Three years of academic course work followed by what was referred to as a 'Year Out' working in an office. Then a final two years of academic studies, followed by another year in a professional office and studying for a final Professional Practice exam.

I went to see Dr Otto Koenigsberger at the University of London, for guidance on what I might do during my 'Year Out'. He was used to postgraduate and research students, rather than an undergraduate like me. Frankly, the meeting didn't go well, but undeterred, and with the urge to get out into the thick of the issues, I decided to look at what was happening in third world countries.

At that time, a London based, international firm of planners and architects, had been commissioned by the Venezuelan Government, to tackle the problems caused by overcrowding of the capital, Caracas. Llewellyn-Davies, Weeks, Forrester-Walker & Bor, with their comprehensive approach and width of design disciplines, had also been appointed as the head consultants for the design of several new satellite towns near Caracas.

I went to a lecture given by Richard Llewelyn-Davies on the recent design of Milton Keynes, a satellite town outside of London. There I met one of the partners and we spoke of their recent appointment to the Venezuelan Government, and I expressed my interest in spending a year there. We made a time for the two of us to meet at his offices the following week. At the meeting he suggested that I should write to their co-ordinator in Caracas, a Dr Jonathon Smylie and send him my CV and availability.

I wrote the next day to Dr Smylie and got a reply to say although he didn't have a position for me, he would ask on my behalf his counterpart in the Venezuelan Government Planning Department, and that I should hear from them soon. A week went by, and nothing came. A month went by and still nothing. I had booked a flight to Caracas via New York where I would stay for three days.

I went to see the Venezuelan Commission in London but was told that I needed a letter confirming a definite position before I could get a work permit. No such letter arrived. Without a work permit, I would only be able to get a tourist visa for seventeen days before having to leave the country and reapply. Time was marching on, and I must admit I had put the issue on the back burner. I had become totally consumed with the preparation of the display of three years of my undergraduate design projects to be judged by a panel of external examiners. The internal examiners had written some favourable comments about my design work but that counted for nothing if the external examiners didn't agree.

* * *

After three full days of the panel looking at and judging of the student's work, the results and grades were finally posted on a notice board. I arrived with some trepidation and found a crowd of other students all looking at the notice board. I finally managed to get to have a look at the results and looked up and down but couldn't see my name anywhere on the list. I thought that they had overlooked my display when someone said, 'Well done Kaspar, you deserve it.' I turned around to see my tutor and was about to tell him that my name wasn't on the list when suddenly I saw it at the top of the list in the Distinction category. I could not believe it. They must have made a mistake.

'Wait till I tell my father,' I thought to myself he certainly won't believe it.

That evening I went home to see my parents and it wasn't until the end of the meal when my father turned to me, asking 'Well aren't you going to tell us how you got on? What did the external examiners have to say for themselves?'

'I passed with a D,' I told him.

He looked rather glum and said 'Well I suppose that is one better than an E.'

'D stands for Distinction. I got a Distinction from the external examiners,' I said enthusiastically.

You should have seen his face. 'D for Distinction, well that can't be bad,' he said. 'We always knew you could do it.'

I had finally got some form of approval from my father. I hadn't realised, how much that it had meant to me. I had always looked up to him and for once I had received approval from him. It would take me many more years before I would earn my Rite of Passage to metaphorically 'Defeat my father'.

I wrote more letters to Dr Smylie and the Venezuelan Director of Planning but didn't get a reply. I spoke with my father about the situation, asking him for his advice. He suggested that the only way to sort out these types of issues, is to be there in person. He told me the story of how he had left Calcutta as a sixteen-year-old boy and arrived in Sheffield for an apprenticeship the day after his application had arrived.

'There is nothing quite like turning up and asking for what you want,' he said, 'Just go there as a tourist and while you are there, go and see this Smylie fellow. See what he has to say. Be prepared to have to go to Aruba or Curacao or even Trinidad to reapply for a work permit. Don't worry if it doesn't work out, at least you will have given it your best shot. The worst that can happen is you come back having had a great holiday.'

By implication, he had told me that he wouldn't think badly of me if I failed in my mission, but he would be disappointed if I didn't give it a go. He had given me permission to fail, as long as I had tried. Better to try and fail than not to try at all.

A few days later, I boarded my Pan Am flight to New York.

* * *

New York in the late 60s was quite an eye opener. I was used to the hustle and bustle of London but was totally unprepared for the sleaze of New York. I had booked in for two nights at a rough hotel near the intersection of Broadway and 34th Street. The Empire States Building was close by, and it seemed much was within walking distance. As I was still on London time, I needed to stretch my legs. I didn't fancy sitting in a confined sweltering bedroom with what seemed endless plumbing noises from all directions, so I decided to take a walk. It didn't matter where I walked as long as I kept walking. I didn't have a map but then Manhattan being on a grid system seemed all very simple to negotiate. I spoke with no one, and no one spoke with me. After what seemed to be at least four hours of walking I decided to make my way home. Unfortunately, my dyslexia kicked in and instead of finding my way back to Broadway and 34th Street, I found myself at the junction of Broadway and 43rd Street. The Metropolitan Hotel was nowhere to be seen. No one had heard about it but most of the people I asked replied, 'Sorry, I'm not from these parts.' I was lost, hungry and extremely tired. It was around 2:15am when I found myself in Time Square. Lurking in the shadows of doorways were drunks, pimps, drug dealers, scantily clothed women and people of undefined gender all hanging around as if waiting for action. As the police car sirens screeched and whined, I felt numerous pairs of eyes watching me. One unsavoury gentleman approached me and in his Bronx type twang asked, 'Do you wanna f**k or do you wanna be f**ked?' In my rather proper British accent I replied, 'Neither thank you, but thanks for asking,' and kept on walking.

Eventually I remembered that my hotel was near the Empire States Building and it was around 3:45am that I crawled into my bed. 'How clean are these sheets?' I thought before falling asleep and didn't wake till 10am to a barrage of plumbing noises.

More walking and then more walking. It seemed endless. I went to see all the sights and many sights that I didn't want to see. Two days without much to eat and very little sleep.

Eventually, I got onto the second leg of my journey and took another Pan Am flight to Caracas, the capital of Venezuela. If I hadn't been prepared for New York, then I certainly wasn't prepared for what was in store.

* * *

I arrived at Simón Bolívar International Airport at Maiquetía and was immediately hit by the smothering, intense humidity. Walking across the tarmac to the immigration and customs hall was quite a struggle. I felt like turning around and going straight back to New York. Struggle I did and eventually after finding my bags, entered the dank immigration and customs hall.

'Welcome to Caracas,' said the customs officer in the local dialect. His beaming smile displayed a perfect set of white teeth. I took the opportunity to practice a bit of small talk in Spanish and he seemed pleased that I was making an effort. He rummaged around in my bags and then asked quite nonchalantly, 'Tienes algun palanca?'

My Berlitz tapes, that I had been using to study Spanish hadn't introduced me to the word 'Palanca'. I hurriedly pulled out my pocket Spanish to English dictionary and found the word 'Palanca' translated as 'crowbar'! Why was he asking me if I had a crowbar?

Realising that something was a bit askew, I told him I didn't have any 'Palanca'. Even if I did have some, I wasn't about to admit it. He smiled and waved me through.

Later, I learnt that Palanca is a colloquial term used as 'Contacts' would be in English. A crowbar is used for leverage, and so my smiling customs officer had asked if I had any contacts who would be able to help if I needed any strings to be pulled or any impediments to be overcome. Venezuela works on 'Palanca'. I was about to find out that mountains can be moved but only if you know the right people.

* * *

My father had advised me to book a hotel room for a week. 'You will need a base until you find your feet,' he said, as if these things cost just small change. 'Don't worry about the cost, just treat it as a holiday. After all you are a man of Distinction.'

Using his attitude, I decided to take a taxi to the hotel. Hang the expense I thought as I stepped outside and back into the oven like heat.

In fact, it was the best thing that I could have done. The antiquated buses into the city were laden with peasants and their various farm animals. Although it looked like fun, I'm sure they would have taken days to get there.

The swarthy Hispanic taxi driver slammed down the boot lid of his 1950s Chevrolet, and off we went with all windows fully open to the blaring sound of heavy-duty Salsa music at full volume. The airport is down on the coast, so we had to climb up the steep mountain side as the driver shouted all kinds of expletives at locals whom he somehow kept swerving to narrowly avoid. More expletives and then turning to me he would laugh his throaty laugh and expose his rather toothless set of gums. I learnt a lot of words that hadn't been covered by my Berlitz tapes, or perhaps I just hadn't got to that chapter.

We climbed and climbed on a rather impressive highway until we got to the ridge and there, laid out in front of us, was the sprawling city of Caracas occupying a vast valley at high altitude. A heat haze hung over the city, so one couldn't see the entirety, but I could make out the hills surrounding the city, littered with shimmering shanty towns, called Barrios.

Slowly we started to descend into the city centre, a ten-lane freeway with sprawling tentacles. The traffic seemed horrendous but the driver singing to the Salsa beat seemed to know the rules. Cursing and swearing we finally got to the hotel. I felt totally emotionally and physically drained.

Luckily, Hotel Tamanaco was like heaven. It was clean, cool and had a large swimming pool. 'Hang the cost,' I heard my father's voice inside my head as I dived into the tranquil pool.

* * *

That evening after a bit of a rest, I walked into the bustling nearby market and found a bar. Dressed in black jeans and a black faded T shirt I blended into the melee. 'Una cervesa por favor' I asked as if I was a local. I had arrived. All I needed now was a job. I suppose a crowbar might have helped.

35

The Sloth

The next morning, having eaten a large breakfast of cereals, tropical fruits and numerous cups of dark Columbian coffee, I made my way to the northern of the impressive twin towers called the Simon Bolivar Towers. At that time, they were the centre piece of the modern cityscape with surrounding, swirling plazas full of exaggerated painted murals. Dr Smylie's office was on the thirty-first of thirty-two floors, and it commanded a spectacular view of the city. Only the Minister of Planning with an office that took up most of the thirty second floor, could boast a better view. I took the lift to the thirty first floor, which was dedicated to managers of the 'Ministerio de Obras Publicas, Direccion de Planeamiento Urbano' – The Ministry of Public Works, Urban Planning Department.

The large internal foyer was clad with marble throughout and housed an impressive semicircular reception desk with enough room to accommodate at least eight receptionists. I approached the sole receptionist, who batted her exaggerated false eyelashes, while maintaining the filing of her thirty millimetre long, lime green painted fingernails. She wore a very low-cut revealing rayon T shirt that exposed much of her more than ample bosom. Her exaggerated red lipstick, and green eye shadow gave her somewhat of a circus clown appearance. Her heavily permed, matt black hair looked like a wig that didn't compliment her sallow complexion.

'Can I help you?' she asked in Spanish slang, still filing her nails.

'I would like to see Dr Smylie please' I asked in my best Castellano, the type of Spanish that they speak in Caracas.

She directed me to sit on a plush armless chair on one side of the foyer and then picked up the phone to speak to Dr Smylie's secretary. Then she asked if I wanted a glass of water and when I replied in the affirmative, she dismounted from her fully extended swivel chair and disappeared out the back while trying desperately to pull down her tight mini skirt so as not to expose too much of her derrière. All five foot of her and in her six-inch platform shoes, she waddled off behind a screen and returned with a glass of water and a big smile.

Eventually, a wizened gentleman came out and introduced himself as Dr Smylie's personal assistant. I followed him into a vast office with full height floor to ceiling glass windows which afforded a magnificent view of Caracas.

'Ah Mr Kaspar, how nice to see you, do take a seat, I'm Jonathon Smylie,' bellowed the rotund man from behind a large mahogany desk. Rising, he shook my hand as if he was trying to crush every bone. 'Hope you had a good trip from London. When did you arrive? Now how can we help?' he rattled off without taking a breath.

I sat down opposite him feeling rather diminutive and asked, 'Did you get my letter with my application for a job?'

'Yes, yes,' he interrupted. 'I spoke with the Minister of Planning yesterday, but he hasn't got back to me yet. But seeing you have come all this way; we can't possibly let you go back empty handed. Let me have another chat with the Minister to see what he has to say. Can I give you a call around 6pm this evening and let you know what transpires?'

I told him that I was staying at Hotel Tamanaco and gave him the number. He gave me a wry smile and said with deliberation 'Then I will call you there.'

We shook hands again, as I took the lift down to the ground level and then back into the furnace outside. Used to walking, I decided to take a roundabout route, slowly making my way back to my hotel. Caracas boasted sumptuous plazas with lush tropical planting. There, local musicians busked gentle love songs, with harmonies to die for. In one square, a young woman sang beautiful melodies while an elderly man accompanied her with an upbeat rhythm on what appeared to be a miniature four stringed guitar, called a 'cuatro'. In the background, another man kept up a syncopated rhythm on a double bass. A small child went around the crowd with a hat. Sometimes the man playing the cuatro would take the lead voice while the woman would harmonise, swaying with eyes closed, to the rhythmic sound of a pumping set of maracas. Elsewhere, a woman played a full-sized harp, the traditional instrument of Venezuela. Music came naturally from the people and the crowds sat basking in it.

* * *

In yet another square, I came across a gathering of people all looking up at a huge palm tree. Up there in one of the fronds was a massive three toed sloth, looking down with a cheeky grin at the crowd below. The sloth, who would have been the size of a fully grown chimpanzee, was slowly making his way to the end of a large frond. I wondered what was happening and why everyone had stopped to observe it. I soon found out. The sloth had a mate in the adjoining tree and wanted to jump from one tree to the other. Sloths are not good jumpers, so this individual was slowly making his way to the very end of the frond, hoping that with an outstretched arm, he might be able to grasp a frond of the neighbouring tree and pull himself across. The gap between fronds must have been at least one metre. The sloth dangled at the end of the frond, appearing to be contemplating how he might bridge the gap.

He seemed to know the strength of the frond he was sitting on and started to bounce up and down, to make it oscillate in a vertical motion. The crowd, some twenty metres below, gasped as he bounced up and down and with one outstretched arm, trying to grab the adjoining palm. He was too slow to grab anything, so had to wait till the frond that he was sitting on, came to a standstill.

More contemplation and then with great force he somehow managed to bounce on his frond but this time, he was ready to grab the frond of the adjoining tree. Eventually, he managed to grasp the frond and hung on tightly. His mate coyly looked on from afar as the crowd below let out a small cheer. His problems certainly weren't over just yet. There he was, with most of his body on the original tree and one outstretched hand grasping the frond of the other tree. Suspended in mid-air between the two trees, the crowd of now about seventy-five people, were becoming concerned. Many stood underneath him ready to catch him or at least break his fall. Slowly, the sloth manoeuvred himself closer to his destination. An outstretched leg managed to grasp the target frond as he tried to slowly transfer his weight from one tree to the other. He hung on for dear life, suspended equally between the trees. He seemed to look down and give a cheeky smile to the horrified crowd of people below. He, like an expert trapeze artist was playing to his audience below. With a slight wobble here, and a step back to safety there, gradually he manoeuvred a second leg onto the target tree. Now all he had to do was let go completely of his original tree and transfer fully to his destination. The frond of the destination tree suddenly took his full weight and swung down towards the ground. The crowd gasped.

* * *

The sloth hung on tightly and when the frond had returned to a stable position, he scampered up towards his mate. The crowd cheered as the two sloths embraced.

36

Blue Underpants

I arrived back at my hotel room about 5pm and told the receptionist that I was expecting a call from a Dr Smylie. I asked her to put him through when he rang.

I went up to my room and turned on the television. I must have fallen asleep as I was suddenly awoken with the television still on and the phone ringing. Half-awake, I answered the phone and the receptionist said 'Mr Kaspar, I have a Dr Smylie on the line for you.' I didn't have time to switch off the television when Jonathan Smylie's voice came through loud and clear.

'Michael, it's Jonathan Smylie here. Now look, I have spoken with Minister Jiménez and told him all about you. He says that he wants you to stay and that I should find you a job, so if you want to come on Monday around say 9:30am we can get you started. Is that okay with you?'

'Yes, of course Sir' I said sounding a bit too much like a schoolboy. 'To whom should I report?' I asked, leaving off the Sir.

'Come and see me first and I can introduce you to the team,' he replied. 'Good to have you aboard' and with that the phone went dead as he rung off.

I took a deep breath and thought to myself, 'Well I've done it. I've got myself a job.' Then, I thought about my father and how he had advised me to take a chance. In my thoughts, I could hear him saying 'Don't worry if it doesn't work out. At least you will have given it your best shot and we won't think any the worse if it fails.'

I wanted to phone my father to thank him for his advice but realised that the time difference would mean it was past midnight in London. Instead, I sat down and wrote my parents a long letter telling them the good news. I was used to communicating by letter, as I had been doing so throughout my boarding school days.

I decided to go for a short walk around the district and find myself a beer. Extremely tired, I curled up in bed around 9:15pm with lots of thoughts simultaneously bombarding my brain. I hadn't told Dr Smylie that I didn't have a work permit. What kind of work would I be expected to do? What would the pay be if any? How should I go about finding somewhere to live? Lots of thoughts but I eventually went to sleep thinking of the music in the squares, the drama of the sloth and what would I do until Monday.

That weekend I walked around the city of Caracas and began to feel its heartbeat. I wasn't used to the equatorial climate but soon learnt that the temperature and humidity grew in intensity until about 5pm each afternoon, then there would be an almighty downpour that would cool things down and clear the heavy atmosphere. Sometimes, it was accompanied by lightning and thunder which of course, like the rest of Caracas, was more exaggerated than I was used to.

I took my sketch book with me and found myself drawing people, buildings and plazas. I was pleased with the sketches, as they reflected the relaxed mood that I found myself enjoying.

* * *

Monday arrived and I went down early for another huge breakfast. The staff were quite sympathetic and even told me to stuff some croissants into my pockets. 'Here take some butter and Jam, we don't want you going hungry in the middle of the day,' said one of the young waitresses. I had booked at the hotel until Wednesday but didn't want to extend the booking until I had sorted out exactly what was expected of me at the Ministry of Public Works.

I was fifteen minutes early for my appointment with Jonathan Smylie and he was fifteen minutes late. I had left my list of questions behind but in the half an hour wait had managed to recall all of them on a new list.

'Come in Michael,' bellowed Dr Smylie as he stood at the entrance to his office. 'Call me Jonathon, none of this Sir nonsense. We're not in the army here.'

I found it difficult and just fell short of saying, 'Thank you Sir.'

All my perceived issues were simply brushed aside.

'We really don't have a job for you, but Minister Jiménez thought under the circumstances that you would be helpful around the office. The pay will be two thousand B's (Bolivars) a month. How does that sound? Oh, and don't worry about your work permit, we can sort all that out. Just bring along your passport and we'll take it down to Departamento de Extranjeria y Migracion. They can issue with the appropriate visa. Anyway, no rush for all of that, but I want to introduce you to the man you will be working with. Follow me.'

I followed him down to the level below to the design studio and was introduced to Aaron Fender, a portly roly-poly man of about forty years old. Aaron was both an architect and town planner from Nottingham and had been working in Caracas for a good five years. We became good friends although I did find him rather odd in both his dress sense and demeanour.

Aaron loved playing tricks and I soon learnt to be rather cautious. He told me that he would guide me through the do's and don'ts of the department. He had organised a job for me and explained what he wanted me to do. He told me that NASA had been contracted by the department to take three satellite stereo photographs every week of the whole of the Caribbean and the northern parts of South America. The resolution of these three photos was so good, that the magnified blown-up prints showed washing on the clothesline. My job was to sort out the photos to form a map of a city called Valencia some two hundred kilometres away. Like a giant jigsaw, I sifted through the photos, placing them appropriately before cutting off any overlaps.

The work was not only interesting, but the pay was about four times my expected pay in a London architect's office.

I decided that the best thing that I could do was to write a dissertation that would serve to highlight some of the planning issues facing Venezuela. My immediate boss and friend Aaron thought this to be an excellent idea and got approval from Dr Smylie for me to carry out such a report. I would need to visit various parts of the Republic and then document my findings. My study wouldn't be a heavy academic study, but somewhere between a travel document and an exposé of the issues that I perceived to be important. They wanted a fresh and positive look at the country as a whole.

Armed with my sketchbook, an expensive camera and an exorbitant number of rolls of film, I set off to explore.

* * *

It was Aaron's suggestion that I should make a trip into the jungle areas to see for myself what was a totally unique, and fragile part of the country. My trip to the southern jungle areas known as Territorio Federal Amazonas would later become the basis of a story that I would use to entertain many dinner guests. I would start the story by showing my guests what seemed to be a piece of cane about three inches long with a red feather sticking out of one end, asking if anyone knew what it was. After wild guesses, I would tell them the following story:

Aaron my immediate boss at the Planning Department in Caracas, organised a government plane to take me south to a place called Tama Tama, a small village which was the gateway to the jungle area of Venezuela. Arriving at Tama Tama, I was met by a local government official who warned me of some of the dangers that I would soon encounter. 'Piranhas fish will eat you in a couple minutes, so be very careful about even dangling a hand in the river,' he said and then added 'Yes, the mosquitoes are really bad but even worse are those missionaries buzzing around trying to convert your soul.' He also asked me if I knew a Dr Emile Kaspar and he thought his wife was also some kind of doctor. I told him I didn't think we were related in any way. It seemed curious as I had also been asked the same question when I went to a cocktail function at the British Embassy in Caracas.

I stayed in Tama Tama for a couple of days and eventually a man in a bongo arrived. A bongo is a sort of boat made from a dug-out tree. He was going to be travelling down the Casiquiare river for about five days and didn't seem to mind if I joined him and his other passengers, an elderly woman with a small child, and a young teenage boy, whom he referred to as Chorro. Also on board were some grains, beans, and a couple of live chickens. We set off deep into the jungle and I soon learnt that we were going to pick up Platinos, a monster banana, as well as some Brazil nuts from a small holding near the intersection of the Casiquiare and Rio Negro rivers.

After a couple of days on the river, we dropped off the woman and child, on the third night we went to the bank of the river where we cooked one of the chickens that Chorro had killed and expertly plucked. On the fourth day we arrived at the Rio Negro and started our adventure along the Colombian border.

At around 5:30pm that evening, we went to the bank of the river and secured our bongo. The man with the bongo told me that he and Chorro would go down stream for a little way to exchange some cargo. He suggested that I should walk up the pathway to the nearby Shebano and that he would meet me there later that evening. I walked for five minutes or so to a clearing in the jungle. There, I found a Shebano inhabited by a tribe of Yanomami Indians. I walked into the central open space and immediately was surrounded by some thirty or so tribesmen who were all decked out in a strange headdress of colourful feathers and twigs. Most of them wore no more than a string around their waist with an attachment to secure their penis and to stop it flapping about. Many had spears and some had small bows with arrows. Soon they had surrounded me and were trying to gently pat me all over. This patting was a way of feeling the vibe I was giving off. In our culture we shake someone by the hand but in their culture, they sense the person through a gentle touch. To say I was petrified would have been a gross understatement. I stood there completely frozen thinking I might soon be tenderised for the pot. I was only wearing a pair of shorts and some of the tribesmen were fascinated by the fact that I had body hair. Then one man behind me, must have felt a coin in my back pocket, curious to know what it was, he started to put his hand in the pocket. Of course, in our culture, this act is perceived as an invasion of personal space. I quickly spun around to see what was happening and immediately all the tribesmen, feeling my anxiety, stepped back a full pace. With spears pointing at me, they were ready should I make a sudden move.

I came face to face with the culprit of my invasion, an elderly, rather strange looking man. Our eyes fixed on each other. The tribesmen became silent but ready. I stood there for what seemed an eternity. Then, from out of nowhere, I started a tittering laugh which came out more like a snigger. Luckily, laughter like crying, is part of an international unspoken language common to all humans, and before I knew it the whole tribe were laughing with me. The elderly man and I became best of friends as he followed me around everywhere. I took the coin out of my back pocket and gave it to him. He looked at it and then dropped it on the ground as it had no value to him at all. I picked it up and put it back in my pocket and this seemed to amuse him a lot.

It was a good hour or two before the bongo man and Chorro came back. He told me that we would have to travel another couple of days to pick up our cargo of Bananas and nuts. That night I had to find a spot outside of the Shebano to swing my hammock as foreigners are not allowed to stay after dark. I was by then used to sleeping in a string hammock but not yet used to the blood thirsty mosquitoes who like vampires would buzz around furiously for blood. I awoke at the crack of dawn to the sound of someone looking through the little plastic shopping bag in which I carried a change of clothes and some other small items. In the half light, I recognised the same elderly tribesman rummaging through my belongings. He smiled at me and then finding a used pair of Marks and Spencer's blue underpants in my bag, thinking that this would make him a rather splendid trophy. I was aware that in the Yanomami culture there are no concepts such as possessions or ownership but that one took whatever you needed. I decided that he should give me something in return, so I pointed to his left ear where he wore through a large hole in his ear lobe, this rather elegant piece of cane with a red feather sticking out of one end. He gave me the object, and then putting my blue underpants on his head he smiled, disappearing into the jungle.

No doubt he too has probably dined out many times on the story of how he came across such blue underpants. But should you ever come across a man with a pair of blue underpants on his head, please let him know that they are mine!

* * *

I worked in Caracas for another six months before deciding to return home to London, but not before venturing on some travels throughout South and Central America.

The journey home wasn't at all planned and ended up taking me just over nine months of some daunting experiences. I was a hardened traveller by then, but I still hadn't prepared myself for what was about to happen.

PART 4

A Journey to the Never Never Lands

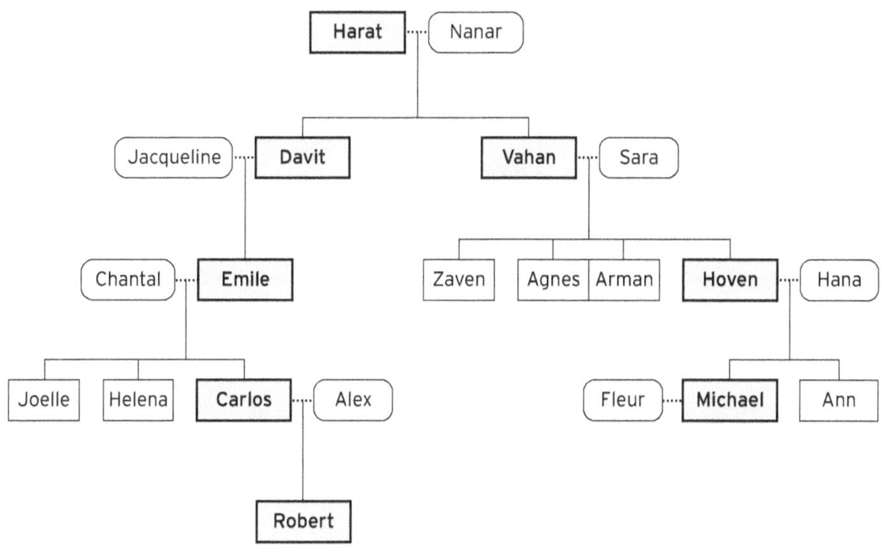

37

Sydney-Australia

Back home in London, I managed to complete the final two years of my architectural studies. It was not without a struggle, as I never really settled back into being a student again. I had experienced so much of life in the real world and couldn't wait to go travelling again.

My father had decided to retire, after selling his business for an offer he couldn't refuse. My parents went travelling around the world for five months staying at the best hotels, when suddenly they decided to return from sunny Auckland, New Zealand to London's bleak February of 1974. The British government had imposed a three-day working week due to the Arabs turning off their oil. It was a winter of discontent.

Both of my parents had been impressed by their six weeks stay in Sydney, followed by an extensive exploration up the east coast of Australia. It felt like my father had become a spokesperson for the Australian Tourism Board by the way he sang their praises. 'It's a land of opportunity. A land that is ripe for development. Once you graduate, you should go there for a year and have a good look around.'

And so it was that once again, I put on my travelling boots, setting off for a year's working holiday in Australia. It's now more than forty years later and I still feel like I'm on an extended holiday.

* * *

I arrived at Sydney airport at 11:45pm and was met at the airport by my cousin Jeremy. He had immigrated with his family some ten years previously. The plane taxied to a halt at the end of the runway of Kingsford Smith airport and immediately, two customs officials dressed in white shorts and long white socks, told us in the broadest of Aussie accents to stay in our seats while they, "Spryed the plyan". They then ran through the aisles of the plane spraying generously to exterminate all the bugs that we had brought with us. I found out later that this ritual was considered the white people's version of "Welcome to Country".

We drove over the Sydney Harbour Bridge at about 1am on the 22nd of September. It was a very full moon that danced on the shimmering waters and made the recently completed Opera House twinkle, like a diamond set in a tiara.

The next morning, I awoke to a brilliant blue sky, with the sounds of laughing kookaburras and chortling magpies. I was to stay with Jeremy and his wife Carol at Frenches Forest, on the North Shore, for a few days until I found my feet. Jeremy had previously sent me a copy of architectural companies listed in the Sydney Yellow Pages phonebook, and I had written to ten of them advising of my impending arrival in Australia. Out of the ten letters, I had received seven replies, which I considered a reasonable response especially as it was a good twenty-five years before the advent of emails. Three companies politely responded to say they didn't have any work for me. Three companies responded that they would put my application on file and that I should contact them when I arrived in Sydney. The seventh response, an architect from Chatswood, told me all about the sudden downturn in the economy and that large construction companies were being sent to the wall. He went on to write:

> *By now you will have probably bought your ticket and it would be too late to change your plans. Don't worry, death by starvation is very uncommon in Australia, so you might as well come and see me when you arrive.*

After breakfast on the first morning, I rang the three companies who had suggested I should contact them and one by one, I got the same response that the economy had taken a nosedive, so they were more likely to be shedding staff rather than recruiting. Then I rang the architect from Chatswood and arranged a time later that day to go and see him.

Arthur Jolly lived up to his name. He was a chubby middle-aged Scottish gentleman, with a broad Glaswegian brogue. As it had just turned 5:30pm, he brought out a new bottle of Glenlivet 18. I felt obliged to partake. The outcome after the third scotch was that he didn't have any work but suggested I should call Barrington Architects, a mid-sized firm in Neutral Bay Junction, as he had heard that they might be looking for some help.

'Speak to Dave Rogers, he's a good mate of mine,' said Arthur in rather slurred drawl. I was soon to find out that 'mateship', is the Aussie equivalent of the Venezuelan 'palanca'.

The next morning around 10am I rang Barrington Architects and asked to speak to Mr David Rogers. The receptionist put me through, but I didn't have to introduce myself as Mr Rogers in his no-nonsense way just said, 'Now Michael, Arthur Jolly has told me all about you and the truth is we could do with someone like you. Can you come over here later today, say around 5:45pm, and we can down a can or two?'

It turned out that David Rogers was a partner in the firm. Originally a Londoner, he had studied architecture at the Architectural Association at Bedford Square, before migrating to Sydney, some twelve years previously. He explained that they had some work but not that much. They were hoping to pick up some more contracts along the way. We arranged that I would start on Monday and agreed on an initial payment of $4,000 per year. Once again, the 'grog', as the Aussies call it, flowed, as we downed a couple more Tooheys together.

That Saturday I got up early and strolled down to the shops to buy a copy of the Sydney Morning Herald to look up the classifieds for second-hand cars for sale and flats to share, at or close to Neutral Bay. I'm not sure how it happened but somehow both the flat and the car jumped out of the page. My cousin Jeremy couldn't believe it. He and his wife Carol had been traipsing all over Sydney for a second-hand car whereas I just stumbled upon the blue mini-GT of my dreams. Jeremy drove me to the dealer's car yard to have a look at it. I only had enough money in my cheque account for a deposit so the dealer said he would keep it for me until I came up with the balance. Although I had opened a bank account with the Bank of New South Wales in Frenches Forest and deposited £500, I hadn't yet received the bulk of my savings from the National Westminster Bank in London. I was still waiting for the transfer to take place and couldn't even hazard a guess as to when the funds would arrive.

On the Sunday, I arranged to inspect, what appeared to be the ideal share flat at Phillips Street, Neutral Bay and wasn't disappointed. The flat mates, Linda and Sally, worked together at the local Commonwealth Bank, and were looking for a man to share with. We seemed to hit it off and agreed on what I thought to be an equitable rent. My room was minute, but that didn't really bother me as I intended to be out most of the time. I paid them a fortnight's rent in advance and told them that I would move in the following Saturday, after picking up my new car.

On the Thursday lunchtime, I went to buy some sheets, a blanket and a Lilo. I reckoned that a blow-up mattress might be more useful especially if I went camping. Besides it was much easier to transport around the place.

At lunchtimes each Friday, a group of the younger staff at the office, played squash and invited me to have a game. Someone lent me a racket and I brought along an appropriate change of clothes. Playing against a young man called Dennis, I soon realised that he was no more than a beginner. Having taken the first game off him, and well into the second, I was up near the front of the court and looked back to see where he was going to hit the ball, when whack it got me straight in the left eye. I fell to the ground holding my eye which swelled up so I couldn't see out of it. I had to stop playing. When we got back to the office, my direct boss Billy told me that I should go and get it checked by a doctor. I waited at the surgery for at least an hour before seeing a doctor. Poking away, he finally said, 'Because of the amount of blood in the eye, I can't see through to the back of the retina. I suggest you see a specialist at the Royal Eye Hospital, over by the Domain.'

I took a taxi to the hospital and phoned the office to tell them where I was. The receptionist said, 'No worries, mate, I'll let Billy know.' Eventually, after more poking and prodding, the eye specialist said much the same as the doctor over at Neutral Bay. 'Because of the amount of blood in the eye, all we can do, is to wait for it to drain and then assess things properly.'

'How long will we have to wait?' I asked quite innocently thinking I would be late for supper.

'If all goes well, it should start to clear in three days and be fully drained in five,' he replied. 'You will have to lie in bed completely still, with both your eyes covered, to give it the maximum chance to drain.'

'Five days and why both my eyes covered?' I exclaimed with a touch of anxiety.

'Any movement in the right eye, will cause the left eye to move and we could end up with a clot in the eye,' he explained in his matter-of-fact monotonous tone. 'You could lose the sight of your left eye if the blood doesn't clear properly, so I have organised a bed up on the third floor.'

After making a call to my cousin Jeremy to explain what had happened, I was bandaged up and blindfolded, taken up in the lift to a ward with four other gentlemen. Some of them not so gentlemanly.

Five days lying in that hospital ward was quite an experience. On the one hand I was worried about what would happen if I lost the sight in my left eye, but on the other hand, some of the other patients in the ward were such colourful characters, and though they were also meant to be lying still, they continued their strong Aussie banter, all day, and all night.

The main protagonist was a young man called Charlie in the opposite bed to mine. Charlie was a live wire to say the least. He introduced himself as 'Charlie Cook, no relation to Jimmy.' It took me quite some time to twig he was referring to James Cook the explorer. Charlie Cook, one night, walking home with a sackful of winnings from the 'Trots' at Harold Park, had suddenly been set upon by a gang of thugs. For once he had won big, but not being able to keep his mouth shut, he had boasted how much he had won.

'Six thousand smackaroos down the gurgler,' he said 'And only a punch in the head did I get out of it. Don't know if I'll see dem ***** again, but if I do, I'll get dem bastards.'

Of course, it wasn't all fun. The darkness, and not knowing the time of day or night, only exaggerated my anxieties. Would I be able to see again? Would I have to return to London? I could imagine myself blindfolded, trying to walk up the steps onto the aircraft.

Being blind for five days did bring some positives. Firstly, I no longer was afraid of the dark. Secondly, I experienced a heightened awareness of some of my other senses. As a child, we had a blind piano tuner, and I now understood why. The third, and maybe the most subtle of the experiences, was learning that things can unexpectedly be turned upside down. There I was, getting myself well and truly organised, when suddenly this happened. I had found myself a great job, a flat within easy walking distance from both the harbour ferry and where I worked. I had arranged to pick up my snazzy, new car the next day, and then drive on to the flat at Neutral Bay. All manner of thoughts surfaced. Would I be able to see again? How long would they hold my job? What about the flat? Would I be able to drive again? A sea of turbulent thoughts with no release.

After five days, I was allowed to leave the hospital and thankfully with perfect vision. All that worry, simply washed away as a calmness returned.

Thankfully, my cousin Jeremy had phoned various people. He had secured the car, arranged about the flat and most importantly, had spoken with David Rogers to tell him what was happening. 'No worries mate, no we won't be replacing him just yet. There's no urgency mate,' had been the response.

All sorted itself out with life just simply delayed a week. Five days of being in hospital hadn't taken the shine off my youthful exuberance but had helped me recognise that the flow of life can be dramatically disturbed by a small incident out of the blue. It also taught me, that my mind plays lots of games, and I desperately needed to develop an 'off switch'.

* * *

The office work wasn't taxing but helped to build up my bank balance and allowed time to explore. At 6.15am each morning, I would jog up and down the golden clean sand at Balmoral beach, before jumping in the water for a swim. A fellow jogger, a wrinkled elderly gentleman told me, 'Don't swim too deep as dem sharks will get ya. And don't swim where they put dem shark nets, cos the baby sharks get in through the small holes, feed on all dem smaller fish, and become too big to get out. Once they have eaten all dem small fish, like Piranhas, they try a bit of human, to see if deys like the taste.'

* * *

I had been working at the office for four months when one Monday morning David Rogers called me on the phone and asked me to step into his office. 'Sit down Kaspar,' he said pointing to a small coffee table setting. David Rogers, who had also been to an English Public School and had then completed two years National Service, always called me Kaspar. Once seated, he said 'We unfortunately are running short of work and will have to let some of you go. We have taken the decision that we will be asking the last three people employed to look for alternative employment. It's got nothing to do with ability but it's just that you were the last to be employed. So, we are giving you a fortnight's notice but will be happy for you to take any time you need to look around for another job.'

'Oh well that's a pity,' I replied, 'I have really enjoyed working here.' Then I asked him if he could fill in my British Professional Practice logbook. 'They require that you work a minimum of five months in an office, but I will have only worked four and a half months, so do you think you could make it five months.'

'No worries, Kaspar' he replied, 'We can sort that out when the time comes.'

The other two young men who were also being fired, were understandably glum and rather despondent. The final Friday came round, and the other two young men slunk off without saying goodbye. I happily went up to the mezzanine level and certainly wasn't going to miss out on my last drinks and nibbles. At around 9:30pm I saw that David Rogers was about to leave, so I went up to him and thanked him for everything. I asked him if he had signed my logbook and if not, perhaps I could pick it up sometime next week, when I had arranged to pick up my pink taxation slip. 'We thought you wanted to work for a minimum of five months Kaspar. Why don't you come back to work on Monday? I'm sure we could sort out things then.'

The next Monday I went back to work as if nothing had happened. David Rogers called me into his office and explained that it was customary to fire the last in. 'Some people have been known to kick up a bit of a stink, if they think that someone, who joined the firm after them, is staying on. 'We want you to stay but frankly the other two blokes were dead wood. However, we really do want you to keep looking for work as times are getting tough out there.'

I worked there for another three weeks, when one afternoon, Rogers called me into his office to tell me that he had been having lunch with an architectural colleague, a partner in a small practice in North Sydney. 'They are looking for some help to finish off a large project, and I suggest that you go straight over there to have a chat.' The next Monday I started working for the firm in North Sydney. The work was more demanding, so I learnt a lot in a short space of time. I learnt about detailing, especially the flashing of some complicated butterfly roofs. What I hadn't realised was that the office had a strong religious bent with some of the staff clutching their bibles from time to time. On occasions, the religious staff members were called into a 'Prayer meeting'. Another heathen, also called Michael, and I were excluded and asked to hold the fort.

One weekend, we had a real Sydney downpour. Lightning, thunder, the complete works. Returning to the office on the Monday, we found the box gutter overflowing, with water cascading onto the drawing office floor. Amazingly, not one drawing had been damaged. 'God recognises the righteous,' said a young religious drafter. It was almost enough for me to start saying my prayers.

* * *

After three months of hard work, the documentation of the project I was working on, was finally completed, printed and sent for tender. It was time for me to say goodbye and make my way up to sunny Queensland and the top end.

38

The Telegram

It wasn't long before Carlos moved into the house at Barnes, with Alex and her mother Jane. Although the house was small, Jane was able to give the two lovebirds plenty of space as she went to her secretarial job in Hammersmith early each morning. Carlos and Alex spent most evenings at the Troubadour Club and other Folk venues.

* * *

Jane was an accomplished violinist, playing a range of classical and modern pieces in a string quartet. She had never really come to terms with the ways of Folk music, with its lack of structure or discipline. She could feel the emotion and admired the immediacy of the occasion; envious of the fact that the sounds came naturally, and with little practice. Some basic chords played with intricate finger picking were all that was required to accompany Alex's delicate voice. The poetry of the words would give a story line and meaning to a song. Sometimes the words would express emotions such as love or tragedy, while on other occasions the song would have a message of a historical or political nature. The era of the 'Protest' song was being explored and brought to the populous. It was all 'Blowing in the wind, as times they were a changing.'

On occasions Carlos would bring out his Blues harmonica and both Alex and Jane were mesmerised by the earthy sounds that he could conjure. At the club, his Venezuelan songs of love and sadness were greatly admired, and the simple tuneful chorus lines were easy for people to join in as they became part of the performance.

Winter in London was bitterly cold that year, but they missed out on having a 'White Christmas' by a day or two. Carlos had seen snow from a distance but had never touched it. The snow melted and spring came with its abundances. Walks with Alex along the river, visiting pubs and cafés became their favourite pastime. Luckily, both liked walking and would get up early to walk along the river for a few hours, often stopping for lunch at the Bell and Crown at Strand on the Green. Evenings, and late into the night, were spent at the Troubadour Club. Even on their nights off they would go and see a favourite performer. Life was easy and Carlos relaxed as he became immersed in his newfound environment. Caracas seemed very far away, but he still exchanged weekly aerograms with one or other of his parents.

Carlos's father Emile would write about the political turmoil that President Perez Jimenez had left in his wake. The political pendulum seemed to be oscillating at an ever-increasing pace, leaving behind a trail of fear and utter confusion. Left and then right, left, right, left, right marched the polemic angst that was tearing the country apart. It was like watching a political tennis rally that gathered momentum leaving the opponents and spectators utterly exhausted.

Carlos's mother Chantal wrote regularly to him about the family and friends. Much of the news was about his two sisters Joelle and Helena. Both girls now had serious boyfriends one of which she approved of but the other was in her eyes a charlatan and leading the young Helena astray. She wrote that Joelle had accepted the proposal of marriage from Gonzales, but they hadn't decided a date. Gonzales was a lawyer and in Chantal's eyes was going to be the saviour of the next generation. Carlos pitied the poor fellow and the burden of keeping up to Chantal's high expectations.

Then in May, Chantal wrote to her son Carlos to say that Joelle and her fiancé Gonzales would be coming to London in early June for three days as part of a European tour.

Carlos wrote back saying that he would invite them to see him performing at the Troubadour club and show them the Isabella Plantation in Richmond Park. 'The Camellias and Rhododendrons should be magnificent at that time of the year. Tell them to bring some sturdy walking shoes.'

Carlos and Joelle had mutual respect. They had completely different personalities but fully accepted their differences. Joelle had a serenity about her. She was a classical beauty, studying ballet from the age of two. Combined with the Yoga, Tai Chi and Transcendental Meditation, people often found her tranquillity daunting. Her long straight blonde hair, piercing blue eyes, and self-assured composure, gave no hint of her South American background, most people thought of her as a detached Scandinavian.

Carlos saw past Joelle's beauty and poise, admiring her kindness and empathy towards others. She in turn appreciated Carlos's robust creativity and, in some ways, felt that she missed out on the spontaneity of life. Although different, they both felt comfortable and relaxed in each other's company. Intrigued, they looked forward to getting to know their respective partners.

The first night of their visit was a complete disaster. Gonzales, dressed in a dark suit, black shirt and diagonal stripped tie, entered the Troubadour club, instantly knowing that this wasn't the place for him. He looked down his nose at Carlos and the only thing that the two men had in common was that they both spoke Spanish with a similar dialect from the streets of Caracas.

The good news was that Gonzales had prearranged a series of business meetings in the "City" during the next day, and suggested that Joelle might like to catch up with Carlos and Alex for lunch somewhere. It was agreed that the three of them should meet at Richmond, where there were some fine English pubs along the river and around the Green.

They enjoyed a splendid day in Richmond, before walking along the riverbank behind Kew Gardens, then all the way home to Barnes for a welcome cup of tea.

Joelle took her leave, saying Gonzales had planned the itinerary for the rest of their stay in London. A driver would take them to Windsor Castle before a quick visit to Hampton Court. Then the following day, the same driver would take them to Oxford and onto Blenheim palace, but because Gonzales had to attend important last-minute meetings, the trip to Blenheim had to be cancelled. Joelle was pleased to have a quiet day to herself, appreciating a pleasant visit to the Royal Academy, a stroll through intimate arcades, culminating in a spot of afternoon tea at the Ritz. Joelle enjoyed her own company. It gave her time to think.

The next day Joelle and Gonzales left for Paris and then on to numerous other European capital cities. When they returned home to Caracas, Joelle went to live with her parents, telling Gonzales that she needed to take some time apart. Joelle felt somewhat in limbo and didn't have the courage to cut all ties. She deferred broaching the subject of calling off the wedding, preferring the path of least resistance.

* * *

It was about four weeks later at 4:49pm, on a damp Wednesday afternoon, when Carlos was woken from reading his book, by a knock on the front door. Carlos went to see who it could be and there on the porch was a young delivery man from the Post Office. 'Telegram for a Mr Carlos Kaspar' said the young man in a high-pitched voice. 'I will need some photographic identification. Passport if you have one.'

Carlos went to fetch his passport and then signed the required form. As the young delivery man sped off on his little Honda 50 motorbike, Carlos went back into the house, to find an appropriate implement to open the telegram that would completely change the rest of his life.

< URGENT-NEED-TO-TALK-WITH-YOU >
< WILL-CALL-YOU-AT-6-PM-BST >
< WOLFGANG-BERNSTEIN >

Wolfgang was the business partner of his father, Emile. 'What does he want to talk about that is so urgent,' thought Carlos. He made himself a cup of tea, as the English do when they want to kill some time and spread out on the sofa to continue with reading his book. He was reading Jamaica Inn by Daphne Du Maurier and had become fully engrossed when the phone brought him back from darkest Cornwall. It was Wolfgang from Caracas. On the dot of 6pm.

'Carlos, I have some tragic news to tell you,' said Wolfgang, in a rather solemn voice. 'Your mother, father and two sisters have been killed in a plane crash.' Carlos heard the words but couldn't respond. 'Are you there?' said Wolfgang thinking that the line had dropped out.

'Yes,' replied Carlos 'What do you mean were killed?'

'There was a terrible accident in the mountains near Merida,' replied Wolfgang with a tremble in his voice. 'It appears that their plane lost altitude. Emile was flying them to a skiing holiday, but something must have gone terribly wrong.'

Time stood still as Carlos failed to register the magnitude of the disaster. He was completely stunned and couldn't speak. His world took leave, as the moment froze into a cold emptiness. Wolfgang felt the silence to be deafening and realised that he wasn't likely to get a response from Carlos at that time. 'Perhaps I should ring you back in say an hour and we can talk about it,' suggested Wolfgang.

'Yes, that might be a good idea,' replied Carlos, abruptly putting the phone back on the hook.

Before the hour was up Alex had returned home to find the stunned Carlos, looking blankly at his cold cup of tea. No tears had been shed, but his eyes were bloodshot. Carlos managed to convey the tragedy that had occurred, asking Alex if she would take the forthcoming call from Wolfgang. In her cool and calm manner, she took the call in the bedroom, asking Wolfgang all the right questions. How, When, Where and what needed to be done? She could then relay the information to Carlos when he was in a fit state to take such dreadful news.

Carlos slept sporadically for three days but even then, found it difficult to do anything except sit and stare into space. Life seemed to escape him; time lost its meaning.

It would be Wolfgang and the other medical partners who would make the necessary arrangements for death certificates, funerals, and numerous other items. Carlos was in a daze and stayed put in Barnes totally incommunicado. Alex saw her fiancé sliding away but could do little about it. It was a full three months before Carlos decided that he wanted to go to Caracas to see for himself what was happening.

Alex went with him, and they stayed at the Bernstein's for a total of six days before Carlos decided that he could take it no more. He closed the unhappy chapter of his life, going back to London, hoping to patch together some sort of existence.

Emile and Chantal had made mirrored Wills leaving everything to their surviving children. They had also stated that they wanted a funeral ceremony to be held by a Yanomami chieftain in Territorias Amazonas. This ceremony was duly carried out. Their charred bones were pulverised to a pulp with certain fruits from the jungle being added to make a concoction, that was then ceremoniously drunk by the fifty strong tribe's men and women.

The first item on Emile and Chantal Wills, that of leaving everything to the surviving children was never carried out, Carlos received nothing but sad memories. The house and all their worldly chattels were spirited into thin air and never fully accounted for. As Wolfgang Bernstein explained to Carlos, 'There were countless sharks circling around gorging on every morsel.'

It didn't help that a few months later, Alex gave birth prematurely to their first child. The boy was still born and so was whisked away without either parent having seen him. If the child had lived, they had agreed to call him Davit. Perhaps under the circumstances it had been for the best as the situation was not conducive for the upbringing of a baby. On the other hand, a child might have symbolised a new beginning and brought Carlos out of his despondency. As it was, this unfortunate incident, only threw Carlos deeper into despair.

It would be seven years later that Alex would give birth to a delightful and much cherished little boy. Like all the males of the family, Robert was born with the familiar birthmark behind his left ear. This birthmark was to play an important identification role in time to come.

* * *

Carlos died of a brain tumour and a broken heart when Robert was just 11 years old. Robert and his mother Alex continued to live in the small house in Barnes, not knowing what was to unfold.

39

The Top End

Having left my suitcase full of city clothes with my cousin Jeremy, I bought myself a cheap rucksack and headed north. I took a bus up to Brisbane where I stayed for a couple of days before moving further north to Bundaberg. There, I stopped for three weeks to help some friends of my father, sort out a small holding that they had just bought. Then on to my destination Cairns in the far north of Queensland.

* * *

It was May 1975, and in those days, Cairns was a sleepy outback town. I stayed in a youth hostel, where I heard from others about a small youth hostel near Tinaroo Dam in the Atherton Tablelands.

I took the tourist train to Kuranda, then made my way to the Youth Hostel at Tinaroo, a house with three large bedrooms. It could sleep a maximum of ten people, but there was also plenty of space outside to pitch a tent. A woman in the nearby town, kept an eye on the place, taking the money from the hostelers. When I arrived, there were only a couple of people staying at the hostel, but they left the next morning, having already stayed their allowed three nights. I had the place to myself.

Near to the youth hostel was a National Fitness camp, a large rather dilapidated building. I went to look around and got chatting to one of the painters who had just started painting the whole building. It transpired that he was employed by a RED employment scheme. He told me that if I wanted a job, I would have to sign on at the Commonwealth Employment Offices in Atherton. The next day I started work. The woman running the youth hostel said that because I was working, I wasn't considered a hosteller, so allowed me to stay longer than the three days. In return I ran the youth hostel for her, so she only had to visit on a weekly basis.

By day I was a painter, but by night I was a youth hosteller. There was a party every night, but I had to go to work at 8am the next morning. I received a travel allowance to walk all of fifty metres to work. As the middle of July approached, more young people came to stay at the youth hostel to get away from the winter down south.

After a couple of months, I was pleased to see that the painting job was nearing completion and it would soon be time for me to be moving on.

* * *

One evening, some new people arrived at the hostel. A young man called Peter had travelled all the way from Perth in an old Land Rover, via Adelaide, Melbourne, and then up the east coast of Australia, picking up hitch hikers along the way. Over a barbeque and a bottle of red from the Barossa Valley, he told me that he intended to go back to Perth via Darwin, the Kimberley's and then down the west coast of Australia back to Perth.

'Any chance of a lift,' I said with a cheeky smile.

'No worries mate, only I've got to go up to Cooktown but will be back on Tuesday. How far are you thinking you want to go?' he asked matter of factually.

Peter, true to his word, returned from Cooktown on the Tuesday afternoon with a couple of young hitchhikers that were also subjecting themselves to a trip of a lifetime across the top end and down the west coast of Western Australia, some four thousand five hundred kilometres to Perth. Unwin, a softly spoken young man from Toronto in Canada with his totally inappropriate suitcase and helpless demeanour contrasted with the other hitchhiker, Bazza the outback bushy type from somewhere but nowhere in particular. On the Wednesday we stocked up with supplies from Atherton, and in the evening cooked up a gigantic dinner over which we discussed our route to Darwin. Unwin declared that he was a vegetarian but ate eggs and drank milk for protein. Bazza in stark contrast, declared that he didn't eat vegetables and usually just ate the animals that he caught and skinned. Peter and I were the two omnivores who could eat and drink anything that happened to come our way. It was agreed that we would share the cost of petrol, food and general supplies but any repairs to the vehicle would be at Peter's expense.

Thursday morning at the crack of dawn the four of us with ample supplies for the next three days, set off in Pete's long wheel-base Land Rover that had a winch at the front to get us out of difficulties. Bazza had his sizeable knife to skin and cut up his prey, Unwin had his various labelled containers with copious amounts of organic dried fruits and an assortment of different cereals. Peter had all the functional things like toilet paper and cooking utensils while I had my sketch pad and a small blues harmonica in the key of C.

We loaded up the roof rack with what seemed huge amounts of necessary stuff, most of which belonged to Unwin, and set off inland towards Chillagoe to see the caves. I sat in the back with Unwin, Peter drove, while Bazza sort of navigated.

In the evening we camped off road and made a fire. After dinner, Peter would read a Mickey Spillane novel, I discussed *War and Peace* with Unwin, promising not to spill the storyline, while Bazza went walkabout. I continued to plough my way through some of the German writers such as Thomas Mann and Hermann Hesse. I was particularly struck by Hesse's *Narcissus and Goldmund*, and how he introduced the interplay between the intellect and the creative.

The sealed roads became treacherous dirt tracks, forcing us on many occasions to dig our way out of 'Bull Dust'. Thankfully, we had that winch at the front of the vehicle to use as a last resort.

Soon communication between the four of us became strained. Liaisons were formed. Bazza communicated with Peter, who in turn communicated with me, but I was the only one who conversed with Unwin, as outright hostility developed between Unwin and Bazza.

Like a little dinghy, becalmed in an ocean of outback desert, we all began to show signs of disintegration.

I sat in the luggage compartment in the back of the Land Rover and played my blues harmonica while watching the road, like life, vanish into the distance. Spinifex as far as the eye could see.

We made our way to Fitzroy Crossing before the September rains came. From Broome, south to see the wildflowers. Sometimes we would pitch camp in the dark, only to wake up to a sea of colour as far the eye could see.

On the last night before we got to Perth, we decided to have a final dinner and a few drinks together. It was then that I brought up the subject of the discordance between the four of us. Suddenly everyone started voicing their feelings, clearing the stale air. Even Bazza expressed his views on the matter, but just fell short of apologizing for his behaviour.

The next day Peter drove Unwin and me to the Youth Hostel in Perth. We never heard from each other again. It was as if the trip of a lifetime had been marred by the conflicts between the differing personalities.

* * *

The four thousand, five-hundred-kilometre drive soon melted into the past as my attention turned to Perth and getting a job to replenish my depleted bank account.

Finding a job in an architect's office never seemed to be much of a problem for me. I looked in the local paper and found a plum job, close to the main gates of the Botanic Gardens at Kings Park. I then found a flat nearby, taking over the last three months of a lease from a young British couple who wanted to return to the UK.

With a good job, and a flat in easy walking distance, the next thing seemed to be acquiring a car. Public transport wasn't the best and there was a lot to see at the weekends. I had met a young man called Ron in a pub who told me that he did up and sold used cars. Ron was an East End cockney, who had come out to Perth on a £10 sponsored ticket and was trying to save enough money to get back home. I told him that I was in the market to buy a car, but it was difficult to get around to inspect what was on offer. I would spend hours getting there only to find that it wasn't worth the trip. Either the car was hopeless, or it had been sold. Ron told me that he would bring a car to the office for me to try at lunch time. Sure enough, the next day at midday there was Ron on the opposite side of the street leaning against some brute of a car for me to test drive. 'But Ron the gears are totally stuffed, you can't expect me to drive this,' I said after trying to get the gear lever to work.

Eventually one lunch time he turned up with a beaten-up 1961 VW Beetle. I could hardly keep a straight face as I said, 'Blimey Ron, they are getting worse.'

'Don't judge a book by its cover, me ol dad used to say,' he replied, grinning. 'This car has a good ticker. She ain't a good looker but she's cheap and will get you around to have a look at other cars you might want to buy.'

His logic made sense. At least I could get around to find something I really wanted. I realise now that I had been a bit spoilt by having a father in the 'Motor Trade', and I had a lot to learn about cars and their mechanical idiosyncrasies.

Some would say the car had a rustic charm, but I didn't quite see it that way. A straight galvanised pipe acted as a front bumper – Roo bar. The lack of rear seating left a big void; good for carrying luggage but no good for passengers. Major dents in each corner of the car and bodywork that had been hand painted yellow and purple, with what must have been washable paint, had left a psychedelic mess where the colours had merged. The car looked a proper sight.

'Ok, ok, let's give her a go,' I said trying to be positive.

Ron handed me the keys and a screwdriver saying 'You'll need this to open the driver's door. Just poke it in the hole and give it clockwise turn.'

Sure enough, the driver's door didn't have a handle, but the screwdriver did the job. I sat in the driver's seat and adjusted the cracked mirror. I gingerly turned the ignition key and immediately that familiar Beetle sound belted out of the back, but because of the gaping hole in the exhaust system, the sound was magnified, and was able to be heard in the neighbouring suburb of Subiaco. Apart from the horrendous noise, the car drove beautifully and the gears although a bit sloppy, worked smoothly.

We went back to the office to negotiate a price. Ron wanted $250, saying that he would throw in some muffler bandage and the screwdriver.

We agreed on $200, and he could keep his bandage, but I would take the screwdriver. We had a deal. I counted out the cash in new $20 notes and we did the relevant paperwork. I noticed that the car had South Australian registration plates and asked Ron if the car had been stolen. He assured me that he knew the young girl who had previously owned the car and she had recently driven back across the Nullarbor Plains. He told me that when her mother saw the car, she was so appalled, that she asked Ron to sell it. It sounded all good to me and anyway I had Ron's phone number. I was pleased to now be the owner of what turned out to be a truly beautiful relationship, between a man and his car. Betsey and I formed a very fruitful interdependency that lasted the test of time.

I drove my new car, well new to me, to the back of the office and down the ramp into the underground parking area. The noise from the blown muffler was horrendous. The senior partner, Duncan Law, was aghast as he saw this apparition of a yellow and purple VW Beetle, but the senior associate calmly guided me into a parking space between his green Daimler and David Stern's brand-new blue Jaguar.

'Nice car,' said Duncan as I rather embarrassedly alighted from Betsy. 'That would be a 61 model, I think. You might want my friend Hans at Lannocks Motors to have a quick look at it. He was trained in the VW factory in Wolfsburg and knows everything there is to know about VWs. Tell him I sent you. By the way Stern, being Jewish, won't be too pleased you have bought a German car but take no notice of him.'

Early the next morning I took my Betsey round to Lannocks and met Hans. To my surprise he had a doctor's stethoscope around his neck as he had just been listening to some gear grumbles in a Karman Ghia.

'Not a problem Michael,' said Hans in his strong German accent. 'Vee vill have a good look at everythink and vill get back to you soon.'

I told Hans about the missing door handle and that he would need a screwdriver to open it.

'No vurries myte. Vee has plenty of screw drivers and I has zee 61 handles also. By ser vay are yous related to Emile Kaspar.' Once again, this name surfaced but I just brushed it aside as unimportant.

I hurried back to my office, leaving Betsey in good hands. Around 11:30am Hans called me to say that they would fix the muffler and then do a tune up and service and that I could pick up the car around 6:15pm that evening.

Hans did warn me that spark plug number three was rusted in but seemed to work ok. He told me that this was a common problem with Beetles as the filter tower prevented the cool air generated by the fan to get to number three spark plug. He warned me that one day and completely out of the blue I would hear a big bang as number three spark plug would erupt out of its socket and hit the underside of the hood. That would be the best time to get it fixed, but in the meantime, he had done a complete service in terms of grease, oil change and timing. He had fixed the exhaust system as well as put a new door handle on the driver's door. Betsey was totally rejuvenated and purred to show her appreciation.

I decided not to cause any angst with David Stern, so kept Betsey near my flat and walked the seven minutes to work. Betsey couldn't help being German and I had no intention of renaming her Berta. It would only confuse her, and besides, she had enough problems of her own.

* * *

After a year of exploring Perth and its surrounding areas, I felt it was time to move on and see more of Australia. I had really enjoyed Perth and thought it would certainly be a place to come back to. I carefully chose a time, when we were in between projects and twiddling our thumbs, to explain my desire to my boss Duncan. He was more than understanding, not only assuring me that there would always be a job for me if I ever came back to Perth, but also gave me the name of an architect to see when I arrived in Adelaide. On my last Friday, Duncan signed my British Professional Practice logbook, before we all went out for drinks and dinner.

I had planned to leave for Adelaide on the Saturday but due to a rather pounding hangover, it was the Sunday morning around 6:15am when Betsey and I said farewell to Perth and headed off towards Adelaide. It would be a new adventure for me but of course it would be just a homecoming for Betsey.

40

The Harbour Bridge

I set off for Adelaide early on Sunday morning. I wanted to beat any traffic and the midday heat. It was early in November and the days were getting longer.

I had decided to continue my travels around the coast in an anticlockwise direction. 'Just keep the water on your right and you will eventually get back to where you started,' had been the advice given to me by an elderly gentleman before I left Sydney.

Betsey, being originally from South Australia seemed to know the way and undaunted kept up a steady pace. She rattled a bit here and there but nothing to worry about. I wound down all the windows to feel the wind. Although we had travelled around Perth and its environs together, this was the first time we had shared the open road. The sense of freedom was exhilarating.

* * *

You could be forgiven to think that Nullarbor is an Aboriginal name, but it is in fact a name derived from the Latin – "Null Arbor" meaning "No Tree". It certainly did live up to its name, as the newly built fully sealed highway traversed endless miles of nothing but spinifex either side. Betsey ploughed forth effortlessly as if in a hurry to get to the South Australian border, just passed Eucla. At the border, a sign about not taking fruit into South Australia was there to greet us. As we crossed into South Australia the road became a potholed nightmare.

On the way into Adelaide, I decided to have a look at the newly created satellite town of Elizabeth just to the north of Adelaide. Naming the new town Elizabeth after Queen Elizabeth II, seemed to be no better than naming a town Adelaide after Queen Adelaide. The Australians still revered the English monarchy even though the British had cut the ties with Australia by joining Europe. It's a bit like the grown-up child who still lives at home.

* * *

It was the 19th of November when Betsy and I rolled into Adelaide. Little did we know that it would become home, and in my case for more than forty years.

I'm not exactly sure what happened when I arrived in Adelaide, but it seemed like my searching was over. I needed a rest and where better to stay than the sleepy backwater town that Adelaide used to be. The city of churches with a pub on every corner seemed to be in perfect harmony. The gridded city centre, with parklands surrounding the central square mile, gave a sense of order, like a well-tempered Bach fugue. The river Torrens meandered gracefully along the edge of the city. A central square, with two perpendicular axes through the middle, divided the city into four quadrants, each with their own smaller square. To the east, the Adelaide hills, and to the west, the beaches and Spencer Gulf, formed limits to a city of less than one million inhabitants. It was a city where one could breathe.

It was mid-November, and the Jacaranda blossom was in full flight, giving off a gentle indigo haze. Ducks with a dozen baby ducklings were waddling around everywhere and there were even the pictorial street signs warning drivers of their presence.

* * *

Once again, my work ethic kicked in and I decided I needed a job. I printed out my CV and thought I would drop it in to a variety of offices around the city. A lot of businesses are pushing to complete projects before the Christmas break, and it is usually all hands-on deck. Duncan

Law, my boss in Perth, had given me the name of some architects that I should visit when I got to Adelaide. I followed up a couple of names without much success except for a handshake. Then I tried a firm at Palmer Place in North Adelaide, and I asked to speak with a Mr Vale the head of the company. I presented my photocopied 'Letter of Reference' from Duncan Law to the receptionist and was asked to wait in the plush reception foyer.

Finally, I was ushered into Mr Vale's office, and we talked for a while. I showed him some of the sketches that I had made while travelling around Australia, he seemed suitably impressed.

'I would love to be in a position to offer you a job,' said John Vale, 'but the only position I have at the moment is in Sydney. We have set up a satellite office in Paddington and we need to get a big project out before Christmas. It's the first stage of a large shopping centre out at Camberwell. I can only offer you a couple of weeks work, but you never know it could lead to something else after Christmas.'

I declined the offer saying, 'I had hoped to stay a bit longer in Adelaide and would keep trying.' I thanked him for his offer and went across the road to sit on a park bench to write an aerogram to my parents back in London. I wanted to let them know that I had left Perth and had made it across the Nullarbor to Adelaide. I started to write about Mr Vale's suggestion and then mid-sentence paused and wrote 'I wonder if his offer still stands. I think I will go back and ask him.' I stopped writing the letter, walked back into the office, and asked to speak with John Vale again. He was somewhat surprised to see me and even more surprised when I asked him if the job was still available.

'Yes, as far as I know the job is still available,' he replied. 'When could you start?'

'I could leave straight away and drive through the night,' I replied enthusiastically. 'It's 3.45pm now, and I reckon I could be in Sydney by 9am tomorrow morning. As they are half an hour in front of us and allowing for a couple of hours sleep along the way, I should be able to start work at midday tomorrow. Is that okay?'

'I admire your enthusiasm but let me make a phone call to Sydney and tell Drew Chambers that you are coming over. Don't forget to take those sketches of yours as I'm sure Drew would love to see them.'

'I have all my possessions in the back of my car, so of course I will have to take them with me.' I replied with a smile.

I'm not sure what John Vale thought as he came out to see me off. There was a slight hesitation in his voice as I introduced him to Betsey. He shook my hand with vigour as he said, 'Do drive carefully young man, and try to avoid those big red kangaroos.'

Once again Betsey and I were on the road but this time driving through the approaching night and into the darkness of the Australian outback.

* * *

We crossed the Hay plains as the sun was setting, and then on to Wagga Wagga. No big Reds in sight and Betsey coasted without missing a beat. We rested for a couple of hours and then cruised through the morning light, and onto Sydney. Luckily, I had made really good time and managed to catch both Linda and Sally my old flat mates in Neutral Bay, before they went off to work.

I explained my sudden reappearance asking if I could sleep on their couch for a few days.

'No worries mate,' said Linda as she made some toast and marmalade for me. 'Make yourself at home. You will need a front door key.' We agreed to catch up that evening as they both were in a rush to get to work.

I was at the office by 11am and Drew Chambers was pleased to see me, they were desperately trying to get a large project out to tender before Christmas. 'We need to get our architectural drawings and specification all sorted out by the 10th of December so we can get the consultants sets of documents back for checking by the 17th,' he explained while showing me around the small office of just five staff and a receptionist-cum-typist. It was all hands on deck.

That evening, I could hardly keep awake, so we decided to postpone our night out at the pub until the weekend. During the next couple of days, I seemed to do nothing but work. I phoned my friend Dennis at Barrington Architects, the first office I had worked at on my arrival in Australia. I reminded him about the squash ball in my eye and he jokingly said he was up for a rematch. I declined his offer and told him that one injury was enough. He invited me to have a drink with him at the office on Friday evening. 'I'm sure you would be most welcome; we would love to hear all about your trip up north. Hope you took lots of photos,' he said, and I wasn't shy in taking up his offer.

* * *

I asked some of the staff at the Paddington office, where I could get my VW Beetle tuned and serviced. I told them about the car I had bought in Perth and how I had driven all the way to Sydney without a problem. Apparently, there was a Lannocks, VW centre in Bondi Junction, so I called them and as it happened there was a vacancy on Monday morning.

I got there at 8:15am and told the head mechanic that I had just driven over from Perth. He just laughed. I told him not to bother about the problem with number three spark plug and he said he would just have to do the best he could. I took a taxi back to Paddington and was there by 9am. That afternoon I got a call from the garage, telling me that my car was ready to be picked up. I took a taxi back to the garage and paid the money, which was almost double what I had paid for a similar service in Perth. As I drove back to the office, Betsey spluttered once or twice. I thought perhaps it would be something with the three new spark plugs or perhaps she didn't like the electronic tuning. I didn't think too much about it.

We were asked to work late that night as the boss was rather worried about keeping in front of our schedule. He thought it would be better to put in a couple of late nights earlier on, rather than waiting until the final few days, and having to put in all-nighters. The boss took us out to get something to eat, and we were back in the office around 7:30pm. Around 1:30am it was decided to call it a night, as we had entered the realms of diminishing returns. Betsey seemed not be her normal self and didn't start immediately. We were driving over the Sydney Harbour Bridge back to Neutral Bay, when out of the blue Betsey spluttered what seemed to be her last breath and died.

I decided to start walking and found one of the emergency phones that are positioned every two hundred metres along the length of the bridge. I was still a member of the NRMA from when I had previously

308

lived in Sydney, but they weren't allowed to come onto the bridge to attend to broken down vehicles. A man from the bridge authority towed me off the bridge and told me that he would call the NRMA breakdown service for me. Unfortunately, it was at least twenty-five years before the advent of mobile phones. At about 3am in the morning an NRMA mechanic drove up and I showed him my driver's license and NRMA card. I explained that I had driven Betsey all the way from Perth and had that day, taken her to be serviced at Lannocks at Bondi Junction. The man burst into laughter. The mechanic asked me to open the bonnet at the back of the car and start the engine. He seemed to immediately know what the problem was and opened up the distributor and fiddled around for no more than ten seconds. He asked me to start her up again. Betsey roared back to life.

'It's really simple mate,' he said still laughing. 'They hadn't tightened up this little wire in the distributor. This one connects the points to the condenser.' It was all mumbo jumbo to me, but I was glad that he knew what he was talking about, but even more pleased that Betsey was back to her normal bright self.

As I drove back to the flat at Neutral Bay, I thought to myself I should really know a bit more about cars. My father had always told me not to fiddle about with my car but to bring it in to his garage as it would still be under warranty. Betsey was way past her warranty date but certainly not past her "use by date". I decided that when I got back to Adelaide, I would enrol in an eight-week car maintenance course for beginners that had been advertised at the YMCA. That course and also the one I did on Transcendental Meditation were to prove most useful in stressful times ahead.

* * *

With all the documents for the project in Sydney completed, collated and copies sent off to the various tenderers for quoting, I returned to Adelaide just in time for Christmas. I had picked up my suitcase and some other belongings that had been at my cousin Jeremy's garage and was pleased to head back to the relaxed, yet festive atmosphere that Adelaide had to offer.

The years slipped by, and I was too busy to stop what I was doing. The architectural work fell in a hole as an economic recession hit hard. It didn't seem to bother me, as it gave me time to pursue other interests.

Betsey and I found a comfortable studio flat with a lean-to carport on Waterfall Gully Road and as long as I kept my expenses down, I could happily live on the income from my house in London. I was in Mr Micawber's chosen country and heeded well his advice on happiness.

Annual income twenty pounds, annual expenditure nineteen pounds nineteen and six, result happiness. Annual income twenty pounds, annual expenditure twenty pounds, nought and six, result misery.

* * *

I would spend my days walking in the Adelaide hills or along the endless sandy beaches. I played a bit of tennis and started to learn some basic cooking. I thought of becoming vegetarian but most of the vegetarians I knew looked so emaciated and besides I really loved the taste of meat.

41

The Missing Spark

I seemed to be floating along, enjoying the glorious summer weather, the cricket, the tennis, and time at the beach. On Boxing Day each year, I booked and made a rather crackly phone call to my parents to tell them that I was still alive and that all was well. On Australia Day, 26th January 1976, I became a true Aussie, taking up Australian citizenship by swearing allegiance to the queen of England. Somehow, I only needed to be in Australia one year before I could apply for citizenship. My father had always told me to take whatever citizenship I could get as long as I didn't have to give up my British passport. Life was good and I kept putting off the need for looking for work.

* * *

Eventually I decided to look for a new job. The economic recession over, I had no difficulty finding a job and started work in an office housed in a heritage mansion in Brougham Place, North Adelaide. Isaac Lovedale ran a tight ship with a crew of eight people. Both Isaac and his associate Peter Sloane had separate rooms upstairs while the rest of the staff comprising of, a recently graduated Architect, three competent drafters, a secretary and an interior designer were all housed downstairs in one large room. I was introduced to the staff and was told that I would oversee the detailed design of a large Tourist complex to be built at Wirrina, on the way to Victor Harbor. I was given a set of preliminary sketch design drawings to mull over as well as some of the previous schemes that had been archived.

'You might like to familiarise yourself with the project, as I have arranged for the Structural Engineers to fly over from Sydney tomorrow morning for the first consultants' meeting,' said Isaac Lovedale. 'Don't hesitate to ask if you have any questions.'

That afternoon the office had a gentle hum as the drafters, and the rather cute secretary called Suzie, were busy doing their work. Some classical music played softly in the background. Then suddenly the door burst open and in strode the forbidding figure of a man who hurled down an eighty-page Specification onto the secretary's desk. It landed with a thump and was followed with a booming voice saying, 'This just isn't good enough, there are fourteen spelling errors, and you will need to correct them immediately. I haven't marked them off, so you will just have to go through it yourself.' With that he turned around and left the room slamming the door behind him.

Poor Suzie burst into tears as the drafters huddled around her desk in a consoling manner. This was my introduction to the tyrant called Peter Sloane. After a few minutes, one of the drafters, called Barbara, turned to me and asked, 'Did you see that? What do you think? He's the most despicable man on the planet.' She obviously wanted me to join in on his condemnation and frankly it would have been easy to do so.

I was put on the spot but felt I needed to respond. As it was my first day and I wasn't too sure of the lie of the land, I answered by saying, 'You know I have worked in a number of offices, and they all seem to have one thing in common, that is, there is always a difficult person that people talk about behind their back. One day when I am working in an office and there is no one that is being talked about, I shall start to get very worried.' I paused and observed the questioning frown on all their faces. 'You see,' I continued, 'when there is no one who is being talked about, I will start to think that perhaps it is me that they are talking about. I'm more than happy that you talk about this Peter Sloane, but he needs to be confronted rather than tolerated.'

* * *

Architectural work in Adelaide became sporadic. I had tried my luck with Project Homes but found the work so boring and repetitive that I thought it would be better to become a contract architect rather than a full-time employee. I didn't have a family to support and with the rent that I received from my house in London, I could afford to take 'time out' rather than wasting my life chained to a drawing board.

* * *

Then one Sunday afternoon and completely out of the blue, I had a phone call from my old school chum Billy Mollett. Billy had been with me at Prep School, Public School, Art School and had also lived in my house in London. He was now living in Melbourne working as an art director for a prestigious advertising agency. Billy had married his sweetheart Carly and together with his two young children had moved to Melbourne.

'What are you doing here in Oz?' I asked Mollett. 'You seem to be following me everywhere like a bad smell,' I laughed even though I had used this same joke numerous times over the years.

I was invited to visit them in their mansion in Toorak. I had only known Carly as Billy's girlfriend and after I left for Australia, Carly moved into my house with Billy and an architect colleague of mine, Janek Novotny. After a year or so Billy and Carly had married and moved to Clapham leaving Janek in charge of the house.

Once again, Betsey my little VW Beetle and I hit the highway. As we climbed up into the Adelaide hills on our start to Melbourne, I could feel Betsey was happy to be on the open road again, taking the steep ascent comfortably in third gear. We were nearing Tailem Bend and I was sort of entering a transcendental state, when suddenly there was a startling bang from the back of the car. It was like a shotgun or a mini explosion.

I immediately stopped the car and went round the back to see what had happened.

I opened the bonnet to expose that number three spark plug had finally decided to rip itself free. I had been warned that this could happen at any time and the only thing that could be done was to drive slowly to a garage to have it looked at. It would need someone to drill a new thread into the engine head. I had also been told that Betsey would be able to continue on the other three cylinders, as long as I blocked the hole that the freed spark plug had left behind. I wound a rag around the old spark plug and pushed it into the hole as hard as I could. We continued all the way to Melbourne, some six hundred and thirty kilometres, at forty kilometres an hour, as if nothing much had happened.

I enjoyed Melbourne with Billy and his family. Billy was at work during the day, so I found myself playing on the swings with the children in the local park.

I drove slowly back to Adelaide, reflecting on the situation. My major priority was to get Betsey up and running and then perhaps consider a trip back to London. When I finally got back to Adelaide, I bought myself a self-help book on how to repair VW Beetles. From California, the book was full of cartoons and quirky comments; it was just what I needed. The book, entitled *How to keep your Volkswagen alive: A manual of step-by-step procedures for the complete idiot*, started by stating which end was the front of the car and which end was the back! The engine being at the back makes it necessary to clarify such matters.

I followed each step with great precision and patience. It took me ten days to extract the engine block and have a new helicoil insert for number three sparkplug. I also had a full valve grind with new seatings and was ready to go.

As I turned the ignition key, the sound of Betsey spluttering to life again became a pivotal moment for me. My father had always thought of me as totally useless as far as practical matters were concerned. Here some ten thousand miles away, I had managed to prove him wrong. I could do it if I put my mind to it.

* * *

Buoyed by my success I felt it was time to return to London to face my father. It is said that in order for a young man to become a true individual, he must go through a 'Rite of Passage' in which he must defeat his father. I metaphorically had my boxing gloves on, ready for the fight.

I had been away three years or so and had travelled around Australia, bought a house, and most importantly fixed my car. I knew that my father was disappointed that I hadn't got married and had children. I would simply tell him that I hadn't met the right girl yet.

Another reason for the trip was to sign some papers for the sale of my house in Kingston. Janek had decided to buy a flat in Richmond and was leaving the house. To my amazement he had found a buyer for the house and my father's solicitor had organised the conveyancing. They could have sent me the papers to sign, but I thought it a good excuse to travel back to see what was going on. Besides Bob Dylan was to perform at the Hammersmith Odeon.

I arrived weary and worn out at Heathrow airport and was met by my mother. 'Where's Dad?' I asked after giving her a big hug.

'He's parking the car,' she replied. 'I'm afraid to say that he isn't the same man that you left behind three years ago.' This turned out to be one of my mother gross understatements. There in the distance, shuffling along the concourse towards us, was a hunched up old man that looked like a much older version of my father. He smiled a grinning smile as he shook my hand profusely.

As we shuffled slowly to the carpark, I realised that the fight was over before it had started. My father, having forgotten where he had put the car, had to call a special carpark attendant to help us find it.

* * *

My dad had certainly gone away and left behind a shadow of himself. Although this shadow smiled and had a softness about him, I think I would have preferred the brusque joking father that I used to know. Gone was the spark and gone was his Middle Eastern vitality that could be so annoyingly stubborn.

Perhaps he too needed a helicoil and a new set of spark plugs.

42

The Completed Circle

I returned to Adelaide with a heavy heart. No one could say how long my father would live, but my mother urged me to go back home to Adelaide, assuring me that she could manage.

'Don't worry if I need you, you'll be the first to know,' she would repeat time and again, later it became 'I'm happy that you enjoy living in Australia, but I do wish it wasn't so far away.'

Each time I went back to London, my father's health had deteriorated. Each time I left London; I wondered if that had been the last time, I would see my father.

* * *

In the May of 1985, my mother and father moved to a smaller house in Ealing. She couldn't manage looking after such a big house and my ailing father. The process of moving must have been a nightmare. Their house in Acton was eventually bought by an Indian gentleman who was a central figure in the diamond business at Hatton Gardens. The new house in the Brentham Estate would have been a quarter of the size of the house in Acton and consequently it felt very cramped.

On my visit back to London in 1987 my father had become immobile and just sat in a chair. In some ways it became easier for my mother, as he could no longer get up to so much mischief. My mother had kept my father's car in the garage and had filled it up with junk that she wanted to get rid of. I would arrive home around 7:45am and even though I had just had breakfast on the plane, I sat with them and enjoyed another one. We discussed plans for my holiday. It was just like coming home from boarding school, as out came the fatted calf. The only difference being that I was no longer considered the little boy; I was now the head of the family *in abstentia.*

'I feel the first thing we should do after we have finished breakfast is to empty the car at Greenford rubbish dump,' said my mother. 'Then we can have the car to make use of and do as we please.' She didn't drive a car, so decided to sell the car after I had gone back to Australia.

By 10:30am my mother and I were at the dump throwing all kinds of stuff onto the pile of rubbish. 'Oh, look at that,' she would cry. 'That's just what I was looking for,' and before I knew it, she was scrambling on the pile to get something. We usually came back with less than we had taken to throw out, but I must confess, it was sometimes a close thing. Her childlike exuberance contrasted greatly with my father who at that stage would sit on his chair, looking into space.

* * *

Back in Adelaide, I worked on a number of research items. None that one would call proper architecture. I was busy writing some papers regarding the work I was doing on the sensory perception of spaces. I had become interested in this subject from the time I had been hospitalised with both my eyes covered. I was aware that with the loss of sight, some of the other types of perception became heightened. I set up some workshops to explore what happens when people are deprived of a particular mode of perception. Many architects design solely from a visual premise. Blind people are very aware of spaces through sound and touch. This work, together with some papers I had written for an art and architecture symposium, became noticed by the new professor of architecture at Adelaide University. He invited me to join the staff as a part-time design tutor in his department. I enjoyed being a design tutor and from there became involved with numerous interesting projects.

One such assignment, was being the co-ordinator of an Oral History project funded by the Heritage Department to investigate the development of building techniques in South Australia. This entailed interviewing a selection of elderly gentlemen who had witnessed the changes to building methods that had taken place during their lifetime. Brick makers, carpenters, architects and building suppliers to name a few. I found the work fascinating and learnt a great deal about the making of Oral History, as well as the technical developments that had taken place in the Building Industry.

* * *

Another area that I became involved with was that of 'Trees'. Together with some colleagues of mine, I went one evening to a lecture that was given by an elderly gentleman called Richard St Barbe Baker. He had recently turned ninety years old and was still a fine figure of a man, speaking with great eloquence. In 1922, he had been a young man in his early thirties and having completed his qualifications as a botanist, had travelled to Kenya where he started an organisation called 'Men of the Trees'. He had recognised the need for a worldwide reforestation, and set out, with the help of remote tribesmen, to plant as many trees as possible. Cleverly he incorporated the planting of the trees to be part of a ritual, rather than an obligation. He had noticed that the tribesmen performed a dance routine to initiate any collaborative activity. The stamping of their feet and the singing of a song inspired the tribesmen to a greater sense of community. It was soon after the two-hour lecture given by this impressive ninety-year-old, that a small group was formed to establish a South Australian branch of 'Men of the Trees'. I was happy to join the committee and as a design tutor at the university, I would discuss with some of my students, the desperate need for reforestation of the Australian outback. Each time I mentioned the name of newly formed South Australian branch of 'Men of the Trees', I would receive a barrage of derogatory comments such as 'What about Women of the Trees?' Or other comments insinuating that we were male monkeys swinging in the trees. I spent more time combating the ridicule than explaining the need for trees.

At one of the following committee meetings, I vocalised my frustrations and suggested that we should change the name. One of the committee members was against the idea of changing the name saying that it held sacred and cultural significance. Luckily, the committee

318

chairperson suggested that we could hold a public debate to discuss the matter with all the members. I spoke for the motion to change the name and when the woman who opposed the motion arrived at the lectern, all she could say was, 'I don't know what to say, I think Michael is quite right.' A deafening silence was broken by much clapping and applause. The motion was carried unanimously, and the rest of the evening was then spent deciding what name would be appropriate. After much wrangling, the name 'Trees for Life' was formally adopted, and the organisation has grown from strength to strength. I would like to think that in part the success is due to the change of name.

* * *

It was around this time, that I met and fell head over heels with a feisty French woman called Fleur. We met by chance at the birthday party of a mutual friend called Alice. At Alice's request, I started playing the piano and then, tongue in cheek, invited anyone who wanted to learn to come and play with me. To my pleasant surprise, the most beautiful of the guests there, said she wanted to learn and sat beside me on the piano stool. I told her that with both of her index fingers she should play only the black notes, while I filled in with bluesy chords on the lower registers. We seemed to play well together and had a lot of fun. By 11pm the other guests had left the party and it was time for us to go. A week or two later, I invited Fleur to dinner but instead of just ringing her, I made a drawing of a fish on a circular plate and sent the invitation card to her through the mail. I know for certain that it wasn't my cooking of the dinner that attracted her to me, but like to think that it was the music we played together. We married a few years later and since then, Fleur has taken over the evening cooking duties on the understanding that I serenade her with improvisation on the piano. I have always felt that I get the better deal as she is the most excellent cook and I'm not that good at playing the piano. She seems to be able to make a splendid meal out of thin air and often quotes to me Shakespeare's opening lines of *Twelfth Night*.

* * *

It was mid-April of 2011 and I was preparing for my annual trip to London to see my mother, when out of the blue I received an email

319

from a good friend called Georgina Elland. I had first met Georgie at the Adelaide School of Art where she had been studying painting. After completing her final year, she had gone to Sydney in pursuit of a painting career and an older man. Things hadn't worked out for her on the romance side of things, but she had decided to stay in Sydney, as it offered her further career opportunities.

Her email told me that she had been spending time at a studio in Rome, where she had bumped into a young artist from London called Robert Kaspar. Apparently, Robert was completing his two-year stint in Rome, working on his scholarship at the British Academy. *'He says that he is of Armenian origin but has never come across you. I am just wondering if you are in some way related?'* she questioned in her email.

I immediately wrote back to Georgie to tell her that I hadn't come across this Robert Kaspar, but I would perhaps try to catch up with him. I asked for his email address so I could arrange to meet up with him while I was in London.

I got a reply from Robert saying he would love to catch up. He told me that he would be back in London from 1st May and gave me his UK mobile number.

I flew to London and gave Robert a call. We arranged to meet at the top of the ramp that goes down into Tate Modern at 11am the following Tuesday but, if it was raining, we should wait just inside the entrance doors.

Luckily it was a beautiful day and Robert was already there waiting at the top of the ramp. He looked striking with his completely shaved head, a bushy black beard and sporting a heavy rimmed set of Ray Ban sunglasses. We shook hands and I suggested that we should get ourselves a coffee. We found ourselves a table overlooking the river and the conversation seemed to flow. We found so many commonalities, but nothing to suggest that we were in anyway related.

Robert, some thirty years younger than me, seemed extremely mature for his age. He had started his Art education doing his foundation year at Kingston but had then gone to Central School of Art to study painting. After three years of post-graduate studies at the Royal College of Art, he had been awarded his Rome Scholarship. He told me that he had been promised some part-time teaching back at Kingston, but all he really wanted to do was further his career as an artist. Teaching was only a matter of paying the bills.

He spoke of his late father Carlos from South America and I spoke of my own father Hovan from Putney. We had no recognition of the names. Somehow, we spoke of playing Backgammon and shared numerous other common interests. We spoke for a while and then it suddenly happened.

Robert took off his Ray Ban sunglasses and as clear as daylight against his shiny baldness, there behind his left ear, was the family birthmark. The marking that had been carried down through the ages.

I began to dig deeper and started to talk about my grandfather Vahan, and how he had had an identical twin brother called Davit who had been blown up in an explosion in Constantinople. Robert gasped as I said the name 'Davit'. His father Carlos had always talked about his own grandfather Davit having an identical twin called Vahan, who they thought had been blown up in the explosion.

The drinking of coffee went on for hours that day, as our handed down stories unfolded. The stories seemed like a mirror image. A parallel universe that had finally come back together.

* * *

These revelations threw up more questions than answers and it obviously needed a lot more research. We agreed that as I had formally retired and had more time on my hands, I should research further and write down our story.

I remember saying to Robert, 'This could be the basis of a really interesting book,' and him replying, 'Perhaps a blockbuster film.'

'Hang on a minute,' I replied, 'let's get down the facts and then see where it takes us.'

43

Epilogue by Robert Kaspar

London – October 2017

It has been just over six years since I first met Michael at the top of the ramp at Tate Modern in London. We immediately formed a close bond as he worked tirelessly on researching our separated but reconnected pasts.

After our first meeting at Tate Modern, Michael returned to London with his wife Fleur on several occasions and together we have discussed the book that he was writing, sometimes well into the early hours of the morning. Michael and Fleur bought a small garden flat in Richmond as a pied-à-terre and have certainly made good use of it. Fleur is the most exquisite cook, she could somehow out of nothing create a scrumptious feast. Being French doesn't necessarily mean that one knows how to cook, but in her case being French has certainly helped. She has many relatives dotted all over France and would usually go to visit them during June and July. Michael and I would take the opportunity to travel to all kinds of remote places in search of details to be included in his book.

I last saw Michael a couple of months ago, when we travelled together to Yerevan the capital of Armenia. He was keen to follow up on some documents that could possibly enlighten him on unresolved queries.

Why had there been the explosion at Harat and Anar's house in Constantinople? Why had there been the fire at the island of San Lazzaro near Venice? What had caused my grandfather Emile's, plane to crash at Merida in the mountains of Venezuela?

There seemed to be a fragile thread that connected these vile acts of destruction. It felt like a treacherous vendetta, but by whom and why?

* * *

Last August, Michael and I travelled around Armenia together, in search of a letter that Abbot Artoush, the head monk at San Lazzaro, had given to his sister Miriam in Venice, asking her to forward it to their brother Haig Sarkissian in Yerevan. Michael had been convinced that this letter would be the key to revealing many answers that had been eluding both of us. At the last minute, Michael had heard that a descendant of Haig Sarkissian, living in a town called Gyumri, a hundred kilometres north of Yerevan, might have some clues as to where this letter might be.

I had commitments back in London, so I left Michael to go alone to see this Narek Sarkissian. Michael and I said our goodbyes as I took a taxi from our hotel to the airport.

'I will let you know what this Narek says about the letter. Please give my love to your mother Alex,' were Michael's parting words, as my taxi drove off.

I was aware that Michael intended to then go to Istanbul, and on to Moscow for a few days, to check up on some items. He felt that he needed to add some further description to make the cities come alive and as he would say "Live in the page". He would then fly back to Adelaide to continue polishing up his manuscript before sending it out into the marketplace for publishing.

It was two days later that I received his email from Gyumri, Armenia:

From: Michael Kaspar
Sent: Tuesday, 26 August 2017 7:45pm
To: Robert Kaspar
Subject: Meeting with Narek Sarkissian

Dear Robert,

I trust you got home safely, and you have sorted out your lecture programme for the first semester.

Thanks to Narek, who is quite delightful, I feel that we are now close to finding out some truths about our family's history:

Before he died, Artoush Sarkissian, the Abbot of the monastery at San Lazzaro, sent an important letter to our relative Harat Kasper in Constantinople, with a copy to his brother Haig Sarkissian in Yerevan, Armenia. Both letters were written in code, but the letter sent to Haig Sarkissian was later deciphered by a senior monk at the Holy Church at Etchmiadzin, Armenia. Apparently, the original coded letter is now safely held under lock and key in a secret vault somewhere in Switzerland. However, Narek Sarkissian was able to show me a transcript of this letter and it certainly opens up a Pandora's Box of intrigue.

The transcript alludes to a long-lost family map, that traces the connections all the way back to Christ and beyond. The key to this lineage seems to be the shared birthmark behind the left ear.

References are made to various early manuscripts – 'The Codex Sinaiticus' and in particular an ancient text called 'The Dilijan Codex', that has been secreted away and hidden in one of the many churches in Armenia. It doesn't specify which of the churches conceals this document for fear that it might be stolen or destroyed. It is imperative that this precious document doesn't fall into the wrong hands.

The search is on. Tomorrow, I intend to go to the small town of Dilijan, near the northern end of Lake Sevan in central Armenia, and then if time permits, I'll walk through the National Park to Goshavank Monastery, to investigate the whereabouts of the hidden codex. This journey could be fraught with danger.

I have attached a PDF copy of a final draft of my book. Please remove the PDF and this email from your hard drive but keep copies of both on a USB stick in a safe place. Someday, it may be necessary to reveal the contents of both items and shed light on the concealed manuscript.

I'll be flying out to Istanbul on Wednesday for a few days and then on to Moscow for a couple of days before going back to Oz. I will give you a call when I get back home to Adelaide.

Give my love to your mother Alex and tell her to keep in touch. Fleur says to tell her that her latest volume of poetry is simply out of this world.

Cheers Michael

* * *

London – November 2017

We know that Michael left for Istanbul a couple of days after sending me the email, but he hasn't been seen since. No one knows what happened and where he might be. He has obviously gone into hiding. His wife Fleur has been quite beside herself for the last couple of months, so I went to see her in Adelaide to help her through some very difficult times. Apparently, Michael had a private Swiss bank account and must have been operating under a different identity.

A few weeks ago, I received a short-handwritten note from Michael. The postmark on the stamp was from Mexico City, but of course that doesn't mean anything. At least I knew that Michael was still alive.

The note was sharp and to the point.

Dear Robert,

You will no doubt be surprised and hopefully relieved to be receiving this note from me. Yes, I'm still alive.

I think I have found the location of the lineage map that I am looking for, but with it comes not only great responsibility but also grave danger.

I trust that you have kept the 'Draft' PDF of the book and my last email to you. If so, please contact my friend Eugene Black in Adelaide; he will be able to help you with publishing the documents. Tell him not to worry about proofreading or other niceties, but to just get the information out into the public domain.

I won't be able to surface from my hidden identity until the lineage map has been publicly exposed and, even then, it may be necessary to remain undercover for quite some time.

I suggest you shred this note.

Don't try and look for me. However, I may be able to make contact from time to time.

Take care,

Cheers Michael

www.ingramcontent.com/pod-product-compliance
Lightning Source LLC
Chambersburg PA
CBHW021230060726
47590CB00005B/1699